William Malpas has written books on land art (including land art in the U.K.), Richard Long, and three books on Andy Goldsworthy (his first study of Goldsworthy, *Andy Goldsworthy: Touching Nature*, was published in 1994).

CONTEMPORARY ART
FROM CRESCENT MOON PUBLISHING

The Art of Andy Goldsworthy
by William Malpas

Andy Goldsworthy: Touching Nature
by William Malpas

The Art of Richard Long
by William Malpas

Constantin Brancusi: Sculpting the Essence of Things
by James Pearson

Alison Wilding: The Embrace of Sculpture
by Susan Quinnell

Eric Gill: Nuptials of God
by Anthony Hoyland

The Erotic Object: Sexuality in Sculpture From Prehistory to the Present Day
by Susan Quinnell

Minimal Art and Artists in the 1960s and After
by Laura Garrard

Land Art: A Complete Guide to Landscape, Environmental, Earthworks, Nature, Sculpture and Installation Art
by William Malpas

Andy Goldsworthy In Close-Up
by William Malpas

Land Art In Close-Up
by William Malpas

Colourfield Painting: Minimal, Cool, Hard Edge, Serial and Post-Painterly Abstract Art From the Sixties to the Present
by Stuart Morris

Mark Rothko: The Art of Transcendence
by Julia Davis

Jasper Johns
by L.M. Poole

Brice Marden
by Laura Garrard

Frank Stella: American Abstract Artist
by James Pearson

Maurice Sendak and the Art of Children's Book Illustration
by L.M. Poole

Sacred Gardens: The Garden in Myth, Religion and Art
by Jeremy Robinson

Sex in Art: Pornography and Pleasure in Painting and Sculpture
by Cassidy Hughes

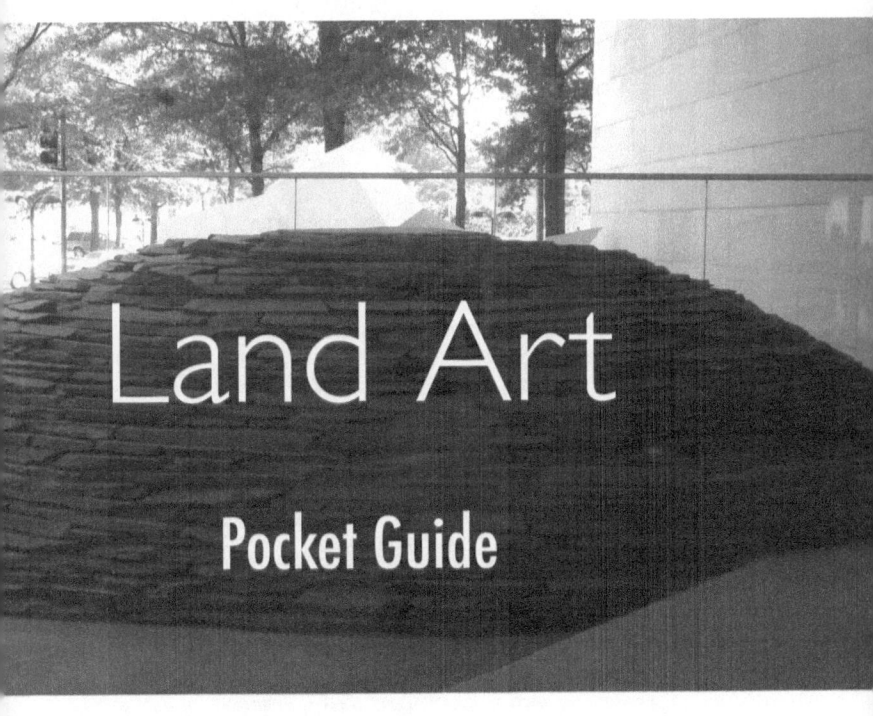

Land Art

Pocket Guide

William Malpas

CRESCENT MOON

CRESCENT MOON PUBLISHING
P.O. Box 1312, Maidstone,
Kent, ME14 5XU,
Great Britain
www.crmoon.com

First published 2007. Third edition 2012.
© William Malpas 2007, 2012.

Printed and bound in the U.S.A.
Set in Helvetica Neue Condenséd 9 on 11pt.
Designed by Radiance Graphics.

The right of William Malpas to be identified as the author of
Land Art and Land Artists: Pocket Guide has been asserted
generally in accordance with sections 77 and 78 of the
Copyright, Designs and Patents Act 1988.

All rights reserved. No part of this book may be reprinted or
reproduced, stored in a retrieval system, or transmitted, in
any form or by any means, electronic, mechanical,
photocopying, recording or otherwise, without permission
from the publisher.

British Library Cataloguing in Publication data

Malpas, William
Land Art and Land Artists: Pocket Guide – (Sculptors Series)
1. Earthworks (Art) 2. Installations (Art) 3. Environment (Art) 4.
Sculpture, Modern – 21st Century
I. Title

709'.040476

ISBN-13 9781861714039 (Pbk)
ISBN-13 9781861714046 (Hbk)

Contents

Acknowledgements 6
Illustrations 7

1 Introduction 15
2 The Alchemy of Matter: Land Art Aesthetics 21
3 The Birth of Land Art In 1960s Culture 51
4 Land Art, Gender, Sexuality and the Body 59
5 Land Art and Religion 66
6 Land Art and British Culture 73
7 Robert Smithson 77
8 Carl Andre 85
9 James Turrell 92
10 Dennis Oppenheim 96
11 Robert Morris 101
12 Nancy Holt 105
13 Alice Aycock 108
14 Mary Miss 112
15 Michael Heizer 114
16 Walter de Maria 117
17 Other Land Artists in the U.S.A. 121
18 Chris Drury 125
19 David Nash 138
20 Richard Long 144
21 Andy Goldsworthy 159
22 Land Artists in Europe 194

Illustrations 209

Notes 243
Bibliography 255

Acknowledgements

Thanks to Peter Redgrove; Andy Goldsworthy; Chris Drury; Viking Press, London; Penguin, London; Thames & Hudson, London; Anthony d'Offay Gallery, London; Henry Moore Centre for Sculpture, Leeds.

Thanks to the authors quoted and their publishers.
Illustrations © the artists.
Thanks to the copyright holders of the illustrations:
Musée d'Art Moderne de la Ville de Paris. Tate Modern, London. Royal Mail Group. John Weber Gallery, New York. Chinati Foundation, Texas. Lisson Gallery, London. Howard Lipman, Connecticut. Hamish Fulton. Andy Goldsworthy. Chris Drury. Anthony Gormley. Nancy Holt. Carl Andre. Peter Randall-Page. James Turrell. Christo. Walter de Maria. David Nash. Michael Heizer. Robert Morris. Frank Stella. Gordon Matta-Clark. Alexander Calder.

Images are used for information and research purposes, with no infringement of copyright or rights intended.

Anna Mendieta, Tree of Life series, 1977

Alice Aycock, Maze, 1972

Andy Goldsworthy, Cracked Line, San Francisco

Dennis Oppenheim, Parallel Stress, 1970

1

Introduction

Most land artists have their favourite motifs, practices, materials and styles, instantly recognizable: Robert Smithson with his giant spiral earthworks; Michael Heizer carving up the Nevada desert; Dennis Oppenheim's Conceptual borderlands and concentric circles; Walter de Maria's lightning fields; Nancy Holt's celestial observatories; Christo's vast wrapped structures; the Roden Crater and 'skyspaces' of James Turrell; Hans Haacke's steam, fog and ice ephemeralities; Alice Aycock's underground labyrinths of nightmares and childhood memories; Richard Long's stone circles and rows; David Nash's wooden figurative sculptures; Andy Goldsworthy's arches, walls, snowballs, body prints, splashes and holes; and Chris Drury's shelters, medicine wheels and baskets.

The term 'land art' is used here as a shorthand to refer to many kinds of art, including landscape art, earth art, earthworks, nature art, green or ecological art, and installations. Land art was part of modernism and, in particular, 1960s art, the time of late Henry Moore, Robert Morris, Yves Klein, Anthony Caro, William Tucker, Tony Smith and Phillip King. It was the 1960s-70s era of what Rosalind Krauss called 'expanded field' sculpture, the High Renaissance of land art.[1] Krauss's 'expanded field' sculptors included Robert Irwin, Michael Heizer, Richard Serra, Walter de Maria, Sol LeWitt, Bruce Nauman, Alice Aycock, Mary Miss, Dennis Oppenheim, Nancy Holt, George Trakis, Richard Long, Hamish Fulton,

Christo and Joel Shapiro.

I have concentrated on some of the more well-known land artists, such as Robert Smithson, Christo, Walter de Maria, Michael Heizer, Richard Long, Robert Morris, David Nash, Hamish Fulton, Hans Haacke, Nancy Holt, Alice Aycock, Mary Miss, Carl Andre, Dennis Oppenheim, and James Turrell. There are, of course, many more artists working with place, site, landscape and the environment. What is written here about the more well-known land artists also applies to the other artists cited above, plus many others.

Performance art, live art, body art and action art has many links with land, environmental, nature and installation art. In performance art, the field is vast. There isn't space in this study to consider them all (there are plenty of other studies). There are artists who talked to dead hares in their arms (Joseph Beuys), artists who carried out weird post-Catholic rituals or cut up sheep carcasses (Hermann Nitsch), artists who performed nude with film, video and installations (Carolee Schneemann), artists who drew on their bodies (while naked, of course), artists who sat in rooms and menstruated (Catherine Elwes), sculptors who stood and sang in suits (Gilbert & George), artists who replayed the physical martyrdom of saints (Ron Athey), groups who threw paint and food over each other while singing vaudeville songs (the Kipper Kids), artists who painted gallery floors with their long hair (Janine Antoni), artists who examined their genitals and masturbated before an audience (Annie Sprinkle), artists who had themselves bound and gagged in a gallery, holding a pig's heart (Tania Bruguera), artists who masturbated (while naked, of course) with cuddly toys (Mike Kelly), artists who meditate, chant, sing and play music (Caryle Reedy), groups who burn US flags and protest against war while naked on Brooklyn Bridge (Yayoi Kusama), artists who re-enact car crashes at a happening (Jim Dine and Judy Tersch), artists who douse themselves in water (Nam June Paik), artists who shoot guns at paint-filled balloons (Niki de Sant Phalle), artists who burn books (John Latham), groups who stage a protest 'blood bath' in a New York street (Guerrilla Art Action Group), artists who sat on horses in galleries (Jannis Kounellis), performers who locked themselves in rooms for six days while covered in paint (Stuart Brisley), artists who hung themselves upside-down in galleries (Jill Orr), creative couples who walk and bump into each other for an hour (while naked, of course), artists who scrubbed cow bones (Marina Abramovic), artists who stand against trees (nude, of course), covered in mud and plants (Ana Mendieta), artists who set themselves on fire (Tomas Ruller), or ignited gunpowder charges (Roman Signer), groups who sit naked in healing baths (Cai Guo Qiang), performers who had their clothes cut off by the audience (Yoko Ono), artists who signed semi-nude women as 'living sculptures' (Piero Manzoni), artists who hid under wooden ramps in galleries and masturbated while speaking to visitors (Vito Acconci), artists who hung between bridges (Dennis Oppenheim), and artists who crucified themselves on the roof of a Volkeswagen (Chris Burden).

Some of the key writers on land art include Rosalind Krauss, Lucy Lippard, Michael Fried, Kenneth Baker, John Beardsley, Lawrence Alloway, John Coplans, Diane Waldman, Harold Rosenberg, Stephanie Ross, Robert Hobbs, David Bourdon, Mel Gooding, Germano Celant, Alan Sonfist, Baile Oakes, Jeffrey Kastner, Andrew Causey, and Gilles Tiberghien.

Key land art shows include *Earth Art* (Andrew Dickson White Museum of Art, Cornell University, 1969), which showed Jan Dibbets, Richard Long, Robert Smithson, Dennis Oppenheim and Robert Morris, *Land Art* (Hanover, 1970), *Earthworks* (Dwan Gallery, 1968), *The New Sculpture, 1965-75* (Whitney, 1990), *Qu'est-ce que la sculpture moderne?* (Paris, 1986), *Virginia Dwan, Art Minimal, Art Conceptuel, Earthworks* (Paris, 1991), *Earthworks* (Seattle, 1979), *Conceptual Art, Arte Povera, Land Art* (Turin, 1971), and many of the Documenta exhibitions at Kassel. At *Earth, Air, Fire, Water* (Boston, 1971), Hans Haacke, Christo, Robert Smithson, Dennis Oppenheim, Richard Long, Alan Sonfist, Douglas Huebler, Peter Hutchinson, Andy Warhol and Michael Heizer showed works.

Some of the best places to see land art *in situ* are in sculpture parks and gardens. in the U.S.A., these include Grounds For Sculpture in New Jersey, Rockerfeller Estate, New York, the Storm King Art Center, New York, Empire State Plaza Art Collection, Albany, New York, Abington Art Center Sculpture Garden, Pennsylvania, Hirshhorn Museum and Sculpture Garden, Washington, DC, Des Moines Art Center, Iowa, Walker Art Center, Minneapolis, Laumeier Sculpture Park, St Louis, Sheldon Sculpture Garden, University of Nebraska, Lincoln, Florida International University, Oakland Museum, California, Franklin D. Murphy Sculpture Garden, UCLA, L.A., Los Angeles County Museum of Art and the Museum of Outdoor Arts, Colorado. Any visit to land and environmental art displays in the United States would take in many of the above sites, with Donald Judd's transformation of the Army base at Marfa being near the top of the list. Further essential sites include Michael Heizer's *Double Negative* in the Nevada desert, Walter de Maria's *Lightning Field* in Quemado, New Mexico, James Turrell's volcano transformation, *Roden Crater,* near Flagstaff, Arizona, Robert Smithson's *Spiral Jetty* in the Great Salt Lakes and Nancy Holt's *Sun Tunnels* in Lucin, Utah.

Although it may appear that land artists tour the whole globe making art, they actually stick to a small number of countries (tending towards the Northern hemisphere, and the Western world). For instance, there are few major land artists who have made significant work in Africa, or large parts of South America, or mainland China, or Russia. There are few Western land artworks in Egypt, for instance (perhaps because the competition is pretty fierce there from some of the most wonderful structures humans have ever made – the tombs, temples, cities and pyramids of the ancient Egyptians. Of course, there are also social, political, cultural and ideological reasons for the lack of major land art in Islamic and Middle Eastern territories).

Europe's a favourite location, but not Eastern Europe. Favourite places tend to be America and Western Europe, obviously, and Japan, and occasionally Australia. Occasionally also India (if it's India, it's usually the scenic parts to the North, in Nepal or the Himalayas). But even in America, birthplace and chief centre of land art, artworks tend to be clustered around the East (New York, Washington, DC, Chicago), the South-West (New Mexico, Arizona), the Mid-West (Colorado), or California.

Some negative criticism: for some critics, the worst kind of land art is that which avoids political or 'important' or problematic issues, such as AIDS, poverty, 'Third World' debt, globalization, colonialism, war, terrorism, and so on. It romanticizies the natural world. It's conservative. It's nostalgic (for a vanished agricultural, working class past that never existed in the first place). It's escapist. It's self-indulgent. It's élitist. It's repetitive and lacks imagination. It lacks formal experimentation. It over-simplifies its subjects. For the naysayers, land art is a romantic retreat into escapist, nostalgic fantasies about nature, with nothing to say about the anxieties, problems and challenges of living in the contemporary, 21st century world. It's hippy, tree-hugger art which panders to the middle class's nostalgia for nature, seen from the perspective of neurotic city dwellers who hanker for the peace and quiet of the countryside. It's an art that flatters and assuages the bourgeoisie's liberal guilt over wrecking the natural world with its ceaseless, massive consumption and pollution. It doesn't seem to say much about the late capitalist world, the technological, post-industrial, consumer society.

Land art is very much the product of the privileged, relatively wealthy First World, a world in which the Northern hemisphere is superior to the Southern; American, Eurocentric ethics are dominant; bourgeois/ 'imperialist' politics pre-dominate; and the racial 'colour' of the art is not black, brown, red or yellow, but definitely white. Though 'post-colonial', land art is distinctly not 'politically correct' when it comes to issues of ethnicity or economy (although there is a strain of land art that engages with political, financial and ecological issues).

2

The Alchemy of Matter: Land Art Aesthetics

SPIRIT OF PLACE: LAND ART, NATURE POETRY AND NATURE MYSTICISM

For the land and site artist, the whole planet can be an artist's studio. The land artist ranges over the whole globe. A desert, a beach, a field, a hill, a valley, a forest becomes a studio, a place of creative activity. The landscape itself is crucial in land art. That's obvious. Or is it? This means the very texture and colour and shape and dampness and springiness and strength and size of moss, for instance. Or a stone. Or a crevice in a rock wall. The way the light falls on a clump of grass, the little bits of dead, yellowish grass on top of the newer, green grass. Pine cones, closed-up. Flowers turning sunward in the late afternoon.

These are the things land artists deal with in making art. These are the actualities that artists employ when they create artworks. To fully appreciate land art, then, one has to look really closely, to grasp the details, as well as the overall conception and the grand design. This is true of small sculptures, as well as the larger American earthworks. Then there are the many layers of human history to consider, the social uses of the land, ranging from industrial and agricultural usage to the private, intimate experiences of individuals. The amount of history embedded in the landscape in Britain, in every square foot, is incredible.

For David Nash, land art is about getting as close as possible to nature: the land artist does not paint nature like the painter, at a distance, with a paintbrush or watercolour block in front of her or him. The sketchpad or easel is a wall, a veil, a barrier between artist and world. The land artist, rather, dives in, 'gets right in there', as Nash says. The land artist does not use oil or pastel or ink to 'represent' nature. Rather, she or he works directly with nature, getting her or his fingers dirty with mud, snow, animal waste, stone, ferns and wood.

Land art gains much of its power (its meaning, its value, its presence) from particular places. Many land artists, for instance, work away from urban areas. Some, like Michael Heizer and Walter de Maria, work in what are regarded as 'exotic' locations – deserts and mountains. The glamour of the locations aids the sculptures. Some land art is overpowered by the Romantic settings. Some of Richard Long's stone circles, for instance, look feeble in their desert or snowscape locations.

THE LAND ART SUBLIME: LAND ART AND ROMANTICISM

Land art and land artists seem to have much in common with Romantic art and Romantic artists. The marks of late 18th / early 19th century European Romanticism include: exalting nature; going to extremes; the cult of solitude; the predominance of subjectivity; rebellion; the artist as outsider; infinity; the sublime, and so on. Contemporary artists (such as Mark Rothko, Robert Smithson, David Inshaw, Anish Kapoor, James Turrell and Thérèse Oulton) express some of the marks of Romanticism cited above.

Land art in its grander moments echoes the gestures of High Romanticism – the Blakean, Wordsworthian, Goethean, Turnerian gestures – which have become so familiar in Western art. 'The Romantics' awe in the face of nature is hard to revive in a culture as estranged from nature as ours', remarked Robert Hughes, 'but, enfolded in distance and immensity, such works of land-art [by Michael Heizer and Walter de Maria] are saturated in nostalgia for it'.[1]

The 'Land Art Sublime' (*pace* Robert Rosenblum's coining of the term 'Abstract Sublime' to describe Barnett Newman's and Mark Rothko's paintings) might include the snow and stone circles made in the wildernesses of Scotland, Nepal and Peru of Richard Long; Christo's islands surrounded with pink polypropylene; the stone circles of Nancy Holt; and of course Robert Smithson's *Spiral Jetty*. The sheer *scale* of some of the works of land artists is of itself visceral and erotic (Walter de Maria's *Lightning Field,* Christo's *Running Fence,* Viet Ngo's *Lemna System*).[2]

The land artist has a special, fetishistic relation with her/his materials: they are not simply bits of matter to be wielded in a particular way. They are treated with respect. Wolfgang Laib dusts the Earth with pollen, to form an enormous square layer of brilliant yellow. The delicacy – and potency – of the sculpture is immediately apparent. This is the sort of sculpture that exerts a synæsthetic power over the gallery-goer: the pollen affects not only the visual sense with its incandescent hues, but also affects smell, taste and touch. Another of Laib's installations was *The Passageway* (1988-93), made up of huge panels of beeswax. 'I believe that the impossible, the invisible and visions can become reality if one really wants to make the effort', said Laib.[3] Anya Gallaccio made large installations using flowers: thousands of red roses in *Red On Green* (1992), 101 sunflowers in *Preserve Sunflower* (1991) and 1,600 zinnias in *Untitled* (1992). Gallaccio's flowerpieces emphasized beauty and decay, sensuality and death.

Andy Goldsworthy, Wolfgang Laib and Chris Drury collect leaves, berries, pollen, honey and other natural elements and weave sensuous artifacts that are ephemeral and intricate. Dennis Oppenheim worked with snow and circles in his *Annual Rings*, a series of concentric circles that straddled the Canadian/ American border, and with burning circles onto grass in his *Branded Mountain*. In fact, Dennis Oppenheim was the first land artist to work with snow on a grand scale.

LAND ART AND GARDENS

'Land art' is a term that includes a wide variety of artistic forms, like the term 'garden'. Gardens are not a single form with a single set of characteristics. Gardens can be so various that some critics have suggested that the word 'garden' is as broad and vague as words such as 'art'.[1] It's a term so general it's practically useless.

Gardens can be very small or very big; they can be flat or terraced; they can be circular, square, or narrow; they can be organized around a 'natural' plan or a strict geometric plan; they can be 'wild' or 'tamed'; they can be enclosed or open; they can contain lakes, ponds, streams, fountains, statues, trees, statues, lawns, shrubs, rocks, walls, fences, benches, flowers, stones, follies, ruins, grottoes, temples, paths and many kinds of environmental art.

A traditional Japanese (Zen Buddhist) garden, with its stones and sand raked into patterns, is quite different from, say, an English kitchen garden in Chelmsford, or a suburban yard in Iowa. Gardens can be vast displays of state and regal power, such as the gardens at Versailles or Hadrian's Villa, or modest attempts at cultivating food in a backyard. Gardens have been made for many reasons: in the pursuit of decoration, finance, medicine, religion, contemplation, play, sport and food. Sculptor Isamu Noguchi thought of gardens as

> sculpturing of space: a beginning, and a groping to another level of sculptural experience and use: a total sculpture space experience beyond individual sculptures. A man may enter such a space: it is in scale with him; it

is real. (1968)

For some critics, the most interesting aspect of land art is its connection with gardening and landscape design.[2] But for the chief land artist – Robert Smithson – art degenerates as it approaches gardening.[3]

If there can be 'found art', can there be 'found gardens'? Perhaps an artist, working in the Conceptual and environmental art mode, could simply claim any piece of land as their 'found garden', just as artists such as Marcel Duchamp, Kurt Schwitters and Robert Rauschenberg took found objects and exhibited them as art (and Gordon Matta-Clark bought tiny pieces of land and it became an artwork). When does a garden start becoming a garden? How many objects are required to make a garden? Is a single blade of grass a garden? Are two plants on a window ledge a garden? Or five plants, or ten plants, clustered together in pots? Is an overgrown path a garden? Or an allotment dedicated to growing tomatoes and potatoes? Is a couple of yards of grass behind an abandoned gas station a garden? Is a municipal park, consisting only of children's swings and slides on grass, a garden? Is a farmer's field a garden? Or a farm?

And when does a garden stop being a garden? Is a garden of a hundred years ago that can barely be seen amidst piles of refuse still a garden? How much of the human touch is required to make a piece of land a garden? If sand raked into a pattern can be a garden for the Japanese Zen Buddhist, is any piece of raked sand a garden? Are the patterns made in the sand by the receding tide a garden? Is the sea making gardens with every tide? Or the wind, or erosion, or earthquakes or other natural forces? Does a garden have to have the 'human' touch to make it a true garden?

Environmental or land or garden art can include American earthworks (such as those by James Turrell and Mel Chin); ephemeral interventions in the environment (such as those by Andy Goldsworthy, Hans Haacke and Michael Singer);

architectural installations (such as those by Alice Aycock, Mary Miss and Nancy Holt); land art as performance art (Richard Long, Hamish Fulton and Christo), even if the artist is the only audience; land art that involves landscaping and garden art (such as Alan Sonfist, Patricia Johanson, Robert Irwin and Ian Hamilton Finlay); and sculpture or art parks. There are 'video gardens', too, such as Matthew McCaslin's *Bloomer* installation: 12 TV monitors played tapes of flowers blooming in time-lapse. The TV sets were arranged in groups like plants, with the cables tangled on the floor (at St Louis Art Museum).

'TRUE CAPITALIST ART'?: THE COST OF LAND ART

Not all but much of land art is very expensive. That is, it is costly moving tons of earth around. Taking a motorbike out into the desert and drawing lines with it is one thing (as Michael Heizer had done in *Circular Surface Displacement* [1968], North of Las Vegas), but making a 40-mile 18-foot high fence (Christo) is another. Much of land art requires patrons, sponsors, co-ordination with galleries, lawyers, public administrators, helpers and industry. The costliness of land art may explain why much of it is American.[1] Land art requires investment with no immediate return. Patrons are crucial to land art. In American earthworks the key patrons were the DIA Art Foundation, Robert C. Scull and Virginia Dwan, director of the Dwan Gallery between 1966 and 1971.

Richard Long perhaps speaks for many British sculptors when he writes of his aversion to American earthwork art:

> In the sixties there was a feeling that art need not be a production line of more objects to fill the world. My interest was in a more thoughtful view of art and nature, making art both visible and invisible, using ideas, walking, stones, tracks, water, time, etc, in a flexible way... It was the anti-thesis of so-called American "Land

Art," where an artist needed money to be an artist, to buy real estate to claim possession of the land, and to wield machinery. True capitalist art.[2]

Although Richard Long (and others) may despise the amounts of money spent by the American earthwork artists, isn't he also part of 'true capitalist art'? Doesn't he also live off his art? Doesn't he just wander around the planet on his sacred 'walks', putting a few stones into a pile, and taking a photo of his efforts? Isn't Long (and Andy Goldsworthy, David Nash, Shirazeh Houshiary, Rachel Whiteread, Richard Wentworth, Bill Woodrow, Helen Chadwick, Alison Wilding, Hamish Fulton and Richard Deacon) also a part of the 'capitalist' art world?[3] Don't Long's artworks sell for lots of money, a lot more money than the materials cost? Isn't Long being hypocritical when he criticizes the bombastic aspects of American land art when he himself benefits from the hugely over-priced art gallery system, where even mundane art it seems (such as artists' prints) are sold for 'silly prices'?

It's easy to view the Christos' wrapped buildings or Walter de Maria's $500,000 *Vertical Earth Kilometer* as expensive, pointless art. This sort of land art may be 'true capitalist art', an art of excessive cost and excessive waste, but then, art has been full of idiot amounts of money for ages. What about Christo's wrappings? They cost a bomb, for sure, but, as Christo says, he pays for it himself, with money made from selling smaller works. Christo's *Running Fence* cost $2.5 million; *The Umbrellas* in Japan and California cost $26,000,000. Christo says his art 'has to do with things that are very simple'.[4] This definition can also apply to other land artists; they, too, transform ordinary things.

When these transformations of the ordinary cost so much, and require 200 rock climbers, as Christo's covering of the Reichstag in Berlin needed, then commentators wonder about the 'importance' of such artistic productions. There is something right and homely about Andy Goldsworthy and his couple of stonewallers building a wall in the Northern wildernesses of Britain. They toil away in true grimy, stalwart, Eric Gill-like craftsman style. But there's something cynical and obscene, perhaps, about Michael Heizer or Walter de Maria carving great gashes in the American desert, or Christo making artworks that cost 26 million dollars yet only last for two weeks. Surely that money would be better spent on a hospital? Or on feeding needy groups or countries? Surely artworks that cost millions of dollars but only benefit a (relatively) tiny amount of people are wasteful? Isn't famine relief a better alternative? Perhaps one could make famine relief/ earthquake relief/ medical supply/ housing, and other 'charity' and 'aid' projects, an art event? Perhaps if Christo spent $26 million on providing food for the needy instead of wrapping a building in Berlin in a bit of plastic, people would not be so angry? When artists spend such vast amounts of money on art, it's no wonder people find this obscene. But then, if spending millions of dollars on art were outlawed, we'd have no Hollywood, no movie industry, no television, no advertising, no media. These are the hypocrisies and ambiguities that surround art. How can one 'justify' a $26,000,000 Christo wrapping? Or a typical Hollywood feature movie (cost: $45 million, with a typical advertizing budget of $5-15 million)?

LAND ART AND PHOTOGRAPHY

In land art photography, the viewer is not offered a *range* of viewpoints of a work, although land artists clearly take more than one shot of each work they make. No artist takes just *one* photo out of a 36 exposure 35mm film, or one frame out of a twelve shot 120mm format film, or one image out of 100s available on a digital camera. No, an artist, like an photographer, takes a range of shots, at different, bracketed exposures, from different viewpoints (much as the trendy advertizing film director of today shoots twelve hours of footage for just one thirty second advert).[1]

Each land artist, then, must select this or that viewpoint, behind this bush or next to that tree. The land artist is therefore also a photographer, selecting views, reframing their works, making choices about lighting, angles, lenses, film stock, etc. Land artists will make decisions about exactly *when* to photograph their work. Some works are ephemeral, and last only moments, so the photograph must be taken immediately (but even when a work lasts only a few seconds or minutes, there are still choices about which moment to select). Other works, such as Robert Smithson's *Amarillo Ramp* or Nancy Holt's *Star-Crossed* (1981), last longer. The land artist as photographer can therefore wait for a certain combination of sunlight and clouds. This is particularly crucial in cloudy places like, say, Florida or Britain, where lighting can vary so dramatically over a few minutes. As anyone who has been in Dartmoor or the Sierra Nevada will know, the sunlight can burst through the clouds at one moment, then a moment later there'll be dark, sombre clouds, looking as if it's going to rain. A moment later, it *will* rain, and afterwards, facing away from the sun, one might see a rainbow. Much of the world's weather is this changeable, so every land art photograph is a highly selective and subjective view of a particular place.

Another critical aspect of photographing land art is not only deciding what to *include*, but choosing what to *exclude* from the composition. Visiting a land artwork in the flesh, one can see it from all sorts of angles, with all sorts of backgrounds, in all sorts of conditions. Knowing a land artwork only from a photograph, one knows only *that* particular viewpoint, and no others. The land artist will take great care in framing the images, to show the artwork from the best vantage points. Many aspects of the surroundings might be elided from the final published photographs – an apartment block, a row of cars, trash, people, power lines, and so on.

Land artists must also oversee the journey of the images

or pixels they've shot from development through printing to framing. As anyone who has taken a photo will know, all manner of details can affect how one reads a photograph: how it is printed, light, dark, soft, hard, cropped, full frame, more red, more blue, burnt in, dodged, touched up, glossy or matt paper, and so on. The size of the photo affects it very much, as does the frame. Go into any framer's store and one'll see a plethora of different types of frame. All these things the viewer might take in at one glance in a gallery, but the artist has to make decisions all the time about all these matters, and many more. Land artists/ sculptors, then, must be accomplished photographers. Their work must be high standard, for it is exhibited in high art locations, such as the city gallery, or glossy coffee table art books.

In land art, the commentary, the written records, the obsessive documentation, is just as important as the artwork itself. Often, it *is* the artwork. The land artist's life becomes part of the artwork. Andy Goldsworthy said '[m]y art will always be a reflection of my way of life.'[2] Brilliant late 1960s sculptor Eva Hesse spoke in Romantic, emotional terms of her art, employing words such as 'essence' and 'soul'. She spoke of wanting to emphasize 'soul or presence or whatever you want to call it.' Although Richard Long is not as openly emotional in his descriptions of his art, these words of Hesse's could apply, with some minor revisions, to Long's (and other land artists') art: 'I think art is a total thing. A total person giving a contribution. It is an essence, a soul... In my soul art and life are inseparable.'[3]

Jan Dibbets said that documenting the work wasn't important: 'I've done lots of works without taking photographs'.[4] But most land artists record their activities (e.g.: 'walk this morning; made a snow sculpture; it wasn't successful; back home for lunch'). Ultimately, *any* activity can be land art. Going to the stores can be a piece of art. One might drop a stone on the path as one goes, or perhaps not. Either way, you've just made a work of art. Is, then, walking to

Gilmor's corner store for a pint of milk and a pack of cigarettes a fully accomplished and thoroughly authentic work of art? Where does authenticity end and artifice begin? Or, rather, where does life end and art begin? Clearly, they are a continuum in land art.

Richard Long says that '[n]ot all walking is art'. That is, a walk becomes art when it is conceived as art. The conception of the walk, made before the walk, is crucial, even if there is no 'reason' at all for the walk. 'A walk, and place, can be chosen for any reason'.[5] Long also says, though, that '[a]nything an artist makes, is art', but adds: '[n]ot everyone is an artist.'[6]

The relation between outdoor and indoor works, between stone cairns in some remote zone and a stone cairn in a Western gallery, is resolved simply in land art by being regarded by the artist as a continuum. One can see how for the land artist both indoor and outdoor works are one, i.e., part of the same thing. But the viewer might see them as separate, because the viewer (usually) can't see many land art outdoor pieces (Richard Long likes to keep his locations secret and anonymous).[7] The viewer only knows land art outdoor pieces from photos and texts. So it's always an odd relationship with land artworks for the viewer. For the artist, it's great, because the big photos and writings relate to her/ his own experiences, of working outdoors. S/he knows the work inside out: *s/he lived it*. The viewer, though, gets a different experience: s/he sees odd phrases, titles, dates, measurements. Odd snippets of info. Or photos. So people love land art not because they love the photographs, or the writings. They love it, perhaps, because of *what it suggests.* Land art persuades people to look outwards, away from cities, towards the landscape, towards stones and water and all the rest of it. Perhaps that's why people love land art, and nature poetry, and all things to do with nature, from gardening to walking the dog to vacations in wildernesses. As Hamish Fulton put it, 'I walk on the land to be woven into nature' (1995).

The outdoor work itself isn't present in land art's text pieces or photos. The work isn't 'in' the gallery. No, the work is *elsewhere*, and it is to that *elsewhere place* that people want to go. Land art creates *desire* in people, as the work of J.M.W. Turner or Aleksandr Blok creates desire – for travel, for other places. Richard Long spoke in a Santa Fe interview of feeling refreshed and renewed after a good walk: that's the experience, perhaps, that viewers wish to gain from land art, from all art.

Land art, then, whether by Alice Aycock, Kazuo Shiraga, Chris Drury or the Christos, is part of a postmodern trend in self-reflexivity, the *mise-en-âbyme* commentary so familiar now. Art about (the artist's) life.

It's about reality. Land artists like what they see to be real, to be the object in and of itself (the 'thing-in-itself' of Existentialism, or Rainer Maria Rilke's *Kunstding*, 'thing of art'). They dislike illusionism. For land artists, their sculpture doesn't symbolize or represent nature, it *is* nature, a part of nature. As Jasper Johns remarked: 'I find it more interesting to use a real fork as painting than it is to use painting as a real fork.' Similarly, one can see how, for James Turrell, Patricia Johanson, James Pierce, Michelle Stuart and other land artists, it's much more interesting to use a stone as a stone rather than as a representation of something else. Robert Smithson's definition of an earthwork is pertinent here: 'instead of putting a work of art on some land, some land is put into a work of art'.[8]

INSIDE — OUTSIDE

Sometimes it's odd to see land art in a gallery, because the mound of soil, the cairn of stones, the slate circle, demands the viewer to look outwards, to nature, to the wildernesses from whence this art comes. Richard Long's stone circles are familiar now, having been seen in art galleries and museums, but one is always aware of the place of their origin, and how odd they look.[1] Those sticks and stones are tiny parts of nature, bits extracted, chopped up, re-arranged, as all art is nature chopped up and reformed according to the artist's æsthetics. Land art creates an ambiguous continuity with the world of nature that exists outside the gallery. Sometimes this ambiguity works against the art on show in the gallery space.

Land art sites, in the first wave of land (late 1960s/ early 1970s – land art's 'golden age'), tended to be wildernesses, deserts, post-industrial spaces, waste grounds, quarries and dumps. One of the reasons for going far from the gallery, the city and the pretty countryside spots was because land artists wanted to avoid the 'pastoral' and the 'picturesque' at all costs.[2] Land artists, asserted Dennis Oppenheim, wished to go beyond the picturesque (while British land artists, such as Richard Long, had some relationship with the picturesque [ibid.]).

David Nash discussed this indoor/ outdoor problem in a 1978 interview:

> An object made indoors diminishes in scale and stature when placed outside. The reverse happens when an object made outside is brought inside, it seems to grow in stature and presence. It brings the outside in with it. The object outside has to contend with unlimited space, uneven ground and the weather. The sculpture I show inside is meant to be seen inside, it relates to the limited space, the peculiar scale, and the still air.[3]

The indoor-outdoor dialectic much concerned Robert Smithson, who said 'I don't think you're freer artistically in the desert than you are inside a room'.[4] In fact, Smithson said he 'liked the artificial limits that the gallery presents'.[5] One of the problems land art must address is the age-old relation between the 'real world' and art, between objects as they are in the everyday world, and objects as they are represented in art. Land art makes the viewer look again at the natural world:

not just at the beauty of it, but at the multitudinous variety of forms in nature. Land art/ sculpture is a poetry of natural forms, in which notions of 'representation' are sidestepped, because it uses things 'as themselves' (the use of photography, though, sees a swift return of confusions over the politics of representation). An object such as the snowball in Andy Goldsworthy's *Snowballs in Summer* (1989 and 2000) is not plastic masquerading as a snowball, but a real snowball. Similarly, the twigs and stalks and needles and pebbles folded into the snowballs are real. What's amazing is the actuality of nature: the variety of forms; the way the branches twist, for instance. Land artists would have the viewer look closely at nature again. By using 'real' objects, land artists aim to demolish notions of representation and mediation. Instead of a picture of snow, one has snow itself; rather than paint pebbles, or sculpt them in bronze, land artists use real pebbles.

Of course, there are problems with using objects as objects – Marcel Duchamp with his readymades confronted this problem. The problem is partly one of context: for, placed in a museum, so obviously as items to be studied, the natural forms become art. The objects may not be on pedestals, but they are perceived as art objects. If you're looking at land art in a book or a gallery, one is already anchored in a gallery/ art/ æsthetic mode of viewing.

Ephemeral, land art aims for an eternity in one place: the soul. As Lawrence Weiner, the Conceptual/ Process artist who exhibited 'statements' (texts on a wall), said: '[o]nce you know about a work of mine, you own it. There's no way I can climb into somebody's head and remove it.'[6] Thus, much of land art exists in that socio-cultural space which is actually inside people's heads. Thus, anyone can 'own' land art: simply by thinking about it. Once thought about, land art, Conceptual art or Process art is 'possessed' by the viewer, in Weiner's system. Indeed, some Conceptual art requires the existence of the viewer to make the work work at all. The viewer brings the work alive.

Working inside was problematic for Andy Goldsworthy, he confessed, because he was disconnected from the natural world outside, with its changes, its seasons, animals, people, history. The outside world was alive, while the gallery or public space could all too easily begin to feel dead after a while. 'I am not not sustained by working indoors. I have too much control inside, and after a while I am drained of reasons for being there'.[7]

CHANGES, CYCLES, SEASONS

Critical in land art is the concept and reality of change, for these works in wood, snow, ice, leaves, water, slate, grass and so on, do not stay around. They are not 'permanent', in the way that, say, bronze, marble, steel or stone can be. The soil in Walter de Maria's *Earth Room* dries out and alters; Robert Morris's steam works and Hans Haacke's balloons are blown away by the wind; Christo's plastic wraps stay on for two weeks. Joseph Beuys emphasized process, evolution, change: his sculpture, he said, was not

> fixed and finished. Processes continue in most of them: chemical reactions, fermentations, colour changes, decay, drying up. Everything is in a *state of change*.[1]

The notion of decay and entropy was an important element in Robert Smithson's earth art.[2] It's the same for Richard Long: 'my work is partly about change or disappearance, invisibility... all these strange states of matter'.[3]

Some land artists enjoy the impermanence of (their) art, and exploit it. As politicians know, words such as 'permanent' are difficult to define, and even more difficult to maintain. Artists with a large vision of life know that nothing on Earth will be truly 'permanent'. After all, 'civilized' humanity is only

10,000 years old, or 40,000, or three million (depending on how one measures 'civilized'). And the planet itself will not last forever: millions more years, perhaps, but not forever.

Andy Goldsworthy said he is not against long-term art:

> That art should be permanent or impermanent is not the issue. Transience in my work reflects what I find in nature and should not be confused with an attitude towards art generally. I have never been against the well-made or long-lasting.

Domination and *penetration*. These are familiar terms describing patriarchal actions or constructions or ideologies used by feminists. Is Goldsworthy, seemingly so delicate in his touches, dominating nature?

Yet, clearly, land artists (and not just the American earthwork artists – Michael Heizer, Walter de Maria, Robert Smithson, Charles Simonds, Christo, Alice Aycock) do dominate nature. James Turrell's *Roden Crater* or Heizer's gigantic *Double Negative* will clearly be around for a long time, unless someone or something destroys them. Andy Goldsworthy's stone pieces, too, may stay around for a while. There is a sense of gloating when Goldsworthy says '[f]ourteen years ago I made a line of stones in Morecambe Bay. It is still there, buried under the sand, unseen. All my work still exists, in some form.'

Daring not to change or affect nature, land artists do just that, all the time. They 'interact' with nature, but their 'interactions', however small scale, can't help changing nature. 'I like the idea of using the land without possessing it', said Richard Long, ever the idealist.[4] Andy Goldsworthy's aim is to 'touch' something in nature, the essence of nature itself, to understand it, and the identification of himself within nature.[5] Thus, about the lake pieces, the stick and stalk sculptures he was commissioned to do in the Lake District in 1988, he remarked: 'I felt I really got through in the lake pieces. I had touched it, and understood it'.[6]

Some environmental/ action/ Conceptual artworks had a built-in impermanence, such as Allan Kaprow's *Fluids* (1967, Pasadena, California), large structures made from blocks of ice, which were left to melt. Barry Flanagan's *Hole in the Sea* (1969) was a cylinder embedded in a beach: Flanagan filmed the water covering the hole as the tide came in. Hans Haacke produced impermanent works, such as ice freezing around an element.[7] He wrote of an artwork which would be as majestic and as transient as birds gathering in the sky: 'I would like to lure 1000 seagulls to a certain spot (in the air) by some delicious food so as to construct an air sculpture from this combined mass.'

In "Natural Phenomena as Public Monuments" (1968), land artist Alan Sonfist suggested building 'museums of air' in cities, which would 'recapture the smells of earth, trees and vegetation different seasons and at different historical times, so that people would be able to experience what has been lost' (1978). Sonfist also suggested monumentalizing the natural world with sounds: '[c]ontinuous loops of natural sounds at the natural level of volume can be placed on historic sites' (ibid.).

There are bronze and marble sculptures still looking remarkable from the Græco-Roman period, and stone figurines from the Palæolithic period. Michael Heizer's scars in remote deserts will endure, but not Robert Morris's steam works or Hans Haacke's *Grass Grows* (1969). Indeed, ephemerality, transiency and change are key components in land art. The bulk of some land artists' work is ephemeral. As Barry Flanagan writes:

> Truly sculpture is always going on. With proper physical circumstances and the visual invitation, one simply joins in and makes the work... there is a never-ending stream of materials and configurations to be seen, both natural and man-made, that have visual strength but not object or function apart from this. It is as if they existed for just this physical, visual purpose – to be seen.[8]

LIVING PLANTS

Many land artists have used living plants at some time or other.

- Some artists have installed trees upside-down (Vito Acconci) and plants upside-down in galleries (Michael Blazy, Henrik Håkansson, Sam Kunce).
- Some artists have trained plants to grow at odd angles (Hans Haacke, Cartsen Höller).
- Some artists have forced plants into vacu-formed moulds (Laura Stein), and rubber foam (Ingo Vetter, Annette Weisser).
- Some artists have lined rooms with cages of bay leaves to produce an aromatic environment (Giuseppe Penone).
- Some artists have planted seeds on their naked bodies (Teresa Murak).
- Some artists have planted clover fields in galleries (Nikolaj Recke), and made couches from grass (Daniel Spoerri).
- Some artists have built parks running up the sides of buildings (Vito Acconci).
- Some have made enclosed indoor gardens (Knut Åsdam).
- Other artists have made portable orchards (the Harrisons); portable indoor vegetable gardens (N55); and crammed hothouses (Lothar Baumgarten).
- And some have let roses run riot over cars (Silvie Fleury).
- Herman de Vries is a close competitor with Andy Goldsworthy for the artist who's created the most works with living plants.

Plenty of land artists and sculptors have used real flowers: Anya Gallaccio employed roses (1992), sunflowers (1991) and zinnias (1992); Herman de Vries (who spread thousands of lavender flowers on a gallery floor in 1998);

Wolfgang Laib with his pollen floor spreads; Richard Long, who pressed flowers flat in a field in *Brough of Birsay Circle* (1994); Jenny Holzer's *Black Garden*, a war memorial garden of very dark plants and flowers (1994); Gary Rieveschl, who planted *Heart Wave,* a line of 12,000 red tulips, in 1980; Daniel Buren also made a row of tulips, *11,000 Tulips* (1987, Holland); Peter Hutchinson, who planted 'thrown ropes' of flowers (1996); also: Annette Wehrmann; Shelagh Wakely; Mark Dion; Meg Webster; Carsten Höller; Paula Hayes; Peter Fischl; David Weiss; Tobias Rehberger; Lothar Baumgarten; Brigitte Raabe; and Olaf Nicolai.

TREES IN LAND ART

Many sculptors and land artists have worked with trees: David Nash, Giuseppi Penone, William Jackson Maxwell, Robert Irwin, Jackie Winsor, Daniel Buren, Alan Sonfist, Harvey Fite, Peter Walker, Giuliano Mauri, Nils Udo, Luc Wolff, Maria Nordman, Sjoerd Buisman, Cosima von Bonin, Stefan Banz, Vito Acconci, Jørn Rønnau, Buster Simpson, Jan Dibbets, Helge Røed, Lars Vilks, Andy Lipkis, Herman de Vries and Mel Chin. Using trees means working within a long and celebrated religious and cultural tradition.[1] For example, trees have since time immemorial been associated with spirits and religions. The Greeks believed that trees had spirits; there were the apples of immortality and trees of eternal life; Daphne turned into a tree when pursued by Zeus; Actaeon was transformed into a stag in the forest when he spied Diana bathing nude; deities such as Athena, Artemis, Dionysus, Apollo, Orpheus and Cybele are associated with trees and woods.

Constantin Brancusi, more influential on land art than Pablo Picasso, Jean Arp, Alberto Giacometti, Auguste Rodin, Henri Matisse or Aristide Maillol, worked notions of shamanic flight into his *Birds in Space* sculptures, and most especially in his *Endless Column*, which is cited by many key sculptors (Donald Judd, Carl Andre, Robert Morris) as an important inspiration. Constantin Brancusi's *Birds in Space* aimed to express the essence of flight, the moment when a quivering verticality is released from the chains of gravity and flies upward. One only has to look at David Nash's *Tripods*, Chris Drury's cairns of rocks, Barnett Newman's *Broken Obelisk*, or Donald Judd's ladders, to see how important Brancusi's sculptures were, with their shamanic, World Tree associations.

Planting trees has become a favourite with land and environmental artists: Alan Sonfist created several solid circles and rings of trees (*Circles of Life* [1986], *Circles of Time* [1987]); Mel Chin planted trees and plants on a landfill site in St Paul, MN (*Revival Field*); Joseph Beuys led the planting of oak trees at Documenta 7 in Kassel in 1982; Andy Lipkis planted trees in urban areas (such as L.A.), and organized fund-raising marathon runs for trees (1979); Andy Goldsworthy has planted dwarf oak saplings in the Holocaust memorial in New York; Giuseppe Penone placed a long white crystal in tree trunks (*Light Traps*, 1994); Vito Acconci constructed a tower of trees (1996), one above the other, all of them upside-down; Robert Irwin installed nine plum trees in Seattle, WA (1983), separated by blue screens; and Buster Simpson planted willow trees in drinking fountains (1993).

Daniel Buren constructed one of the most compelling of all treeworks: an olive tree standing atop a huge cube of soil in a gallery (*Untitled*, 1999), a truly spectacular (and enigmatic) work, with the tree and earth in proportion, quietly dominating an ornate room at Castello di Rivoli.

HOLES

Many land artists have dug holes, cracks, caverns, tunnels and underground labyrinths in the Earth. Maybe there's more to this than just the æsthetic dimension of creating new spaces. Andy Goldsworthy, for instance, has an anxious, ambivalent attitude towards holes in the ground which recall the views of (usually male) philosophers on the negativity of holes and voids, which are associated with the sexual identity of women. These fears and ambiguities are found in much of Western culture: in Sigmund Freud's castration myth; and in the belligerent, misogynist theology of St Augustine, Tertullian, St Paul and Origen. In this view, women are vampires and loathed witches, sucking up masculine desire and energy. Another religious view sees women as Mother Goddesses, identified with nature, the seasons, vegetation and the powers of the Earth. One deity which some feminists and British poets (such as Robert Graves and Peter Redgrove) have worshipped (though they would not use that term) is the 'Black Goddess', a divinity of darkness, night, the unknown and the supernatural.

STONE CIRCLES: LAND ART AND PREHISTORIC ART

The circle motif, one of the primæval symbols of eternity, cycles, time, rebirth, and so on, is employed throughout much of land art. Circles in land art are made from slate, timber, snow or by walking in a circle; they seem to be gentler, more eco-friendly kinds of sculpture. The circle shape itself speaks of organic forms, and, in some religions, evokes the feminine and the Goddess. Not a few sculptors and land artists have made the circle crucial to their works: Alison Wilding, Richard Deacon, Stephen Cox, Mary Miss, Anish Kapoor, Peter Randall-Page, Robert Morris and Dennis Oppenheim.

Land art based on circles includes Vijali's *World Wheel* (1987), Alan Sonfist's *Circles of Life* (1987) and *Pool of Virgin Earth* (1975), Adam Purple's *The Garden of Eden* (1975), Charles Jencks' *Snail Mound* (1992-94), Michael Heizer's *Circular Surface Planar Displacement Drawing* (1970), Stan Herd's *The Circle* (1992), and Mel Chin's *Revival Field* (1993). Many of Nancy Holt's works are circular: *Annual Ring* (1981), *30 Below* (1980), and *Sun Tunnels* (1976).

Donald Judd produced two circular steel bands, 180 inches in diameter, as well as a concrete circular 'wall'. Robert Morris made gigantic circular works, such as his *Observatory* (1971), which was a huge earthwork recalling the megalithic structures of ancient times, such as Avebury stone circle. His *Labyrinth* (1974) was a maze-size sculpture, the kind of maze one finds in theme parks and country houses, except that Morris' *Labyrinth* used the ancient pattern of the Cretan labyrinth, itself a motif some see as distinctly feminine, speaking of Goddess mysteries. Herbert Bayer's *Mill Creek Canyon Earthworks* (1979-82), was a series of earthworks recalling ancient monuments. Robert Smithson's *Closed Mirror Square* was like an Aztec ziggurat, while his *Amarillo Ramp* recalled the massive embankments found at Neolithic earthworks in the British Isles such as Maiden Castle, or Iron Age hill forts such as British Camp on the Malvern Hills.[1]

Some artists have produced stone circles which look very much like Stonehenge, such as Nancy Holt's monumental *Stone Enclosure: Rock Rings* or Alan Wood's *Ranchenge* (1983), a wooden Mid-West American version of Stonehenge. Vida Freeman's *Installation* (1981) in an L.A. gallery comprised white porcelain and stoneware stones with white pillars emerging from them. Michelle Stuart constructed cairns and circles in *Stone Alignments/ Solstice Cairns* (1979). Margaret Hicks fashioned three concentric circles from oak and sandstone in Texas (*Hicks Mandala*, 1975), intended for a 'Ritual of Giving'. David Harding cast his *Henge* (1972) from nine foot tall slabs of concrete, while Donna Myars' *Dream*

Stones (1979) were cast and carved from cement. Michael McCafferty built his *Stone Circles* (1977) on a beach in Oregon, where they were flooded at high tide. Marlene Creates' interventions on prehistoric earthworks included laying rows of paper over them (*Paper Over the Turlough Hill Cairn*, 1981).

The spiral and snake employed by so many land artists down the ages (in ancient Peru, or on the doors of Neolithic tombs, or in the Mid-West of America) is associated with Goddess cults and with the energies of life. The circles and spirals of David Nash, Dennis Oppenheim and Robert Smithson are also those of the Goddess, the ancient Earth Mother. In the eco-neo-pagan view, the land artists, then, make marks upon Mother Earth, upon the surface or skin of the Goddess. Andy Goldsworthy inadvertently evoked phallic penetration when he said: 'I want to get under the surface... At its most successful, my 'touch' looks into the heart of nature' (WH).

Land artists, then, penetrate or cut into nature. The Earth, which is regarded as female in this particular religious/pagan worldview, is penetrated – by Michael Heizer gouging vast chunks out of the American desert, by Walter de Maria thrusting a kilometre-long brass rod into the Earth, and Andy Goldsworthy, seemingly so gentle, has cut trenches into the earth, or smashed slabs of slate or pebbles or leaves, to make lines of broken, shattered material on the earth. He has torn leaves apart to form a line, and has fractured pebbles, making a line, like a fault line in continental structures (*Leaves Torn in Two*, 1986, *Broken Pebbles*, 1987). These are violent gestures, destroying the organic make-up of the natural forms he so adores. All land artists – all artists – must break up and reform materials.

Land artists often use circular forms, which hides the aggression of their gestures. The spiral or circle is a kind, organic, even gentle shape, seemingly in tune with earth energies. Circular structures (igloos, huts, stone circles, tombs, earthworks, pools) seem to be in harmony with nature, echoing the circle shapes of the planet itself, or suns, eyes, blood cells, orbits. The circular structures suggest primitive, archaic, more 'authentic' ethics, the 'back to nature' syndrome. There is, then, not only a mystical side to land art, to David Nash, Robert Smithson, Dennis Oppenheim, Hermann de Vries and Herbert Bayer, but also a nostalgic element (nostalgia is a key element in any religion). Looking *back* to the land, land artists also look *back* to a former, even ancient era which was, patently, better (to a golden age which is and was imaginary, which never existed). This is the hidden subtext in the writings of the land artists, this nostalgia for the better times of archaic cultures, when people lived 'in harmony' with the earth. This is, of course, a widespread nostalgia, not backed up by the evidence, which is that for ancient and prehistoric peoples life was as hard, if not harder, than it is now.

Many land artists have made mounds which recall prehistoric burial mounds (apart from the ones cited above) including Charles Jencks (*Snail Mound*, 1992-94), Judy Varga's *Geometry of Echoes Converge* (1980), Maya Lin's *Wave Field* (1995), Peter Walker's *Turf Mountain* (1993) and James Pierce (*Burial Mound*). These (Minimal) sculptures are ambivalently related to ancient monuments, however, as Samuel Wagstaff remarked of Tony Smith's works:

> They are related to early cultures intentionally or through sympathy – menhirs, earth mounds, cairns… [and] to this culture with equal sympathy – smokestacks, gas tanks, dump trucks, poured concrete ramps.[2]

Land artists, then, consciously or slyly invoke ancient, prehistoric monuments. Michael Heizer, Robert Smithson, Anthony Gormley, Robert Morris and Nancy Holt make references to ancient earthworks. Gormley likened the *Angel of the North* site to a burial mound. (What separated Hans Haacke's earth mound from gardening? My *intent*, Haacke replied.) The famous *Serpent Mound* in Adams County, Ohio, dating from the 10th century AD, is an obvious ancestor of Andy Goldsworthy's *Lambton Earthwork* and landscaped art by Michael Heizer, Herbert Bayer, Robert Morris and others.

Some land artists work in megalith-rich landscapes (such as Richard Long in the South-West of Britain). There are over nine hundred stone circles in the British Isles. Long too makes connections with prehistoric art in terms of manufacture: the cave paintings at Lascaux, Long said, were made by people's hands on the rock. Long has made references to some of the key sacred/ religious/ prehistoric sites of Britain: to Silbury Hill, the largest humanmade mound in Europe, so the guidebooks say; to the ithyphallic Cerne Giant in Dorset; to Glastonbury Tor, mecca for hippies, occultists and 'New Age' travellers; to Windmill Hill, and so on. Long even put a picture of himself with a backpack in Africa right next to one of the famous ancient hill figures of England, the 'Long Man of Wilmington', 231 feet tall, in Sussex. This is one of those prehistoric sites that some see as being an alien, or St Paul, or a Roman emperor, or King Harold. Long ironically compared himself with another 'Long' Man.[3]

Locations such as Great Serpent Mound, Ohio or Mesa Verde (an Anasazi site) in the U.S.A., or Silbury Hill and Glastonbury in Albion, have long been revered by people as holy sites, 'places of power' as they are called. Land artists capitalize on the mystery of such places. One of Richard Long's works is a walk between two prime magical centres of Britain, Stonehenge and Glastonbury, both deeply associated with prehistoric astronomy, ancient priesthoods, Arthurian legend, Merlin the Magician, the Age of Aquarius, ley lines, Druids, geomancy, and so on:

ON MIDSUMMER'S DAY
A WESTWARD WALK
FROM STONEHENGE AT SUNRISE
TO GLASTONBURY BY SUNSET
FORTY FIVE MILES FOLLOWING THE DAY[4]

The photograph that goes with this text is the sort of picture postcard view one finds in newsagents and heritage centres around Great Britain: Glastonbury Tor at sunset. Like St Paul's, the Tower of London, Big Ben, Buckingham Palace, Beefeaters, the changing of the guard, red buses and telephone boxes, this is one of the archetypal images of Britain. And, typically, it is Glastonbury Tor that Richard Long chooses to photograph, not the stores nearby, the electricity cables and poles, the junk yard behind the highways, the rows of garages, and the housing estates.

Land artists' stone circles often recall prehistoric stone circles. While they may deny it verbally, Nancy Holt's *Stone Enclosure*, Robert Morris's *Observatory* and Richard Long's circle sculptures evoke famous sacred sites in Europe such as Delphi or Carnac, or the great circles of Britain: the Rollright Stones in Oxfordshire, Boscawen-Ûn and the Merry Maidens in West Penwith, Cornwall, Castlerigg in Cumberland, Stanton Drew in Somerset (a huge and little-known set of circles, and the nearest large circle to Richard Long's home in Bristol), and of course the mother of all stone circles, Avebury.

Some land artists, such as Richard Long, maintain that their stone rings are subjective, private, individual works, quite different from the public, social art of the prehistoric stones circles. The ancient stone rings were made by a group of people, a society, constructed, perhaps, according to the plans of a priestly élite. Land art circles are (usually) the work of one person, but a major contemporary artist is no less a member of the cultural, æsthetic élite. Prehistoric stone circles may have been made for religious rituals, perhaps connected with the position of certain astronomical bodies or celestial alignments. The circles in stone, snow, dandelions, trees and concrete of land art are made for private consumption, for the artist alone, or for an onlooker who wanders into a gallery or a space then out again, back into the chaos of the city. Yet the ancient sacred sites and land art/ Postminimal earthworks have much in common, because art and religion join at so many points.

Land artists benefit from the allusions to ancient monuments, because the atmosphere and magic of prehistoric stones rubs off on their own work. In stressing the importance of megaliths, the land artists not-so-subtly imply a continuity between themselves and these prehistoric relics. The æsthetic continuity that's emphasized also implies religious affinities. Thus, the land artist is the contemporary equivalent of the priests and hieratic sects who created Stonehenge, the lines in Peru, the Pyramids, and Australian aborigine 'songlines'. A spirituality is affirmed in land art, which only a few land artists actually speak about. But this religious feeling is definitely there, definitely a part of the discourse of Michael Heizer, Turrell, Robert Smithson, Hamish Fulton, Robert Morris and Nancy Holt.

MAZES

Mazes and labyrinths are favourite land art forms. Robert Smithson, Richard Fleischner and Alice Aycock created large earthwork mazes in the late 1960s/ early 1970s. Andy Goldsworthy designed a maze (at Burham in 1988), and an earthwork which was a curving ramp, exactly like Robert Smithson's *Armarillo Ramp*, though on a much smaller scale. Richard Fleischner created a *Sod Maze* in 1974, in the turf at Newport, Rhode Island, an enormous *Zig Zag* (1972) in grass (370 feet long) and a *Chain-Link Maze* (1978), 61 feet square. Michelangelo Pistoletto built an interior maze from large pieces of corrugated cardboard laid out across the whole gallery (*Labyrinth,* 1991). In *Monumental Ikebana* (1990), Hiroshi Teshigahara made a giant arched path from bamboo in a gallery space. For Vong Phaephanit's bamboo installation (*What Falls to the Ground Cannot Be Eaten*, 1991), a forest of bamboo sticks was hung from the ceiling of a London gallery, approached through a monumental black doorway.

The mazes of land artists can be seen as a part of the resurgence of interest in mazes which occurred in the 1980s (aligned, as ever, with green/ ecological/ occult/ New Age trends). Mazes were commissioned for country houses, zoos and theme parks. A maze became seen as one more feature for visitors to enjoy: apart from the country mansion or palace or museum interior and formal gardens, the public could visit a maze, and perhaps an adventure playground. Some mazes were set beside children's play areas, emphasizing the sense of play, rather than ritual. At country houses in Great Britain, such as Ragley Hall in Staffordshire, the maze was part of the adventure play area, and was conceived as something of a gym or assault course: there were walkways and bridges over some of the passages in the brick maze, which were climbed via ropes and ladders. Probably the most famous maze in Britain is at Hampton Court.

LAND ART AND CONSTANTIN BRANCUSI

It was Constantin Brancusi's project to strip away the detritus that had accumulated around sculpture, Henry Moore said, and to offer the pure, simple shape. What Brancusi did was 'to concentrate on very simple shapes, to keep his sculpture, as it were, one-cylindered, to refine and polish a single shape to a degree almost too precious.'[1] This is what many contemporary sculptors have done, keeping their shapes simple and purified: Andy Goldsworthy, Alison Wilding, Richard Deacon, Stephen Cox, David Nash, Richard Serra, Donald Judd and Robert Smithson.

Quite a few artists (not all of them sculptors) have expressed admiration for Constantin Brancusi's photographs, the way he would set up his sculptures in his studio and photograph them at particular times of day, when the lighting was just right. Andy Goldsworthy said he admired how Brancusi created the conditions in his studio so that his work 'comes alive at a particular time of day as the light momentarily touches it'.[2] For Andy Goldsworthy, Brancusi's works were at their best when they were arranged by the sculptor in his studio and photographed.[3] Somehow, it wasn't quite the same when they were displayed in modern art museums (such as the Pompidou Centre in Paris or the Museum of Modern Art in Gotham). The Brancusian ethics, of simplicity, purity, smoothness, interiority and organic form are found in the Minimal sculptors, as well as the Constructivist notion of working with materials in a 'natural' way, so that the material dictates the form one creates with it.

LIGHT AND SPACE

Light: one recalls the reported dying words of Romantic artists like Johann Wolfgang von Goethe, who called for 'more light!', or J.M.W. Turner, who said 'the sun is god'. Numerous sculptors, installation artists and land artists have worked with light and lighting: Douglas Wheeler, Hap Tivey, Susan Kaiser Vogel, Larry Bell, James Turrell with his 'sky-spaces', Robert Irwin's reworked gallery spaces, Dan Flavin and his fluorescent tubes, Bruce Nauman, who made very narrow corridors lit by green fluorescents, Maria Nordman's extensions to studio exteriors, Nancy Holt's *Sun Tunnels*, Eric Orr's sound and light environments and DeWain Valentine's acrylic tubes hanging alone from gallery ceilings.

Eric Orr (1939-98) constructed a *Silence and the Ion Wind* installation (1980), a series of dark rooms culminating in the *Golden Room*, 'an allusive structure for an elusive experience', approached through an ion wind.[1] In *Wall Shadow, Sky Lights, Sound Tunnel, Zero Mass, Sunrise, Blood Shadow, The Stone Snake, Prime Matter* and *Blue Void*, Orr deployed sound, light, wind, sand, ice and shadow. In *Prime Matter* (1981), Orr created fog and flames from a twenty foot tall metal column (a larger version was constructed outside the Mitsui Fudosan Building in L.A. in 1991). Orr has fired xenon lasers up into the sky on top of skyscrapers in Long Beach, CA (a permanent installation, *Landmark Lumière*, 1991).

Many artists have taken gallery spaces and reworked them, adding walls or scrims, or curtains, or false ceilings, or doorways, or new windows. Often these light and sound spaces look like empty gallery rooms: Eric Orr (*Light Space*, 1985), Hap Tivey's *Sodium Exchange* (1976), Susan Kaiser Vogel's *Point Conception* (1980), DeWain Valentine's *Curved Wall Spectrum* (1974), Larry Bell's *Leaning Room II* (1988), Bruce Nauman's *Yellow Triangular Room* (1973), Douglas Wheeler's *All Gray Graduating Light* (1976), Maria Nordman's *6/ 21/ 79 One Day Only* (1979), James Turrell's *Second Meeting* (1988), and Robert Irwin's Kansas *Installation* (1979). The forerunners of these light spaces includes Yves Klein's *Le Vide*. Some artists made the reconstituted gallery interior one of their trademarks.

3

The Birth of Land Art in 1960s Culture

THE PRESENCE OF THE OBJECT: LAND ART, MINIMAL ART AND 'OBJECTHOOD'

One can see the body written into, say, Andy Goldsworthy's delicate leaf sculptures, or Constantin Brancusi's extraordinary egg shapes, but not, perhaps, in the giganticism of Michael Heizer's *Double Negative*. Yet, even here, the human body is present – if only by the way it is violently dwarfed by the scale of Heizer's earthwork. Much of land art is vast. As Carl Andre said:

> I once described the change in sculpture in the 20th century as moving in its concerns from form to structure and now having a concern with place... I believe now you can make sculpture you can enter.[1]

In 1970, Michael Heizer said that the old kind of sculpture had been replaced – 'destroyed, subverted, put down' (170). Kazuo Shiraga made works of art with his body, such as smearing mud on pieces of paper with his feet. His body-art was called 'the art of committing the whole self with the body'.[2] Minimal sculptures are not set on pedestals, like Renaissance or Greek sculpture; they sit on the floor, or lean against walls (as in Robert Morris's *Floor Piece*, or Carl Andre's *Cedar Piece*, 1959). The new sculptural space must have 'three, not two coordinates', said Morris. 'The ground plane, not the wall, is the necessary support for the maximum awareness of the object'.[3] Minimal sculptures exist in the same space, on the same plane (the floor) as the viewer. They are, as Morris said, in an in-between cultural space, somewhere between being monuments and being ornaments, between being architecture and jewellery.[4]

MINIMAL ART, POSTMINIMAL ART AND LAND ART

The world of Minimal art was clean, calm, devoid of unruliness, violence, even ambiguity. Something like an airport: white, spotless, spacious. Or a new shopping mall. A row of pristine supermarket shelves, stacked high with new cans of fruit, the labels all turned face-out. Minimal art was an art for the 1960s, an era of commodification of a global scale, and the increasing affluence in the West after the austerity of the 1950s, where mass production created a uniformity to the appearances of so much of street, home, personal, medical, transport and educational furniture (especially in Europe and America). Minimal sculpture, Barbara Rose remarked, looks 'machine-made, industrial, standardized, materialized or stamped out as a whole'.[1]

Many land artworks appear to be 'simple', in that there doesn't seem to be much going on. But, as Donald Judd wrote in his influential "Specific Objects":

> it isn't necessary for a work to have a lot of things to look at, to compare, to analyze one by one, to contemplate. The thing as a whole, its qualities as a whole, is what is interesting.[2]

Some artists make a virtue of simplicity and ease: Jan Dibbets said he liked projects that anyone could do. For example, he chose four sites at random on a Netherlands map and went to each place and took a photo. It was '[q]uite stupid.

Anybody can do that', Dibbets admitted (1970). But Dibbets said he enjoyed searching for the places and photographing what was there. It was also silly for people to buy such works: 'it's stupid for other people to do it, or to buy it from me. What matters is the feeling'. And the feeling of the artist was something that couldn't be bought.

LAND ART AND CONCEPTUAL ART

Land art is related to Conceptual art, and is a part of Conceptual art. Much of land art exists only in photographs, memories, words, and texts which are not the land art itself. Works that can be seen and those that are hidden or 'invisible' can have the same importance for the artist. One of the hallmarks of the 'ideal Conceptual work', as Mel Bochner said in 1974, is 'an exact linguistic correlative, that is, it could be described and experienced in its data and it could be infinitely repeatable'.[1] Land art is often Conceptual art: Dennis Oppenheim's *Whirlpool Eye of Storm* (a jet trail in the sky), Hans Haacke's balloons floating over Central Park and Robert Morris's steam pieces exist now only as photographs, memories and criticism.

By contrast, James Turrell wanted to place the viewer right in the midst of his artworks, so they could experience directly the subject of his art (light, the sky, celestial events) for themselves. It was important for Turrell that his art wasn't a record or a photograph of something that happened elsewhere, that the viewer hadn't seen or couldn't see for themselves. Thus, at Roden Crater, Turrell constructed spaces that the spectator could enter physically, to experience light and the sky directly.

The pictorial or visual aspect of land art was overemphasized by critics and viewers, Dennis Oppenheim argued in 1992. It was 'basically the *idea* of earthworks, the idea of the salt flats' that was important, not the visual element; '[t]he visual quotient is not as strenuous as you think'. Many land artworks were conceptual, mental, not visual or even physical. 'In other words,' said Dennis Oppenheim, talking about Robert Smithson's *Spiral Jetty*, 'it's about the salt, submersions, the jetty, what is around the salt flats. In the end it's about mental configurations' (1992). This presents a problem, because most land artworks are known primarily in a visual form – in photographs. It'd be great if land artworks were visited or directly experienced, as Oppenheim and others intended, but they aren't. For Richard Serra, the 'focus of art for me is the experience of living through the pieces', but the actual work itself, the physical object, was not the whole point, or the whole pleasure, of making art: 'that experience may have very little to do with the physical facts of the work of art'.[2]

One of the pluses of Conceptual art was that art could be just ideas, and the artist wouldn't have to carry around masses of materials. Dennis Oppenheim wrote:

> In 1968 and 1969 I lived in an apartment. I didn't need a studio. Everything that I had done as an artist was contained in one small case of slides. And it accounted for two of the most strenuous years of work in my whole life.[3]

Many sculptors have spoken of the importance of the *making* of the sculpture, its actual construction, with real (and sometimes organic, living) materials. As Barry Flanagan put it: '[m]y work isn't centred in experience. The making of it is itself the experience'.[4] In some artists, the material employed also has a symbolic or added meaning, as in Joseph Beuys' *Fettecke* or 'fat corner', a sculpture with powerful autobiographical and semiotic associations. Beuys emphasized process, evolution, change: his sculpture, he said, was not

> fixed and finished. Processes continue in most of them: chemical reactions, fermentations, colour changes,

decay, drying up. Everything is in a *state of change*.[5]

Land art is meta-art, art about art, art that relies on other art to 'exist'. Land art exists for a brief moment, then becomes myth, gossip, photography, words (or more often, art criticism and journalism). Many of Richard Long's works are simply collections of words, printed in capitals, in Eric Gill's font, Gill Sans, on large pieces of paper. The text of one of Long's works can be printed here, and this text here will be very close to being a Richard Long artwork in itself (although he likes them printed much larger). Thus:

A MOVED LINE

PICKING UP CARRYING PLACING
ONE THING TO ANOTHER
ALONG A STRAIGHT 22 MILE
WALK

MOSS TO WOOL
WOOL TO ROOT
ROOT TO PEAT
PEAT TO SHEEP'S HORN
SHEEP'S HORN TO STONE
STONE TO LICHEN
LICHEN TO TOADSTOOL
TOADSTOOL TO BONE
BONE TO FEATHER
FEATHER TO STICK
STICK TO JAWBONE
JAWBONE TO STONE
STONE TO FROG
FROG TO WOOL
WOOL TO BONE
BONE TO BIRD PELLET
BIRD PELLET TO STONE

> STONE TO SHEEPS' HORN
> SHEEP'S HORN TO PINE CONE
> PINE CONE TO BARK
> BARK TO BEECH NUT
> BEECH NUT TO STONE
> STONE TO THE END OF THE
> WALK
>
> DARTMOOR 1983

That's a Richard Long artwork, and a real piece of land art. It seems as if Long has nothing much to 'say'. Well, he is a sculptor, so he wouldn't be so good at writing or speaking. Wrong. He's a land artist (though he dislikes the term 'land art' — artists often don't like being categorized this way or that), and land artists are always much concerned with writing and written texts. A Richard Long exhibition, for instance, features written texts on display, and photographs, as well as installation works and sculptures.

The texts of land artists also draw on poetry, on concrete or 'visual poetry', or typewriter art. Richard Long, for instance, prints his laconic texts in circles (*Full Moon Circle of Ground*, Dartmoor, 1983), in concentric circles (*Three Moors, Three Circles*, Liskeard to Porlock, 1982), in vertical lines, as in trendy style magazines (*The Isle of Wight as Six Walks*, 1982), and in curved swathes of text (*A Moved Line in Japan*, 1983).

Sixties Conceptual artist Lawrence Weiner produced text works, capital letters on a wall or in a book (Richard Long, Barbara Kruger, the Art & Language group and Michael Craig-Martin have also created post-Conceptual wall works). Weiner's solution to making sculpture was that a sculpture on a plinth has to be 'translated' into language, so that people can understand it. Sculpture is language, and words are language, therefore, Weiner reckons, words can be sculpture:

> when you see a piece of wood lying on the ground with a piece of stone on top of it, you must translate that in your

> own head into language. What I try to do is present
> language itself as a key to what sculpture is about... It is
> a presentation of a piece of sculpture in language.[6]

Like John Baldessari and Sophie Calle, Lawrence Weiner fashions capital letters in short phrases which are about a viewer's relationship with an object. The words are a means or the expression of a relationship with something.

BILLOWING CLOUDS OF FERROUS OXIDE
SETTING APART A CORNER ON THE BOTTOM OF THE SEA

This is a typical Lawrence Weiner artwork.[7] Here's another:

THINGS PUSHED DOWN TO THE BOTTOM AND
PUSHED UP AGAIN

Richard Long commented that '[t]he discovery [Weiner] made that art does not necessarily have to be made, that was a great breakthrough'.[8] Lawrence Weiner is right, of course: words alone can be sculpture, for poets have long known that language is an *experience*, not simply abstractions or concepts. Language really does affect people – otherwise why would they spend so much time consuming language? That is, they consume 25-40 hours of broadcasting per week (in the West – that's over a day and a half spent consuming television and radio per week. So the words on a gallery wall of Lawrence Weiner, Sophie Calle, John Baldessari, Hans Haacke and Hamish Fulton don't seem at first to be 'art'. They are not sensual and graspable in the physical realm, like a marble statue. Yet those words, whether photocopied on cheap paper or printed in high quality typography on deluxe paper, or painted onto the wall, are 'art', they are communication, language – even sculpture.

Laid over Richard Long's walks is the grid of the map: the maps in Conceptual art constitute a new landscape of the soul, as Robert Smithson wrote in 1968:

> A cartography of uninhabitable places seems to be developing – complete with decoy diagrams, abstract grid systems made of stone and tape (Carl Andre and Sol LeWitt), and electronic "mosaic" photomaps from NASA. (1968, 26)

Just about every land artist used maps in their work. Not just in the obvious sense of mapping (and finding) future sites for artworks, but as key elements in the artworks themselves. Jan Dibbets chose places on a map at random, visited them and took a photograph. Dennis Oppenheim made maps a central ingredient in his 2-D Conceptual works, which combined maps, text, photos and sketches. Richard Long based many walks around maps, such as in a circle on a map, or a straight line. Chris Drury cut up and wove maps together (a development of his love of basket-weaving). Robert Smithson made many mapworks, including map games, folded maps, aerial maps, and cut-up circular maps (*Untitled Circular Map*, c. 1968-70, and *Entropic Pole*, 1967). Tom Van Sant collaged satellite maps. John Baldessari spelt out 'California' using maps in *The California Map Project* (1969). Charles Ross made star maps (1975-86). Jasper Johns painted a large map collage painting (1966-71). Nancy Holt buried poems (written for Carl Andre, John Perrault, Robert Smithson, Michael Heizer and Philip Leider) in remote locations, with a map marking the burial site (1969-71).

4

Land Art, Gender, Sexuality and the Body

GENDER AND SCALE IN LAND ART

> *The awareness of scale is a function of the comparison made between that constant, one's body size, and the object. Space between the subject and the object is implied in such a comparison.*
>
> Robert Morris (1966, 21)

Contemporary artists, of all kinds, have made massive art. David Smith's *Wagon I* (1963-64, National Gallery of Scotland) and his *Cubi* sculptures are huge, heavy, chunky, truly colossal pieces which dominate their surroundings. Donald Judd wrote: '[t]his scale is one of the most important developments in twentieth century art' (1975, 200f). One of the largest earthwork projects is James Turrell's *Roden Crater Project,* a series of tunnels and chambers in an Arizonan extinct volcano, begun in 1974 and funded by the DIA Foundation. Turrell said:

> My art is made for one person. I like the solitary experience. Standing alone at night, perceiving the Roden Crater and the moon and stars, you really feel the vastness of the universe and yourself entering into it.[1]

'In sculpture, there's quite a concrete relationship between one's size as a person and/or mass as a person and the mass of a piece of sculpture', remarked Carl Andre (1970, 57). Richard Long's art is not monolithic in scale, usually: but his works can stretch over many miles, far longer than even Christo's fences. Artists such as Christo made pieces that were 24 miles long. Even medium-sized pieces, such as Donald Judd's wooden boxes, are sometimes seen as monumental. A critic in the *New York Times* called Judd's 1977 installation at the Heiner Friedrich Gallery a 'majestic and finely measured presence'.[2]

Lucy Lippard described scale not just as something mathematical, optical, *seen*:

> Most discussions of scale consider it a strictly optical experience ...But a sense of scale is also a *sense* proper. Scale is *felt* and cannot be communicated either by photographic reproduction or by description.[3]

The bombastic, 'monumental', massive and brash 3-D art of modern sculpture was not made exclusively by male artists. Land artists Mary Miss, Nancy Holt, Sherry Wiggins, Donna Henes, Lynne Hull, Patricia Johanson, Alice Aycock and Agnes Denes have all created very large works. Other female architectural sculptors included Jackie Ferrara, Donna Dennis and Elyn Zimmerman. For feminist critics, these women artists were drawn to shelter imagery: the origins of 'shelter sculpture', as Lucy Lippard called it in a 1979 article ("Complexities: Architectural Sculpture in Nature"), were in female biology and the female body.[4]

Mary Miss created a 5 acre scale work in Illinois,[5] Patricia Johanson designed a large lagoon park in Dallas (1981-86), while Nancy Holt produced gigantic *Sun Tunnels*, 18 feet long pipes that were 9 feet high with many holes punched in the side, to let light in.[6]

Helen Escobedo created some huge concrete and steel sculptures which 'attempt to fuse hard-edge geometric forms with nature's organic manifestations', as she put it. Works such as *Snake* (1980-81) rise impressively from the Earth, celebrating the flux and movement of organic forms. Beverly Pepper's *Sand Dunes* (1985), big, curving mirrored slabs of wood buried in sandy beaches, might be seen as a type of 'Earth Mother art', art which worships and works with the Earth, rather than, as in some of male land art, cutting or penetrating it (like Michael Heizer, Robert Smithson and Walter de Maria).

Many of the celebrated products of contemporary sculpture, however, have been made by male artists: Donald Judd's 'specific objects', blocks of aluminium and plexiglass that 'climb' gallery walls;[7] Tony Smith's monumental cubes with their *thereness* (celebrating the primacy of presence, not effect);[8] Dan Flavin's mesmeric fluorescent tubes, a sculpture of light and space;[9] Sol LeWitt's Conceptual cubes and wall drawings like enormous graphs; Richard Serra's huge 'walls' or slabs of steel leaning together;[10] and Carl Andre's plates of steel, copper and zinc laid on the floor.[11]

One of the most exciting developments of contemporary sculpture and art is the installation, the taking-over of a whole space or environment – the floor, walls and ceiling of a gallery, as in Rebecca Horn's *Ballet of the Woodpecker* (1986-87), a room full of mirrors, or Sylvia Stone's *Crystal Palace*. Many land artists' works are clearly related to the art installation: it is an art of environments, where the relatively small addition of a stack of stones forming a cairn sets alive the surrounding landscape. One sees the landscape in a new way: context is all-important.

LAND ART, SEXUALITY AND THE BODY

Much of sculpture in the modern era has been thoroughly traditional (conservative), and patriarchal, in its orientation and expression. Take Henry Moore, one of the most celebrated of Western sculptors, and one of the big names of modern British art. Moore's nudes, though, are no different from the conventional female nude, found in so much of high art from the Renaissance onwards. Moore's polished wood surfaces, so softly rounded and enigmatic, seem so enchanting. But, despite his formal innovation, Moore is as sexist and reactionary a sculptor as Francis Bacon is as a painter.

But when sexuality and gender is addressed, contemporary (male) sculptors have rarely been ironic. Usually, the norms and dualities of male/ female, active/ passive, culture/ nature, good/ evil are exalted. The great or celebrated names in contemporary sculpture – Alberto Giacometti, Henry Moore, David Smith, David Hare, Eduardo Chillida, Pablo Picasso, Isamu Noguchi, Claes Oldenberug, Mark Di Suvero, Jean Tinguely – rarely tackled notions of sexuality in major works of sculpture, or in a questioning manner. When Picasso incorporated gender issues or eroticism, it was invariably heterosexist, as in his *Bust* (1932, estate of the artist), with its gigantic breasts, echoing the "Stone Venuses" of yore. The great works of contemporary sculpture – David Smith's *Cubi XXVII* (1965, Guggenheim Museum, New York), Claes Oldenburg's soft sculptures and giant blow-ups of everyday objects, Alexander Calder's mobiles, Richard Serra's chunks of metal, John Chamberlain's squashed cars (1961, Art Institute, Chicago) – seem to eschew issues of sexuality and gender. Not much of mainstream or 'malestream' contemporary sculpture concerns itself with eroticism without pain or violence, and hardly ever feminism.

The body features occasionally in the art of Andy Goldsworthy in a direct manner. One sees the shape of Goldsworthy's body after a snowfall or rainfall (his *Rain Shadows*), or 'printed' onto frosty ground by his shadow at sunrise. Goldsworthy sometimes appears in photographs, beside his work. Goldsworthy's hands are seen, and other parts of the sculptor, but there is nothing in Goldsworthy's work (or that of Hamish Fulton, Richard Deacon, Stephen Cox or Barry Flanagan) that is as ferocious as feminist and women's body and performance art.

WOMEN SCULPTORS AND LAND ARTISTS

Important contemporary women sculptors include: Nancy Graves, Eva Hesse, Niki de Sant-Phalle, Rebecca Horn and Louise Nevelson, and women land artists such as Mary Miss, Nancy Holt, Sherry Wiggins, Donna Henes, Ana Mendieta, Vijali, Betsy Damon, Phyllis Yampolsky, Jody Pinto, Viet Ngo, Helen Mayer Harrison, Mel Chin, Karen McCoy, Meg Webster, Maya Lin, Martha Schwartz, Dominique Mazeaud, Lynne Hull, Doris Bloom, Patricia Johanson, Constance DeJong, Harriet Feigenbaum, Phyllidia Barlow, Debbie Duffin, Mierle Laderman Ukeles, Gloria Carlos, Agnes Denes and Alice Aycock.[1]

Eva Hesse, who died at the age of 34 in 1970, is especially interesting; her works repay many visits. Hesse was part of the group that included Carl Andre, Robert Ryman, Sol LeWitt and Mel Bochner. She worked in series, like other Process and Minimal artists. She called the repetitions 'sequels' and 'schemas'. Her artworks have an immediate, challenging impact. They hang from ceilings, in rows, made of rubber, latex, cloth, wire and fibreglass, evoking organic forms in ambivalent, sensual ways.[2] Pieces such as *Ingeminate* (1965, Saatchi, London) offer up a mysterious affirmation of life in the form of two coils of cord connected by a long piece of surgical hose. *Sans II* (1968, Saatchi, London), meanwhile, was a dozen rectangular 'compartments' made from fibreglass which hinted at some obscure systematization of flesh and organic form. Hesse wrote: '[i]f I can name the content... it's the total absurdity of life'.[3] As Anna Chave noted, Hesse's forms resemble abstract 'breasts, clitorises, vaginas, fetuses, uteruses, fallopian tubes', articulating a new feminine sexual subjectivity, utilizing the female, not the male gaze.[4]

Sometimes loosely hanging, finding their own form, at other times Eva Hesse's sculptures were bound with wire, as if 'making psychic models', as Robert Smithson said.[5]

One aspect of 'feminist' or 'women's' art was (is) embodied by the figure of the Goddess, the ancient and primæval Great Mother of all, celebrated then – and now – as Isis, Ishtar, Demeter, Kali, and so on. The Goddess embodied aspects of the 'feminine' – love, motherhood, purity, nobility, sacrifice, beauty, hunting, and so on. Since the 1960s, the Goddess has been variously interpreted as fact, experience, idea, æsthetic, cult, religion, pagan emblem and many other things by women artists and writers. There are a host of artists who pursue what one might call 'Goddess art', art that employs the figure of the Goddess as an embodiment of female being or experience: Judy Chicago, Mary Beth Edelson, Miriam Schapiro, Niki de Sant-Phalle, Louis Bourgeois and Helen Chadwick. Edelson engaged in the resurgence of interest in the Goddess in her *Great Goddess* series (1975).

One might see Robert Smithson's spirals and circles as Goddess art, for the circles so clearly evoke Goddess themes such as time, cycles, (Moon) phases, dance, transformation, ritual, initiation, astronomy, and so on. The circle is also a profound shape for alchemists. As the *Rosarium Philosophorum* has it: 'make a round circle and you will have the stone of the philosophers'.[6] Richard Long created, in Ireland, an ancient maze form out of small stones set on grass (*Connemara Sculpture*, 1971), and Robert Morris has also made a labyrinth (*Labyrinth*, 1974). The shape of Long's and Morris's labyrinths directly recall the Cretan labyrinth of initiation and ritual, and the spirals at the entrance to

Newgrange in Co. Meath (Eire), a huge passage grave some 4,500 years old.

Herman de Vries created a circular walled *Sanctuarium* (1997) in Westfalen, Germany. Alan Sonfist planted a maze from oak trees at TICKON in 1993. In Dennis Oppenheim's *Maze* (1970), cattle are lab rats running after corn in a field. Dan Graham combined hedges and mirrors in his *Two-Way Mirror Hedge Labyrinth* (1989). Chris Drury has made circular mazes (some of which are reworked dew ponds). Drury also carved a maze from snow on a Sussex hill (1999). Bill Vazan has fashioned a number of earthworks on the ground, including a *Stone Maze* (1975-76, reminiscent of Richard Long's Connemara labyrinth) and Richard Fleischner, Michelangelo Pistoletto, Hiroshi Teshigahara, and Vong Phaephanit have also created maze structures (Fleischner built a maze from turf in 1974 and one from a chain link fence in 1978). A number of (land) artists have made miniature labyrinths – maze models: Charles Simonds, Terry Fox and Patrick Ireland. Andy Goldsworthy has drawn lines on sand, or stitched grass stalks pinned together, in swirling, spiralling shapes which echo the primæval forms of the snake, the spiral and the labyrinth.

5

Land Art and Religion

It's no surprise that the American form of land art should be sympathetic to Oriental mysticism, because Zen Buddhism and Taoism were particularly prevalent in Sixties culture (in Jack Kerouac, Allen Ginsberg, the 'Beats' and the 'dharma bums', for example). It was a natural development, it seems, from Parisian Existentialism to Californian Zen Buddhism. Many of the chief precepts of Taoism and Zen Buddhism chime with those of land art, not only the American earthworks, but also the land art of Richard Long, Wolfgang Laib, David Nash and others. Matsuo Basho, an important Oriental poet, wrote:

> Go to the pine if you want to learn about the pine, or to the bamboo if you want to learn about the bamboo. And in doing so, you must leave your subjective preoccupation with yourself.[1]

And Makoto Ueda glossed Matsuo Basho thus: 'for learn means to enter into the object, perceive its delicate life and feel its feelings.'[2] These notions of searching for the 'essence' are absolutely in tune with the æsthetics of Constantin Brancusi, Carl Andre, Richard Long and Donald Judd. Andy Goldsworthy spoke in exactly the same terms of trying to find the 'essence' of nature, of going out into the natural world in order to learn about it. Goldsworthy followed Basho's Taoist precepts to the letter. Minimal art pursued the oft-used tenet that 'less is more', a radical reductionism and simplification. Or as Carl Andre put it, ''minimal' means to me only the greatest economy in attaining the greatest ends'.³ Michael Heizer confessed he preferred to see art more as a religion than a recreational activity: 'if you consider art as activity then it becomes like recreation. I guess I'd like to see art become more of a religion'.⁴

The relation between land art and Oriental mysticism, in particular, Taoism and Zen Buddhism, has been noted by many commentators. Zen and Taoism, for instance, speak of *(1)* the 'here and now', *(2)* spontaneity, *(3) satori* or enlightenment, *(4)* intuition, *(5)* nature, *(6)* emptiness/ void, *(7)* change, *(8)* meditation, *(9)* cosmic unity – all these qualities can be applied to land art, and are sometimes elucidated by land artists.

(1) For example, the Zen Buddhist notion of the 'eternal now' or 'now-streaming' (*nunc fluens*) as Alan Watts called it. Zen philosophy makes the present moment primary, the only true reality, and land artists too work in the present. Sculptors continually evoke the transient nature of sculpture: Hans Haacke's fog pieces; Chris Drury's fires; Ana Mendieta's snow and mud body prints; Wolfgang Laib's pollen. Andy Goldsworthy's poppy lines are only there for an instant, then they are blown away by the wind.

(2) Spontaneity: this is as crucial in land art as it is in Zen Buddhism and Taoism. The land artist works with whatever materials are to hand; s/he does not (often) use tools or machines; changes in weather must be accommodated into the artwork.

(3) The experience of viewing land art is not quite Zen Buddhist *satori*, in the strict definition of *satori* or enlightenment, but certainly land artists aim for an 'epiphany', as James Joyce called the æsthetic shock, however brief it may be. In land art as object, there are 'no strings attached', i.e., 'what you see is what you get', as Frank Stella put it. One sees the whole thing there, and that is everything one gets. This instantaneous aspect of land art, as also in contemporary painting, is a Zen-like notion. *Satori*, too, has affinities with the

descriptions of land art/ sculpture that some land artists have given (Robert Morris's objecthood, for example).

(4) Most land artists value <u>intuition</u> highly, as do most poets and artists. The land artist trusts her/ his instincts, and works grow organically. Systems are adhered to, but land artists often veer off into intuitive areas.

(5) <u>Nature</u> dominates Zen Buddhism and Taoism, as it does in land art. One is always encouraged in Taoism and Zen to 'follow one's nature', and to co-operate with the universe. Nature is the teacher in Zen and Taoism, as it is in land art.

(6) Easy to see the lure of the <u>void</u> of religions in land art, in those wildernesses beloved of Michael Heizer, Walter de Maria and Dennis Oppenheim. In the paradoxical bliss of Oriental mysticism, emptiness is also fullness, and to 'have' nothing is to 'have' everything. Zen Buddhism and Taoism thrive on paradox, on the 'not-this-not-that' dialectic of Eastern philosophy, as a way of getting at the unsayableness of the essence. Similarly, Andy Goldsworthy, in a paradoxical manner, speaks of the monumental aspect of sculptures made from leaves: the very small can also be very big, he says.

The imagery of Zen Buddhism and Taoism is also that of land art: stones, mountains, rivers, water, flowers. China has a long tradition of landscape painting, and it is easy to see the many connections between the contemplative aspects of Chinese landscape painting and contemporary land art.

(7) <u>Change</u> is central to land art: all land art occurs within a changing landscape, whether it be the artificial (humanmade) changes in the gallery, or the natural changes of erosion, elements, water, light, season, and so on. Land art thrives on change, and many land artists have deliberately exploited time and change in their works, from Nancy Holt with her *Sun Tunnels*, which change as the sunlight pours through the holes in the concrete tubes, to the transience of Richard Long's *Mountain, Lake, Powder Snow* (1988), which the elements will swiftly erase.

(8) Meditation is clearly not a goal of earth artists – they make no pompous claims concerning mysticism and meditation. Yet, clearly, meditation is a part of their work, as it is a part of all artists' work. Making land art often involves a mild form of meditation. Richard Long's walks, for instance, are meditations of a kind. 'A journey in the wilderness becomes a fantastic focus of concentration. I can get totally absorbed in the place and totally absorbed in my work', Long said.[5] Andy Goldsworthy too speaks of an intense relationship with his subject as he works. The Cornish poet Peter Redgrove said that 'the ideal state for ordinary going about is the first stage of orgasmic arousal'.[6] This is 'walking' in the Taoist sense; that is, walking as another name for feeling ecstatic.

The very activity of walking releases chemicals in the brain that promote pleasure. Joggers get hooked on them sometimes. 'I think the sexual energy or the energy of creativity or the adrenalin energy you get from being on a mountain, sometimes they are all very close', Richard Long remarked.[7] The physical action of walking is soothing.

(9) Land art is close to the cosmic unity of Taoism in its worldview: like Taoists, land artists believe in a holistic view of things, where each part affects the rest. This interconnected worldview (sometimes called 'Gaia-consciousness') is also the philosophy of ecology and the offshoots of the ecological/ green movement: eco-feminism, Goddess religion, animal rights, eco-paganism, direct action, road activism, anti-hunting lobbies, and so on. Art now has a world consciousness, said Isamu Noguchi (1968).

In the Taoist view, inner and outer commingle, the individual and the mass interconnect. Land artists are (usually) very much concerned with ecological issues, and are careful to make sure their artworks do not scar the landscape. There is no trash in their photographs of their artworks. They are ecologically and societally conscientious artists, and thus Andy Goldsworthy has been hailed as the U.K.'s primary ecological artist. Richard Long says, and Goldsworthy would agree with him, that his art is about finding a harmony between the human and the natural world, between the abstractions of humanity and the reality of nature. As Long puts it, his work is 'a balance between the patterns of nature and the formalism of human abstract ideas like lines and circles.'[8]

In *Being and Circumstance*, Robert Irwin proposed four types of land art: 'site dominant', such as monuments and murals; 'site adjusted', in which some considerations are made towards the site, but it's still studio-made; 'site specific', in which steps are taken towards integrating the work into the site; and 'site conditioned', work which responds to its surroundings. The 'site determined' category is the one Irwin preferred: it is also the type of sculpture favoured by many land artists. Irwin defines 'site conditioned' work as an 'intimate, hands-on reading of the site', which results from 'sitting, watching, and walking through the site'; it means being aware of water, weather, sound, surface, movement, history, and so on; such considerations determine whether the response 'should be monumental or ephemeral, aggressive or gentle, useful or useless, sculptural, architectural, or simply the planting of a tree, or maybe even doing nothing at all' (1985).

The land artist orients her/ himself to the four horizons, and to post-Renaissance time. The human level becomes the spiritual centre. The land art of whoever one cares to think of – in the art of David Nash, Peter Erskine, Andy Lipkis, Nancy Holt – puts people, not God or deities, at the centre of the cosmos. Land art, then, can be seen on one level as the reaffirmation of 'home', a re-instatement of the notion of 'homeland'. The 'homeland', though, is not primarily a physical place, but a cultural and spiritual space. Homeland is a state of mind as much as a landscape. Land art may be the manifestation of a spiritual re-orientation. In land art, the 'mythic centre' of one's life is reaffirmed.

Land artists always affirm the 'livingness' of their art, that they *live* their art. Their art, they claim, is not intellectually discussed or made at a critical distance. Rather, the artist is right in the middle of her/ his art, living it. There is no separation of art and life. Land art is a way of mythicizing one's sense of being-in-the-world, a way of making presence visible, tactile, *there*.

Some land artists include autobiographical material in their work. For some land artists, art and life cannot be easily separated (a common philosophy in modern art). One feeds the other, in a symbiotic relationship. One cannot say for certain where some land art ends and the artist's life begins. Land artists like Andy Goldsworthy and Richard Long see art as a continuation of life, where the feelings artists of the past had about nature (for example, J.M.W. Turner and John Constable and the British landscapists) feed on the same source as artists working today (that is, nature itself). Some people made their life their art (or was it the other way around?): Yves Klein, Salvador Dali, Joseph Beuys, Andy Warhol and Carolee Schneemann, among artists, and writers such as Quentin Crisp and Anaïs Nin. Most land artists are not quite larger than life personalities like Anaïs Nin or Quentin Crisp. They often, however, keep a diary, and carefully record the daily progress of their art, and the manufacture of each work. Around each work, then, is an autobiographical residue.

Making land art is a religious activity because simply being in the world is religious. Land art, like all art, replays the primordial myth of Creation: each earthwork or land sculpture re-affirms the Creation. The land artwork, then, remakes the sacred in a profane world: 'the manifestation of the Sacred in any space whatsoever implies for one who believes in the authenticity of this hierophany the presence of transcendent reality', remarked Mircea Eliade.[9] Not only, then, do land artists make sacred spaces, as all artists do, they also create a sense of the 'real', a sense of beingness, a reaffirmation of the transcendent.

For the land artist, most, if not all, of the world is not just potential art material, but beautiful. Land artists, declining to admit to being romantic or emotional, nevertheless create art that is Earth-loving, nature-loving, ecologically-friendly, that is, in short, full of emotion.

Many land artists have their favourite haunts. Andy Goldsworthy, for instance, revisits certain stones 'many times over',[10] and gets very attached to places, which become like homes.[11] He also admits: 'I like touching stones touched many years ago.'[12] Like John Cowper Powys and the Romantic poets, like the archaic shaman, Australian aborigines and 'primitive' peoples, Goldsworthy goes out into the landscape and communes with it,[13] knows every inch of it, knows this stone and that pool, this place for gathering strong grass stalks and that dramatic hilltop viewpoint.

Uncomfortable as they are with notions of 'spirituality' or 'mysticism', land artists such as Richard Long, David Nash, Chris Drury and Robert Smithson are religious artists, sensitive to the emanations of particular places. Long, for instance, concedes that 'art is magical', as of course it is.[14] Art has been deeply associated with magic and religion for at least 40,000 years, and probably millennia more. Land art, like all art, is full of deep emotions. These emotions collect in clusters around certain places. It is understandable, then, that critics and the public see these emotions as potentially religious.

6

Land Art and British Culture

LAND ART AND BRITISH SCULPTURE

Sculpture in the Sixties in Britain was connected with the art schools (St Martin's, Slade, RCA); with teachers and modernists such as Anthony Caro, Philip King, Hans Haacke, Lawrence Weiner, Joseph Beuys and Henry Moore; with American Minimalism and Conceptual Art; with New Realism; and with Italian Arte Povera.

Tony Cragg was known for his coloured spreads of found objects arranged in lines on the floor (such as his *New Stones,* 1978). Cragg's sculptures were constructed from all manner of found objects, each given the same status, in a non-hierarchical fashion, laid out on the floor (anti-hierarchical structures being one of the marks of postmodernism). Cragg's 1980 sculpture *Black and White Stack* contained bicycle tyres, tin cans, car radiator grills, the side of a child's crib and an ironing board.

Tony Cragg's sculptures, like Bill Woodrow's and David Mach's, are not simply sensual modernist objects but ironic, postmodernist commentaries on the social and political uses of commodities (their work is sometimes dubbed 'post-industrial'). In the work of Cragg, Mach and Woodrow familiar consumer durables and industrial materials are represented in an ironic, metaphoric and parodying manner.[1] Cragg, and other sculptors who trawl the dumpsters and junk yards of urban landscapes (David Nash, Nicholas Pope, Anthony

Gormley, Bill Woodrow), make ironic comments on scavenging and ecological recycling. Cragg was not interested, he said, 'in romanticizing an epoch in the distant past', but questioning the massive amount of commodity consumption in a late capitalist epoch.

The humour, scepticism, pathos and irony in the art of Cragg, Woodrow, Mach, Gormley *et al* makes their post-Conceptual, post-industrial sculpture automatically disruptive. They evade categorization and easy definitions. It is this sense of shifting meanings and ambiguity in flux that makes much of New Sculpture and late modernist work disliked by some critics, because the work won't *keep still*. It won't be nailed down as an object of High Modernism, such as a family group sculpture by Henry Moore, or a Pablo Picasso nude.

Postmodern/ post-Conceptual art ignites many important questions, such as: how does one know about the 'authenticity' or 'originality' of something when it is mediated by the mass media? How does one know something is 'the real thing', when all one knows of it is through images and sounds on radio, television, the internet and the press? Does it matter if the 'original' artwork is fake when the mediated product has such 'truth'? Is an artwork that consists of photographs that refer to an artwork, an idea, an experience that exists elsewhere (such as Lawrence Weiner's printed words 'wall statement' *Sometimes Found*) as 'authentic' as a bronze sculpture by Auguste Rodin? Is the artwork that is an 'idea' as sensual or compelling as one made out of marble or oil? The new British sculpture, with its scavenged objects and seemingly 'ordinary' objects displayed on the floor, disrupts modernist/ traditional notions of 'beauty', 'purity', 'tradition', 'objecthood', 'presence', 'value' and 'meaning'.

THE BRITISH LANDSCAPE TRADITION

The influence of American/ New York/ Abstract Expressionist/ Minimal art and European Arte Povera are two strands in British sculpture, but another is the British art tradition, and another is the British landscape. Land art in Great Britain is bound up with notions of Romanticism. For Robert Rosenblum, the Abstract Expressionists (in particular Mark Rothko) were the last in a long line of Romantic artists. Speaking of his book *Modern Painting and the Northern Romantic Tradition*, Rosenblum said

> were I to write a supplementary chapter to it — I stopped with Rothko and Abstract Expressionism — I would probably include earthworks of the late 1960s and 1970s. Those seem in some way to be the last gasp of that tradition of trying to find some sort of connection with the Great Beyond or the Void.[1]

Certainly the works of Hamish Fulton, David Nash and Richard Long *et al*, are part of this Romantic tradition, as expressed in British landscape art. Associated with land art was the group of British artists, the 'New Arcadians' or 'New Ruralists'.

The influence of British landscape on British sculpture is apparent in many, but by no means all, of British sculptors. Specifically *British* landscape, as opposed to other kinds of landscape, occur in the work of David Nash, Hamish Fulton, David Tremlett, Chris Drury, Roger Ackling and Richard Long, as one might expect. It was Carl Andre who noted, quite rightly, that the British landscape is 'one vast earthwork'.[2]

Chris Drury, Hamish Fulton, David Nash and Richard Long, in particular, evoke the British landscape tradition, the tradition of the pastoral, the sublime, the Arcadian. Fulton, Drury, Long and Nash are Romantic, in the sense of British Romantic poetry (William Blake, William Wordsworth, John Keats, Percy Bysshe Shelley and Samuel Taylor Coleridge); in the sense of the British Romantic painters (J.M.W. Turner,

John Constable, Thomas Girtin, John Sell Cotman and Philip Wilson); and in the sense of the Romantic attitudes and aspirations of infinity, nostalgia, mythology, soul, magic, nature and the Gothic. In sculptors such as Tony Cragg, Hamish Fulton, Shirazeh Houshiary, Anish Kapoor, Richard Long, David Nash, Bill Woodrow, Barry Flanagan and William Tucker one can see the elements of British Romantic literature (as well as the Neo-Romanticism of the 1930s and 1940s): the anarchic idealism of Shelley, the luscious sensuality of Keats, the epic nature poetry of Wordsworth, the angelic visions of Blake and the synæsthetic poesie of Coleridge. The Romantic ethics of taking things to extremes, of going to the infinite and the eternal, are very much to the fore in land art, which is an art which quite definitely sustains Romantic myths and tenets.

There is a macho posturing to some land art theory (some of it no doubt unintentional) in which the relationship with nature is seen as 'fundamental', 'raw', 'violent' and 'intense'. American earthwork artists speak of working in nature as difficult, dirty, uncompromising and exhausting. In North America the poetic reference is Walt Whitman, as well as Henry David Thoreau, Henry Wadsworth Longfellow, Mark Twain, Herman Melville and Ralph Waldo Emerson.

7

Robert Smithson

Instead of putting a work of art on some land, some land is put into a work of art.

Robert Smithson[1]

Robert Smithson (1938-1973) was the chief mouthpiece of American earth/ site æsthetics, and is probably the most important theoretician among all land artists (he is also the premier land artist). Robert Smithson's key theoretical statements were published in three essays. In 1966's "The Crystal Land", Smithson recounted a trip he made to a quarry with Donald Judd, the key Minimal artist. Smithson evoked the decayed nature of the quarry, those aspects of entropy which would feature in his own work ('cracked broken shattered earth, of fragmentation, corrosion, decomposition, disintegration, rock crisis, debris slides, mud flow avalanche').[2] In the second article, "Entropy and the New Monuments" (1966), Smithson discussed the important Minimal show *Primary Structures* at the Jewish Museum.

Robert Smithson's themes were entropy in nature and art; he used the science of crystals and minerals as paradigms of the new art. Smithson had collected crystals and rocks as a child. Crystallography, for Smithson, offered 'a way of dealing with nature without falling into the old trap of the biological metaphor'.[3] No wonder, then, that when Smithson saw Donald Judd's pink plastic boxes he compared them to 'giant crystals from another planet' (RS, 19). The dissolution of crystals also provided Smithson with another analogy for his theory of natural entropy. The third piece, "A Sedimentation of the Mind: Earth Projects" (1968), concerned notions of time and place. While sculptors such as Anthony Caro and his ilk still clung to the old-fashioned ideas of beauty, Smithson spoke warmly of artists such as Walter de Maria, Carl Andre, Michael Heizer, Dennis Oppenheim, Tony Smith and Douglas Huebler (RS, 85).

Robert Smithson was also interested in science fiction: the poetic elements of his art thus form a continuum: between the industrial wastelands he visited for his 'non-site' sculptures and the desolate planets of science fiction; between chaos theory in the New Physics and its exploration in postmodern science fiction; between the forms of crystals and Minimal sculptures, and so on.

Robert Smithson's exaltation of lonely post-industrial sites was echoed in the speculative fictions of writers who evoked post- or near-holocaust worlds. J.G. Ballard, for example, wrote of post-industrial desert lands and run-down townscapes (in *The Drought, Vermilion Sands, High-Rise* and *Low-Flying Aircraft*). J.G. Ballard, as one would expect, took an eccentric view of Smithson's earthworks: Ballard mused on what kind of cargo might have been berthed at Smithson's *Spiral Jetty* and *Broken Circle*. Ballard wondered if the cargo was a 'very special kind' of clock... so many of Smithson's monuments seem to be a potent amalgam of clock, labyrinth and cargo terminal'.[4]

In the 1967 essay "Tour of the Monuments of Passaic", itself a sci-fi sort of title, Robert Smithson wrote about 'great pipes, sand boxes, bridges with wooden sidewalks, all standing for the irreversibility of eternity. Under the dead light of the Passaic afternoon, the desert becomes a man of infinite disintegration and forgetfulness' (RS, 56). This sort of apocalyptic imagery is echoed in the work of William Burroughs, J.G. Ballard, Tom Disch and other speculative fiction writers. It's the desolate wasteland imagery of the movie *Stalker* (1979) and other post-apocalyptic visions.[5]

For Robert Smithson, Carl Andre, Walter de Maria, Michael Heizer, Dennis Oppenheim and Tony Smith were 'the more compelling artists today, concerned with 'Place' or 'Site''.[6] Smithson was impressed by Smith's vision of the mysterious aspects of a dark unfinished road and called Smith 'the agent of endlessness'. Smith's æsthetic became part of Smithson's view of art as a complete 'site', not simply an æsthetic of sculptural objects. Smithson was not inspired by ancient religious sculpture, by burial mounds for example, so much as by decayed industrial sites. He visited some in the mid-1960s that were 'in some way disrupted or pulverized'. He said he was looking for a 'denaturalization rather than built up scenic beauty.'[7]

Robert Smithson said he was concerned, like many land (and contemporary) artists with the thing in itself, not its image, its effect, its critical significance: 'I am for an art that takes into account the direct effect of the elements as they exist from day to day apart from representation' (RS, 133). Smithson's theory of the 'non-site' was based on 'absence, a very ponderous, weighty absence'.[8] Smithson proposed a theory of a dialectic between absence and presence, in which the 'non-site' and 'site' are both interacting. In the 'non-site' work, presence and absence are there simultaneously. 'The land or ground from the Site is placed in the art (Non-Site) rather than the art is placed on the ground. The Non-Site is a container within another container – the room' (RS, 115).

> In a sense my nonsites are rooms within rooms. Recovery from the outer fringes brings one back to the central point... The scale between indoors and outdoors, and how the two are impossible to bridge... What you are really confronted with in a non-site is the absence of the site. It is a contraction rather than an expansion of scale. One is confronted with a very ponderous, weighty absence... There is this dialectic between inner and outer, closed and open, center and peripheral.[9]

Robert Smithson proposed a schema for 'non-site' art in his essay "Dialectic of Site and Non-Site" which ran thus:

Site	Non-Site
1. Open limits	Closed limits
2. A series of points	An array of Matter
3. Outer coordinates	Inner coordinates
4. Subtraction	Addition
5. Indeterminate certainty	Determinate uncertainty
6. Scattered information	Contained information
7. Reflection	Mirror
8. Edge	Center
9. Some place (physical)	No place (abstract)
10. Many	One (RS, 115)

The 'non-site' works were permanent, gallery works. Robert Smithson's *Mirror Displacements* (1968) consisted of putting some mirrors in different settings and taking photographs of them before moving them somewhere else. *Mirror Displacements* was documented in Smithson's *Artforum* article "Incidents of Mirror Travel in the Yucatan". Sometimes Smithson put soil on top of the mirrors, to dirty them up, to sabotage 'the perfect reflections of the sky'. Smithson liked dirt, gravel, sand, sludge and sediment – indeterminate, malleable substances. Land artists often sabotaged the clinical nature of much of art – putting soil or horses in the clean, white gallery space. Of his Italian horse piece, Jannis Kounellis said the aim was to increase awareness of the 'basic nature of a gallery, of its bourgeois origin', its economic and ideological aspects.[10]

Robert Smithson's other projects of the time included putting raw, natural materials into Minimal spaces, creating a tension of dialectic between 'site and non-site', as he called it. 1967's *Ziggurat Mirror* was completed by the use of mirrors. The sculpture needed the mirrors to work properly. Using the mirrors to create repetition, Smithson pointed to the delimited nature of the sculpture: with the right use of mirrors, a sculpture could be extended infinitely. Endless repetition was central to Minimal and Sixties art (Andy Warhol, Sol LeWitt, Carl Andre, Robert Morris, Donald Judd, Frank Stella and others took a simple unit and endlessly repeated it).

Before he made the famous *Spiral Jetty* (1970), Robert Smithson had already been considering the scientific notions of rotation and equilibrium. His sculpture *Gyrostasis* (1968) was a 75 x 57 x 40 inch painted steel structure based on the spiral. Smithson explained that *Gyrostasis*, as the title implied, was about how rotating bodies maintain their equilibrium. 'The work is a standing triangulated spiral. When I made the sculpture I was thinking of mapping procedures that refer to the planet Earth' (RS, 37).

Robert Smithson's *Spiral Jetty* is a 'monumental' earthwork, though the use of the spiral motif has connotations with the ancient symbols of the Goddess.[11] Of his *Spiral Jetty*, Smithson wrote:

> As I looked at the site, it reverberated out to the horizons only to suggest an immobile cyclone while flickering light made the entire landscape appear to quake. A dormant earthquake spread into an immense roundness. From that gyrating space emerged the possibility of the Spiral Jetty. No idea, no concepts, no systems, no structures, no abstractions could hold themselves together in the actuality of that phenomenological evidence.[12]

Robert Smithson was impressed by the characteristics of the Great Salt Lake site, the pinkish mud, the faintly violet water surrounded by limestone hills, and the 'crushing light' of the sun. He had been reading about salt lakes in Boliva, where bacteria turned the water red to match the colour of the flamingos. Smithson found out that the Utah salt lakes were also red and pink due to algæ and mineral waste. Smithson and his wife, Nancy Holt, surveyed the area and chose a lake at Rozel Point in Utah, which had a number of cracks in the mud under the shallow water. Smithson's team began building it in April, 1970, excavating 6,650 tons. *Spiral Jetty* was made from rocks, water, mud and precipitated salt crystals. It was 1,500 ft long and 15 ft wide. Smithson was aided by Virginia Dwan and the Ace Gallery of Vancouver. As with many other projects of the time a film was made of the construction of *Spiral Jetty*. Smithson related the work to spiral nebulæ, to salt crystals and microscopic organisms. Smithson thought in terms of eons of time, and mused on how entropy would overtake the site.[13]

Robert Smithson used one of the primary forms of land art, the circle, in many works, combining it with ideas taken from science (such as *Gyrostasis*, which, said Smithson, 'refers to a branch of physics that deals with rotating bodies').[14] Smithson was not adverse to religious feelings about art: when he visited the site of his *Spiral Jetty*, in the Utah salt flats, he experienced a feeling of 'a rotary that enclosed itself in an immense roundness' (ib., 111). The two elements – rational, mathematical, scientific precision and intuitive, emotional, religious feeling – are two of the chief characteristics of land art. On the one hand, land artists talk about measurements, practical details, materials, maps and spatial data. On the other hand, they hint at religious awe, spiritual feelings, prehistoric art and the influx of the numinous into modern art.

Robert Smithson also identified his *Spiral Jetty* with a mythic whirlpool that sprang up from a tunnel connected to the Pacific Ocean. His *Spiral Jetty* was an 'immobile cyclone', it spiralled inwards from the outside: the track leaves the shore and twists round and round to the centre. *Spiral Jetty* was also linked with notions of decay in nature. In "A Sedimentation of the Mind: Earth Projects", Smithson had written: '[e]very object, if it is art, is charged with the rush of time, even though it is static' (RS, 90). Ironically, Smithson's *Spiral Jetty* was itself subject to natural entropy: the water level rose and *Spiral Jetty* was submerged under water.

Robert Smithson's 1971 *Broken Circle* was another large

earthwork using circular motifs that was set adjacent to the land and extended out into a lake. Smithson chose a quarry site near Emmen, Holland. Again, the site had an interesting geological aspect, which was in keeping with Smithson's love of rocks and minerals. Glacial action had formed unusual layers of soil. Unlike *Spiral Jetty*, which was subsequently submerged, *Broken Circle* remains on display, and is maintained by local funds. It is a 140 foot circle comprising one half of soil and one half of water, with a twelve foot wide canal cutting round the earth section of the circle, forming a semicircle. At the centre of *Broken Circle* is a very large glacial boulder. It was supposedly one of the largest in the Netherlands. Significantly, Smithson allowed nothing at the centre of *Spiral Jetty*: the spectator walked round the inward-turning spiral to find nothing. Smithson was exasperated by the prehistoric stone at the centre of his *Broken Circle*, but he let this 'accidental center' stay there, commenting 'it became a dark spot of exasperation, a geological gangrene on the sandy expanse'.[15]

Robert Smithson's last major work, before his untimely death, was *Armarillo Ramp*, one of many land artworks conceived as an observation structure. Nancy Holt worked with one of the major American sculptors of the era, Richard Serra, to complete Smithson's plans. *Amarillo Ramp*, 15 miles North-West of Amarillo in the Texas Panhandle, is a huge inclined ramp or road, made from quarried rocks. The summit of *Amarillo Ramp* is a viewing point.[17]

Taken together, Robert Smithson's three large-scale earthworks, *Spiral Jetty*, *Broken Circle* and *Amarillo Ramp*, all revolve around circular or spiral motifs, a sense of temporality, of decay and transience, and each uses primitive, mythic forms and gestures in a monumental manner. Two of them are set in wilderness spaces, where the marks of humanity are at their weakest. Yet each earthwork of course speaks acutely of the mark of humanity upon the Earth, and a very particular kind of mark: that of late 20th century

American art-making.

Robert Smithson's influence on land art has been immense, probably more than any other single artist. One example would be Andy Goldsworthy's Durham, England earthwork *Maze* (1989, at Leadgate), which draws as much on the legacy of Smithson's art as also on ancient mythology and symbolism. It uses the labyrinth motif. Goldsworthy's *Maze* can seen a part of the resurgence of interest in mazes which occurred in the 1980s (aligned, as ever, with green/ ecological/ occult/ New Age trends). New mazes were commissioned, and 1991 was designated the 'Year of the Maze'. Like *Lambton Earthwork* (but unlike most of Goldsworthy's works), *Maze* was intended to be used by the general public. As with Smithson's *Broken Circle* or the *Armarillo Ramp*, the public was invited to walk around Goldsworthy's earthworks. Both *Maze* and *Lambton Earthwork* were about responses to the energies in nature – thus the public was invited to explore similar things as they physically walked around the earthworks. Goldsworthy also designed an earthwork which was a curving ramp, exactly like *Armarillo Ramp*, though on a much smaller scale.

8

Carl Andre

Since the 1960s, the statements of a handful of artists have proved to be the most illuminating about 1960s art, and land art in particular. Robert Smithson, Donald Judd, Robert Morris and Carl Andre have been among the most lucid of theorists among artists (and Clement Greenberg, Michael Fried, Lawrence Alloway, Bruce Glaser, Mel Bochner, David Bourdon, Lucy Lippard and Harold Rosenberg among art critics). Carl Andre (b. 1935) has many pertinent things to say about sculpture. His mid-1960s summary of the history of sculpture applies directly to land art:

> The course of development
> Sculpture as form
> Sculpture as structure
> Sculpture as place.[1]

Carl Andre's biography is often cited in accounts of his art. He worked on the railroads, as a freight conductor and brakeman (in Newark, at the Pennsylvania Railroad) from 1960-64, and this is used to explain Andre's use of modules and units which join together to form a work. Like Sol LeWitt and Donald Judd, Andre took one unit and multiplied them until he had a line or a square. Before working on the railroad, Andre was 'a wood-carving disciple of Brancusi', carving chunks out of wood beams. For a long time the shadow of Constantin Brancusi lay over Andre's art. When he came to explain his floor-standing works, such as *Lever*, a line of firebricks, he said he was

> putting Brancusi's *Endless Column* on the ground instead of in the sky... Most sculpture is priapic with the male organ in the air. In my work, Priapus is down on the floor. The engaged position is to run along the earth.[2]

The sexualization of sculpture in Carl Andre's remark is no accident: Andre has spoken in interviews that the best creative work is erotic. In a 1970 radio discussion (with Lucy Lippard, Douglas Huebler, Dan Graham and Jan Dibbets on WBAI FM), Andre said desires, not ideas, were important. 'I have very few ideas, but I have strong desires.... I agree with Dr Guillotine that all ideas are the same except in execution... You can't cut off desires except painfully'.[3] Nature was also crucial: Andre said he disliked Conceptual art because it was cut of from nature (ibid.). Andre said his art 'has never been conceptual in any way'.[4]

While he was in New Hampshire in 1965, canoeing on a lake, Carl Andre (apparently) realized that sculpture ought to be level, like water. After this, most of his sculpture was floor-standing and flat. Andre did not make boxes in the usual Minimal manner. Andre's sculptures were modular in the sense that one piece could be removed and put somewhere else without altering the whole (Andre's 'anaxial symmetry'). Lines of bricks or squares made from plates of metal were typical Andre works. Andre's use of materials was not 'poetic' or 'spiritual' in the usual sense of the words. In works such as *Cedar Piece* (1959/ 64), *Pyre* (1971, S. & C. Gilman), *Herm* (1976, Guggenheim), *Stile* (1975) and *Well* (1964), which were made out of wood, Andre was using materials as themselves, but 'not to evoke nature'.[5] Andre did not intend his materials to refer to other things, to be allusive in the art historical or lyrical sense. His Styrofoam planks were not alluding to marble, as some viewers mistakenly thought.[6]

Carl Andre's notion of the 'dematerialization' of sculpture was central to his art, and also to land art. When they were not being exhibited, Andre's sculptures simply disappeared. They were not objects on permanent display, but were made specially for each occasion and space. Most land art is like this. Andre's works outside of shows exist as ideas, photographs, descriptions, memories, and so on, but not as actual works. Much of land art is also this ephemeral, made for a particular occasion then dismantled (the Christos, Chris Drury, Robert Morris). This emphasis on the materiality and dematerialization of his works led Andre to regard his art as non-spiritual. He said:

> My work is atheistic, materialistic, and communistic. It's atheistic because it's without transcendent form, without spiritual or intellectual quality. Materialistic because it's made out of its own materials without pretension to other materials. And communistic because the form is equally accessible to all men.[7]

This is a humble, self-effacing view of his own art. His art was materialistic, Carl Andre stated, because it does not pretend to be anything else other than itself. However, at other times (in interviews, for example), Andre comes across as a warmly Romantic artist. It is this aspect of his art that annoyed people when the Tate Gallery in the U.K. bought, with public money, one of his piles of bricks. The form (a low oblong shape) and the material of the work (brick) seemed available to anyone who visited a household supply store and bought a few hundred bricks and arranged them in a certain way. Yet Andre's art is of course not as simple as that, and not as easy to produce as that.

Carl Andre's *37 Pieces of Work* is a good example of Minimal æsthetic permutations taken to extremes. It is a sculpture that is typical of Andre's art:

> Taken as a whole *37 Pieces of Work* consists of 1,296 plates, 216 each of aluminium, copper, steel, magnesium, lead and zinc. Each metal appears alone in individual six-foot square plains. Then alternates with another, checker-board fashion, in every possible permutation.

> Since each of the six metals in the large piece was laid out in the alphabetical order of its chemical symbol, alternating successively with the others, there are two versions of each combination.[8]

Carl Andre's *Element* series consisted of wood-carved beams that recalled Constantin Brancusi; Andre's *Equivalents* were 'floor-hugging' sculptures shown in 1966. The magnet pieces, which preceded the metal squares, also hugged the floor, so much so that the third dimension was nearly expunged. The floor-pieces neatly rid the sculptor of dealing with pedestals. They became 'place-markers'.[9] They have no space, according to one critic, they have 'no appearance of inside or center. Rather they seem to be coextensive with the very floor on which the viewer stands'.[10] Place, not space or sky, became what matters for Andre. Andre's floor-pieces are viewer-friendly, too: the viewer is invited to (or allowed to) walk over them. Like Donald Judd, Andre wanted his sculptures to be seen from a variety of viewpoints. Instead of a single viewpoint, one could have a number of angles; he compared viewing his sculptures to walking on roads: '[t]hey cause you to make your way along them or around them or to move... over them' (1970, 57).

Carl Andre's works seem to be slight, almost insubstantial, but, simultaneously, 'their matter-of-factness that makes them in a multiple sense *present*'.[11] Frank Stella influenced Andre's way of making sculpture: Andre often stayed with Stella in the early years, and worked in Stella's studio: when Andre was working on a large log, Stella told him that unworked wood could be sculpture too. Andre considered what Stella had said, and thereafter used materials in an untouched state, 'using them as 'cuts' in the space that surrounds them, shaping the space itself'.[12]

Carl Andre's works are extremely sensuous, with their shiny or dull surfaces of copper, zinc, steel or aluminium. Andre's *Sixteenth Copper Cardinal* (1976), sixteen square copper slabs, is a work that could be described as luscious.

People are used to marble and stone being beautiful, and also certain metals – bronze, silver and gold in particular have been central to sculpture for millennia. Why not zinc and copper, too? After all, much jewellery is made from copper.

Carl Andre, like other Minimal sculptors, introduces the viewer to the sensuality of copper, bronze and zinc shaped into nothing more than… a simple shape, like a slab, put on the floor. Andre's slabs are not 'narrative' or anthropomorphic or literal or allusive; they do not 'depict' animals or gods or people; but they are no less beautiful, as objects in their own right. Spectators are invited to walk on his sculptures, offering a new relation with the work.

If land art is in a gallery, one sees it as art (and a particular kind of Western, bourgeois art, the sort of art that is exhibited in Western, bourgeois galleries). Carl Andre explored the relation between real and represented objects with his controversial pile of bricks. The sculpture was 'controversial' because the general public (whoever they are) perceived, via the media, that Andre had simply stuck some bricks into a gallery. Or rather, that taxpayers' money had been used to purchase Andre's bricks. A pile of bricks on a building site is… a pile of bricks. A pile of bricks in an art gallery is… sculpture. Context is everything here. This is what Carl Andre explored, whether consciously or not: the *response*, affected by so much of culture, socialization, physical context, education, and so on, makes objects sculptures. People make art. A leaf simply exists, but if someone puts it in a gallery or an art book, it becomes art (as well as remaining a leaf). If people think something is art, then it's art, as Donald Judd said.

Carl Andre commented,

> The materiality, the presence of the work of sculpture in the world, essentially independent of any single individual, but rather the residue of many individuals and the dream, the experience of the sea, the trees and the stones – I'm interested in that kind of essential thing.[13]

'I will try to have in my work only what is necessary to it', Carl Andre said (1984). Andre's *Stone Field* (1977) was one of his site-specific works of the 1970s, consisting of 26 very large glacial boulders (one of his more obviously land artworks). It was an imposing piece, introducing the idiosyncratic, organic shapes of nature into the 'geometric wilderness' (D.M. Thomas's term) of the city (Hartford, Connecticut). Andre made a line of hay bales, placed end to end, in a field in Vermont (*Joint*, 1968).[14] It was a line like Richard Long's stone rows, or Tony Cragg's floor spreads.

> Many of the activities in farm work are sculptural: stacking the hay bales, ploughing fields, feeding animals; also the marks left behind by the animals or made by farmworkers, tractors... the texture of the land [Goldsworthy remarked].[15]

Carl Andre created one of his floor pieces of slabs of metal deliberately so it would be altered by being outside. It was called *Small Weathering Piece* (1971), and contained a large number of metals (large for an Andre sculpture): lead, zinc, aluminium, copper, steel and magnesium.

One of Carl Andre's most intriguing theoretical statements is this: 'my ideal piece of sculpture is a road'.[16] This applies not only to Andre's lines of bricks or hay bales, but to Richard Long's lines of stones and walks along roads, to Christo's *Running Fence*, to Andy Goldsworthy's stone walls, and to other land artworks. Andre's notion of the ultimate earthwork as a road has a parallel with the famous anecdote of American artist Tony Smith who, when driving along the New Jersey turnpike, was impressed by the 'dark pavements moving through the landscape of the flats, rimmed in the distance, but punctuated by stacks, towers, fumes, and colored lights'.[17] Something in such long stretches of empty roads, as with airstrips (and, more dubiously, a drill ground at Nuremberg), impressed Smith, who wrote '[i]t seemed that there had been a reality there that had not had any expression in art'.[18] Roads are not 'art', not wholly functional either – they have an aura or mystery which Smith tried to explain.

Richard Long emphasizes the functional or workaday aspect of his walks. He sees his walks as hard work; roads, in the Tony Smith view, are also for and about labour and functionality. The road, for the Minimal or Process artist, in the Carl Andre manner, embody materially the sense of a sequence or process. One unit (the foot or brick or slab of tarmac or concrete) is placed next to another, forming a road. Artists such as Andre (and Sol LeWitt, Ronald Bladen and Donald Judd) did exactly the same, putting one unit next to another, creating a line or sequence of units.

The road also may have no obvious end: endlessness was crucial to Minimal, Process and Conceptual art, as it is to land art. Many land artists emphasize art that goes on and on. Christo's fence, for example, goes on and on for 26 miles. One imagines that Christo would love a fence that could run across a whole country, or, even better, a whole continent. Similarly, Richard Long's walks could extend far beyond their limits, and the modular art of Donald Judd, Ronald Bladen, Robert Morris and Sol LeWitt could expand indefinitely, once the basic pattern had been established. The seriality or endless process of art was identified by Judd as the idea of 'one thing after another'.[19] Carl Andre's concept of the road as the ideal artwork fits in with this urge towards endless process and seriality. The road motif also fits in well with stereotypical American culture, with its love of the 'open road', Robert Frank's famous photograph, road movies (*Easy Rider, Duel, Thelma and Louise, Natural Born Killers*), the frontier spirit (in Westerns), and in hippy and beatnik culture (Jack Kerouac's *On the Road*, Allen Ginsberg and the 'dharma bums' who drifted around from state to state).

9

James Turrell

James Turrell's (b. 1943) *Roden Crater Project* – 'skyspaces', tunnels, observatories and chambers in an extinct volcano near Flagstaff, Arizona – is one of the biggest works of land and environmental art. Begun in 1974, it was funded by many different sources and administered by the Skystone Foundation.[1] The first stage of Turrell's on-going *Roden Crater* project involved bull-dozing 200,000 cubic yards of earth from the volcano's rim, 'so as to shape the sky'. Turrell planned tunnels, pools and viewing chambers at *Roden Crater*. There were spaces at *Roden Crater* where clouds were projected onto the floor during the day, which at night were related to the procession of equinoxes. Many of the spaces planned at *Roden Crater* were built around celestial events, such as full moons, solstices, equinoxes, the movement of the sun, or just being able to view stars and some planets. The connection with the heavens was important for Turrell: most of his works have openings to the sky, and the relationship with the sky is the centrepiece of the works. It's important for Turrell, in short, to see the stars.

The *Roden Crater* work was about the relationship between the viewer and the elements, in particular the sky, celestial events, and light. James Turrell said '[m]y art is made for one person'.[2] The environment was a volcano, relating to geological time.

> The work I do intensifies the experience of light by isolating it and occluding all other light. Each space

> essentially looks to a different portion of sky and accepts a limited number of events.

James Turrell explained (1995, 67). Thus, each space at *Roden Crater* was designed to highlight some celestial event. The subject of some spaces was the vaulting of the sky, and the curvature of the world. Some were about daily events, such as sunrises and sunsets, or the movement of the stars.

The North section of *Roden Crater* is about looking North, the North Star, the rotation of the Earth, changing light, and includes a *camera obscura* (which projects whatever is overhead onto a white sand floor), and a seat for viewing Polaris. The Eastern space is for witnessing sunrise, and a 'skyspace' overhead. *Bath Space* projects a magnified image of the sky above onto a white sand floor, using a water bath above a large sphere as a lens. The *Sun and Moon Room* was constructed around the furthest South moonset (every 18.61 years), the furthest North sunrise and the Summer solstice. *Tso Kiva* is a hemispherical space in the centre of the volcano, for observing light, shadows, shapes and the horizon.

The *South Space* is an astronomical observatory and star chart. The *West Space*, as one would expect, is for the sunset, and the 'twilight arch', the projection of the Earth's shadow into the atmosphere at nightfall. James Turrell said he didn't want Roden Crater to be 'a mark upon Nature, but to be enfolded in Nature in such a way that light from the Sun, Moon, and stars empowered the spaces' (1995, 66).

James Turrell's creative task as he saw it was not to impose his own vision or æsthetics on the viewer, but to encourage them to see things for themselves, to create the situation in which they could have their own experience. These were æsthetics common in much of land art. As he said in 1987, the goal was not to turn an experience into art, but 'to set up a situation to which I take you and let you see. It becomes your experience... not taking from nature as much as placing you in contact with it'.[3] Turrell regarded his art as a 'seeing aid', as showing the observer something that was already there but that they might not have noticed.

On the indoor-outdoor debate, which exercised so many land artists, James Turrell said that, instead of bringing nature into the museum, he wanted to 'bring culture to the natural surround as if designing a garden or tending a landscape' (1995, 66). The artwork became something to visit in itself, rather than one of many artworks in a museum to see. The viewer travelled specially to see the artwork, as they visited *Double Negative,* or Marfa in Texas, or Robert Smithson's earthworks.

James Turrell's primary material was not earth or stone or the usual materials of land art, but light itself, what he called 'light in the space itself'. Turrell wanted to use light as a thing-in-itself, which had presence, just as the sculptor used a physical object which had presence. He achieved this, he said, by setting limits on the space in which light manifested itself: 'I give light thingness by putting limits on it in a formal manner. I do not create an object, only objectified perception' (1995, 65). Turrell was attempting to create spaces in which viewers could perceive the subject of his works, light itself, and celestial events. It was important also for Turrell that the viewer was able to enter those spaces physically, not virtually.

James Turrell's art was not about creating illusions or artificial scenarios or a record of the artwork. Turrell called it 'non-vicarious seeing': '[t]he subject of my work is your nonvicarious seeing. You are not looking at a record of my seeing' (1995, 64). Thus, Turrell's art was not about recording some event that took place elsewhere, or taking photographs of his art, or writing down what happened, as in some land art. Rather, Turrell wanted to place the viewer right into the artwork, to have them able to walk into and around the artwork, and to experience of the artwork for themselves.

Many of James Turrell's artworks were about working with not just light, but with the sky. The archetypal Turrell space was an enclosed area (a 'skyspace') which had an opening above onto the sky. Turrell spoke of the vaulting of the sky, how the sky looked when the viewer was standing up, or sitting down, or lying down.

Some of James Turrell's 'skyspaces' – indoor rooms or spaces which are open to the sky above – include *Spaces That Sees* (1992) in Jerusalem, *Heavy Water* (1992, Poitier), and *Razor* (1991, London). *Kielder Skyspace* (2000) is open to the public, situated outside the village of Kielder near the Scottish border. Turrell has also constructed pools of water which combine water and light: in these works (at *Roden Crater*, and Poitier, France), the viewer is invited to dive under the water to reach a space beyond which's open to the sky.

James Turrell emphasized the spiritual aspects of light in his land art. 'I am interested in light because of my interest in our spiritual nature and the things that empower us. My art deals with light itself, the bearer of revelation, but as revelation itself' (1995, 64). The kind of effect Turrell was after in his light works he compared to staring into a fire, a kind of meditation or daydreaming. Turrell encouraged the viewer to sit or lie down and contemplate light itself, and the effects of light in a particular space. Thus, the spaces that Turrell constructed were furnished with viewing platforms, or benches, or places to lie down and look up at the sky. Situating the spectator in relation to the subject of the artwork (light itself) was Turrell's goal.

As well as drifting off by looking at a fire, James Turrell also often spoke of the experience of flight, of being in a plane and rising into new zones of light, different kinds of light. Turrell also spoke of the curvature of the Earth when seen from a plane (and how, between 600 and 3,000 feet, the Earth seems to curve the wrong way). The Roden volcano was chosen partly because of its relation at that particular place in the Painted Desert to the curvature of the Earth. The low mound of the volcano and its relation to the curvature of the Earth and the sky above had the right mixture of components Turrell was seeking.

10

Dennis Oppenheim

Like Robert Smithson and James Turrell, Dennis Oppenheim (1938-2011) was one of the most interesting of American earth artists, an artist who produced an amazing body of work. It's significant, for instance, that Oppenheim was the first American land artist to work with snow on a grand scale. Oppenheim began making snow works in the late Sixties. The only other important environmental artist who regularly used snow and ice, really, was Hans Haacke. But, more than any of the other first generation land artists, Oppenheim made snow one of his primary media.

Dennis Oppenheim's *Annual Rings* (1968), a series of concentric circles that straddled the Canadian/ American border, was made with snow (one of Oppenheim's recurring motifs was the border zone, margins and thresholds in time and space and concept). Oppenheim has drawn a number of snow works with a snowmobile: *One Hour Run* (1968) was a continuous track made in the snow in Maine. Two tracks, side by side, were carved in the snow between Fort Kent, Maine and Clair, New Brunswick, Canada, in 1968, for *Time Line*, a work which explored the different time zones. Oppenheim's *Negative Board* (1968) was a dark cut in the snow and ice in Maine.

Dennis Oppenheim burnt circles onto grass in *Branded Mountain*. *Accumulation Cut* (1969) was made at Cornell University: a hundred foot long cut in the ice, running away from a waterfall. Also at Cornell, Oppenheim took the floor outline of gallery 4 of the Andrew Dickson White Museum of Art and drew it into the snow and ice outside (1969). Another *Gallery Transplant* was created in 1969, transplanting the floor plan of a gallery in the Stedelijk Museum in Amsterdam to a snowy hillside in New Jersey.

Dennis Oppenheim's *Whirlpool Eye of Storm* (1973) was an ephemeral piece of land art in the Hans Haacke vein: a jet trail created in the sky by a plane flying above the desert at El Mirage Dry Lake in California. *Directed Seeding* (1969) parodied Action Painting by harvesting a wheat field. In *Cancelled Crop* (1969), Oppenheim cut a giant 'X' in a field in the Netherlands, and kept the grain, as if he were preventing the material he'd cultivated for his art from becoming the raw material for other (illusionistic) art: 'isolating this grain from further processing becomes like stopping raw pigment from becoming an illusionistic force on canvas'.[1] Another 'X' was laid onto the landscape at El Mirage Dry Lake out of asphalt primer (covering an area 610 yards square), entitled *Relocated Burial Ground* (1978) (The 'X' shape, as Lucy Lippard noted in *Overlay*, was a favourite motif with male land artists: Chris Burden, Richard Long and Robert Smithson also created 'Xs').[2]

Like many land artists, Dennis Oppenheim produced a maze (in 1970). But Oppenheim's *Maze* was just a little different: it was the design of a maze used in a scientific laboratory for rats transposed onto a large field, with cows as the rats, lured around the maze by the promise of food.

Many of Dennis Oppenheim's artworks are conceptual pieces in the great tradition of Sixties Conceptualism. That is, many are works made to be exhibited in galleries, on walls. They comprise photographs, drawings and maps, with Oppenheim's typewritten captions and explanations: *Three Downward Blows* (1977), *Salt Flat* (1969), *Boundary Split* (1968), and *Negative Board* (1968) (maps were central to Oppenheim's art). Many of Oppenheim's land artworks also existed as these framed photo-text-sketch-map works. One of

Oppenheim's specialities was to impose humanmade geometries, symbols and ideas onto the landscape: to transpose map contours, for instance, or the rings of a tree trunk onto snow (in *Annual Rings*), or the International Date Line in snow (*Time Pocket*). Robert Smithson remarked that Oppenheim was 'transforming a terrestrial site into a map'.[3] Generally, Oppenheim tended to enlarge symbols or ideas or images, and recreate them on a colossal scale in the landscape.

In *Time Pocket* (1968), Dennis Oppenheim 'drew' the International Date Line with a diesel-powered skidder in snow in Maine. In *Boundary Split* (1968), Oppenheim carved lines perpendicular to the Time Boundary between Canada and the U.S.A.. *Star Skid* (1977) was Oppenheim's proposal for a series of concrete and glass stars that would look from the air as if they had landed on Earth and skidded to a halt.

In *Salt Flat* (1969), Dennis Oppenheim created a 'salt flat' (a favourite place for land artists to make work in the U.S.A.) in New York City, with a thousand pounds of salt. The rectangle of salt was recreated in the sea in the Bahamas, and in the Salt Lake Desert. In *Directed Harvest* (1969), Oppenheim carved up fields of crops. Oppenheim set off underground explosions in *Three Downward Blows (Knuckle Marks)* in Montana in 1977.

In *Ground Mutations – Shoe Prints* (1969), Dennis Oppenheim created shoe print works over the course of three Winter months (by wearing shoes with a 1/4 inch groove cut in the sole and heel): 'I was connecting the patterns of thousands of individuals... My thoughts were filled with marching diagrams'. The use of shoes and prints links with Andy Goldsworthy's direct use of the body and Richard Long's walks.

Speaking in 1970, Dennis Oppenheim opined that art now 'more concerned with the location of material and with speculation' (i.e., locations or ideas). Now, art was meant to be visited (location) or 'abstracted from a photograph' (conceptualized).[4] Oppenheim moved towards a kind of art that would be discovered or visited by the spectator, rather than 'made' in the old, traditional manner (this was part of the 'dematerialization' of the art object in Sixties art). Oppenheim moved away from the idea of the special, unique art object, towards found objects, and utilizing existing sites. Oppenheim was replacing objects with locations.

The *Site Markers* series (1967) comprised posts in locations which were documented with texts, maps and photos. The maps and photos explained where the posts were situated, so that the location, rather than the object, became the centre of the piece. As Oppenheim pointed out, the *Site Markers* works were intended to be about the sites themselves, rather than the manipulation or replication of an object: 'beginning with the site-markers started in a sense a journey: art is travel'.[5]

One of Dennis Oppenheim's more Conceptual pieces (*Sound Enclosed Land Area*, 1969) comprised four tape recorders buried in cages in Paris enclosing an area 500 by 800 yards. Each machine played a tape loop which had a voice repeating its position (North, South, East or West). *Contour Lines Scribed in Swamp Grass* (1968) transposed contour lines on a map in two different locations (a swamp and a mountain). The use of aluminium filings poured onto grass in concentric circles recalled Richard Long's stone circles.

The contours of Dennis Oppenheim's own thumbprints were the basis for *Identity Stretch* (1970-75), where a truck sprayed white paint on the ground, using the thumbprint (which Oppenheim had elongated) as a guide, within a grid. In 1970 Oppenheim created a performance piece, entitled *Parallel Stress*, made between a collapsed concrete pier and a wall at Manhattan and Brooklyn bridges. Oppenheim stretched his body between the wall and the pier, echoing the New York bridges nearby. The same body position was re-created at an abandoned sump in Long Island.

In later works, Dennis Oppenheim moved into Jean

Tinguely mode, constructing whole rooms full of post-industrial, multi-media structures which were part-Conceptual, part-assemblage, part-kinetic and part-installation. In the *Fireworks* series of these sculptures, Oppenheim built sculptures from butane gas, rockets, flares, ramps, and metal supports, creating fires, explosions, flying sparks and smoke (as in *Launching Structure No. 2: An Armature For Projection*, 1982, Bonlow Gallery, New York).

11

Robert Morris

Robert Morris (b. 1931) was one of the most eloquent theorists of Sixties, Minimal and Postminimal sculpture (along with Donald Judd and Carl Andre). Morris had, like Judd, begun by working in painting, but moved on to sculpture. Morris studied at Kansas City Art Institute, California School of Fine Arts and Hunter College, New York. In San Francisco in 1961 he worked with the dancer Anna Halprin. He was part of the Fluxus school, alongside Yoko Ono, Simone Forte, Walter de Maria and Henry Flynt.

Robert Morris wrote many artistic statements, the most famous probably being the articles published in *Artforum* entitled "Notes on Sculpture" (1966-69). For Morris, one of the things that was new about 1960s sculpture was the object's relationship with the viewer. Before then, Morris argued, the viewer related to the object as something separate; the new æsthetic put the viewer into the same space as the object.

> One is more aware than before that he himself is establishing relationships as he apprehends the object from different positions and under varying conditions of light and spatial context.[1]

This is a crucial concept in Minimal art, which is nearly always viewed in an object-viewer continuous space.

Robert Morris's concept of 'objecthood' was central to his notion of sculpture. 'Morris wants to achieve presence through objecthood, which requires a certain largeness of scale, rather than through size alone', wrote Michael Fried (1967). Just as important as the object itself was the sense of space around it, the spatial context in which it was displayed. Morris wanted to emphasize that 'things are in a space with oneself', rather than the notion that 'one is in a space surrounded by things' (ib., 127). The whole context of the object in its space ('the entire situation') was important to Morris's notion of the new sculpture. One might say the new, 1960s sculpture, like land art, was about the 'thing in itself', a notion borrowed from Existentialism, but also about the 'thing in its space'.

Although Robert Morris denied being an 'environmental' artist, the context was important to his art.[2] For one critic, Morris's sculpture 'redirect[s] the entire environmental experience'.[3] Referring to Donald Judd's "Specific Objects" article, Morris said he did not separate the two, he did not think that something must be either an object or an environment.[4] As he moved towards Postminimalism, Morris advocated doing away with a figure-ground relationship; instead, heterogeneous 'stuff' should be used, an 'accumulation of things or stuff'.[5] In 1975 Morris wrote "Aligned with Nazca", an article in one of the key magazines of the period (*Artforum*) which related earthwork art with ancient art such as the Nazca lines. However, such connections with ancient art had already been made by artists and critics of land art.

Among Robert Morris's stranger concepts was his 'mobile' mausoleum: in an aluminium tunnel 3 miles long a coffin made from iron and suspended from pulleys would be moved intermittently. An attendant with a magnet would shift the coffin from above. By the entrance to the tube would be swooning maidens in marble, carved in the style of Antonio Canova.[6] 'If something is still capable of moving, is it dead?' Morris wondered.[7]

Robert Morris produced some works of a highly 'ephemeral' nature, such as his 'steam piece' (*Untitled*, 1968-

69), which was created out of doors on a patch of grass. How the work turned out was dependent upon physicalities such as humidity, air pressure, wind speed and direction, and temperature. Clouds of steam drifted over the grass.

British artist Rose Finn-Kelcey produced a steam work: her *Untitled* (1992, London) comprised of water placed on a sheet metal base, with an extractor hood hung above it. In between the two was a cloud of steam, made dramatic by the lighting. Some of Hans Haacke's most intriguing works were with ephemeral natural events such as steam, ice, condensation, fog and flooding. Peter Hutchinson made a cloud piece (*Dissolving Clouds*, 1970) using Hatha yoga meditation techniques, trying to dissolve clouds through thought. The work consisted of a sequence of 6 photographs of clouds. Alice Aycock also created a *Cloud Piece* (1971), photographs of cumulus clouds which melted after a few minutes.

In *Pace and Progress*, Robert Morris produced a work by walking a horse back and forth over a piece of grass until a path had been worn. The action of walking the horse rubbed down the grass. One of Morris's largest commissions was the *Grand Rapids Project*, in Michigan (1973-74), consisting of huge ramps leading up to a plateau. Another large Morris sitework was created in King County, Washington (1979), a series of oval terraces recalling Iron Age hillforts.

Robert Morris's later works included felt sculptures, where an element of randomness and chance dictated how the felt strips would hang. Each installation would be different. Some of the later felt pieces used thick felt (such as in *Untitled 1996* [collection: the artist]). Another work entitled *Untitled 1996* (collection: the artist) was modelled, the felt being draped symmetrically over a pole. *Untitled 1996* recalled a human figure.[8]

Robert Morris's wall drawings, meanwhile, were made by the artist covering his hands with graphite and dabbing them on the wall blindfolded. The large areas of smeared graphite (in *Blind Time IV*, 1991, for example) recall Richard

Long's mud wall drawings. The links between Morris and other land artists would include an emphasis on spontaneity, materiality, chance, randomness, change and ephemerality.

12

Nancy Holt

Nancy Holt's (b. 1938) art, with its large, heavy landscaping gestures (such as her *Dark Star Park*), is comparable with the male land artists. The globes and pools of water, though, are traditionally seen as 'feminine' volumes, but here given a new, monumental turn. Holt's art concerns the movements of the heavens. Her sculptures focus the viewer on the motions of the earth, moon, sun and stars. Holt's art is concerned with the notion of time, in particular with geological time, the relation between time and the Earth. Holt was impressed by the desert when she visited it in the late 1960s with Robert Smithson and Michael Heizer.

> Time is not just a mental concept or a mathematical abstraction in the desert [Holt wrote]. The rocks in the distance are ageless; they have been deposited in layers over hundreds of thousands of years. Time takes on a physical presence.[1]

Nancy Holt has said she is interested in 'conjuring up a sense of time that is longer than the built-in obsolescence we have all around us.' Hence she uses long-lasting materials, such as steel and rocks. Using enduring materials does not stem from a sense of vanity, of wanting one's works to last forever, but rather because Holt wants to create a sense of time that extends beyond the human lifespan.[2]

Nancy Holt married the key earthwork artist, Robert Smithson, in 1963. She worked with him on his non-site projects, including the famous *Spiral Jetty* and *Amarillo Ramp*.

While working on Smithson's enormous *Amarillo Ramp* after his death in a plane crash, Holt developed the idea for the gigantic *Sun Tunnels*, 18 feet long pipes that were 9 feet high.[3] She searched for a suitable site – a desert floor surrounded by low hills. The site she chose (and bought) was in the Great Basin Desert of Utah. *Sun Tunnels* was finished in 1976, with holes in the side of each concrete tube 7, 8, 9 and 10 inches diameter. The holes corresponded with star constellations (Capricorn, Draco, Columba and Perseus), as with *Hydra's Head*. During the day the sun creates points of light on the bottom of the tunnels that move. The moon also shines through the holes by night. *Sun Tunnels* links together the movements of celestial objects and the viewer on the planet.

Nancy Holt said she had the idea for *Sun Tunnels* while being out in the desert and watching the sun rising and setting. The flat desert area evoked 'a sense of being on this planet, rotating in space, in universal time' (1977). It is a cosmological piece of land art, something of an observatory, like the Bronze Age stone circles of Europe. 'I wanted to bring the vast space of desert back to human scale' (1977). The astronomical observatory has been an enduring theme in land art (such as in the work of Robert Morris, Michael Dan Archer, Julia Barton and Andy Goldsworthy).

Nancy Holt's *Hydra's Head* (1975) also concerned the relation between the heavens and earth. Next to the Niagara River at Art Park, Lewiston, NY, Holt sank 6 concrete tubes into the soil. Each three foot pipe was filled with water, so they formed circular mirrors flush with the ground. Again, Holt based the position of the concrete pits on a constellation (Hydra). *Hydra's Head* combined the presence and noise of the rushing Niagara River with the reflections of the sky, stars and moon. Holt's concrete pipe sculptures use the prime symbol of change and all things cosmic, the circle. The *Sun Tunnels* are like enormous telescopes or astrolabes, while *Hydra's Head* evokes six fallen stars, the circles of water reflecting the sky and stars.

Nancy Holt's romantic evocations of stellar, cosmological themes in concrete and soil flourished again with *Stone Enclosure: Rock Rings* (1977-78) constructed at Western Washington University Bellingham. Holt's *Stone Enclosure* directly recalled, even emulated, prehistoric stone circles, in particular Stonehenge. Holt used ancient schist rocks, between 200 and 230 million years old (known as brown mountain stone), to construct two concentric rings 10 feet high. In each wall of stone Holt made 4 arches, each 8 feet high, and 12 'portholes'. It was not a large stone ring, in terms of diameter (the outer diameter was 40 feet), but being ten feet high it was much taller than most Bronze Age stone circles.

Nancy Holt's *Stone Enclosure* makes the connections with ancient astronomy and stone circle building explicit, not slyly implied, as in much of land art. Holt is clear that she is dealing with the ancient astronomical realities of weather, seasons, cycles, stars and time. Another work, *30 Below* (1980), a tower with arches facing the points of the compass, was positioned around the North Star. The still point in the heavens, the Pole Star, was also one of the keys to *Stone Enclosure*, which, Holt said, related to a true North, a dead centre.[4] *Annual Ring* (1981) was an 'open hemi-dome' of steel bars, 30 feet in diameter and 15 feet high, constructed in Saginaw, Michigan. Again, Holt built the dome to highlight celestial events: the sun at the Summer solstice, the equinoxes, and the North Star.

One of Nancy Holt's biggest projects was the *Sky Mound*, begun in the late 1980s (the first phase cost $11 million). Situated in amongst Amtrack and NJ Transit train tracks, highways, bridges, the Pulaski Skyway, the New Jersey turnpike, and metropolitan New Jersey and New York, with views over Newark and Manhattan, *Sky Mound* was a converted landfill which Holt turned into an observatory to mark solstices, equinoxes, and the stars Vega and Sirius.

13

Alice Aycock

Alice Aycock's (b. 1946) environmental artworks are much more ambiguous and deliberately problematic than Nancy Holt's or Carl Andre's works. Many of Aycock's land sculptures involve underground passages and spaces. In 1972 she constructed a series of underground spaces in *Low Building Made with Dirt Roof (For Mary)* in Pennsylvania. The spectator entered the 20 by 12 feet work through a doorway thirty inches high. The work was experienced by crawling through it. Aycock's intention was to evoke an experience of claustrophia, of being in a cellar. Aycock's works had titles such as *The Machine That Makes the World* (1979), *A Theory of Universal Causality* (1983) and *How to Catch and Manufacture Ghosts* (1979) – Aycock is brilliant with titles.

Alice Aycock's sculpture explored the rationality of machines and technology and irrationality of ghosts and magic.[1] Aycock's 1972 *Maze* had direct parallels with the observatories and labyrinths of Robert Morris, Nancy Holt, Julia Barton and Michael Dan Archer. *Maze* consists of 5 concentric wooden rings, each six feet high, forming a 12-sided labyrinth. Essentially it is a fence maze, the kind that can be seen at theme parks and country houses. However, Aycock's New Kingston, Pennsylvania *Maze* is intended to be a labyrinth of the ancient type, a structure in which one is meant to get lost. Aycock stated that she wanted 'to create a moment of absolute panic – when the only thing that mattered was to get out.'[2]

Alice Aycock's intentions, then, are quite different from,

say, Nancy Holt's, who wishes to infuse a sense of celestial contemplation, or James Turrell's, who was after light and revelation. Aycock wants viewers to be confused, even frightened, by her underground passages and mazes. Aycock did not want the viewer to be able to get out of her labyrinth easily (it was partially based on a circular Egyptian labyrinth (designed as a prison), the Zulu *kraal* and the Amerindian stockade. Aycock also cited a circular Greek temple at Epidarus, a 'Place of Sacrifice').

Alice Aycock has spoken of the relations between her art and her own childhood dreams and fears. Her works recreate disturbing moments from her childhood, such as when she was trapped in a revolving barrel at an amusement park. Aycock's works deal with such moments of fear, confusion, strangeness and risk. Aycock also remarked that her structures were inspired by visits to the Pyramids in 1970 and the Greek tombs at Mycenæ, and fantasies of being buried alive.

Alice Aycock's *A Simple Network of Underground Walls and Tunnels* (1975) was made in a corn field at Far Hills, New Jersey. It consisted of 6 square wells in two rows of three excavated out of a 20 by 50 foot area. Two of the wells had 7 foot ladders that enabled the spectator to climb down and explore the dark connecting tunnels. Some of the wells were capped, others were open. The effect was a series of spaces that recalled 'ominous historical precedents, caves, catacombs, dungeons and beehive tombs', wrote Roberta Smith.[3]

Alice Aycock's 1974's *Walled-Trench/ Earth Platform/ Center Pit* was a series of three concentric walls built from concrete blocks. A platform of earth was made between the inner two walls: it was possible to jump onto this platform over the outer pit. Only when the spectator is standing on the inner platform does another aspect of *Walled-Trench/ Earth Platform/ Center Pit* become visible: a tunnel which leads into a dark inner chamber.

The fear and fantasy element in Alice Aycock's land and

site work found a new level of ambiguity in her 1976 *Circular Building with Narrow Ledge for Walking*. Again, the spectator was invited to explore this artwork physically (and psychologically). *Circular Building with Narrow Ledge for Walking* was a round structure thirteen feet high. Inside the well were three concentric ledges, only 8 inches wide. The wall went 7 feet into the ground, and was 'no more perilous or threatening than a treacherous cliff', the artist said, reassuringly.[4] Again, the spectator was invited to investigate the work by climbing a ladder outside the building, then edging her/ his way along the ledges. Indeed, the only way to fully appreciate *Circular Building with Narrow Ledge for Walking,* as with Aycock's other works, was to experience it directly.

Alice Aycock experimented with installing guillotines and motorized blade machines in works such as *The Machine That Makes the World* (1979) and later pieces, such as *A Salutation To the Wonderful Pig of Knowledge (Jelly Fish, Water, Spouter...), There's a Hole In My Bucket, There's a Hole In My Head, There's a Hole In My Dream)* (1984).

The structure *From the Series Entitled How To Catch and Manufacture Ghosts* (1980) was a much larger development of the earlier *How to Catch and Manufacture Ghosts*. It was a combination of steel, pipes, spheres and galvanized drums that drew inspiration from early experiments with electricity and magnetism, Marcel Duchamp's *Bachelor Apparatus*, the Montgolfiers' balloon launch pad, and an oil refinery on the New Jersey turnpike. A later work, *Tree of Life Fantasy: Synopsis of the Book of Questions Concerning the World Order and/ or the Order of Worlds* (1990-92), drew on influences from Renaissance illustrations of people walking into the sky to Heaven, DNA helices, ancient Indian observatories, and Walter Gropius's designs for theatres.

With Aycock's bewildering and unsettling catacombs and mazes one had to move 'one's body through them', a process which also involved descending back through time and memory.[5] Confronted with the subterranean passage or the *Circular Building with Narrow Ledge for Walking* it is soon apparent to the spectator that one is not dealing simply with an art object to be admired for its formal characteristics alone. Aycock wants the spectator to become physically involved in the sculpture: the physical actions of climbing and scrabbling over and through the sculpture trigger an exploration of one's own psychology and memory.[6] The physicality of the body as a tool for exploration in Aycock's works soon becomes a pretext or an inspiration for an exploration of personal psychology. Spectators are invited to risk themselves in exploring her works. Her land/ site art offers seductive as well as potentially dangerous spaces. Aycock wants the spectator to enter, but then confronts her/ him with a door that opens onto a wall, or a tiny passage to crawl through, or a ledge over a precipice, or a pit to vault over. Such devices go straight back to childhood, to acts of dare and bravado (such as walking along a high brick wall, egged on by other children).

14

Mary Miss

Mary Miss (b. 1944) attended the University of California at Santa Barbara. In Summer, 1963 she studied sculpture at Colorado College. After graduating in 1966 from the University of California, Miss studied at the Rinehard School of Sculpture at the Maryland Art Institute until 1968.

Early works included a 'water-line': at Fountain Creek in Colorado Mary Miss suspended a double knot of hemp rope 100 feet over a dry riverbed; every twenty feet were lines of rope. At War's Island in New York Miss threw 15 foot long wooden stakes into the water which were weighted with rocks.

In the middle of a wood in Connecticut in 1974, Mary Miss made *Sunken Pool*: it was a circular wooden structure, 10 feet tall, filled with one foot of water in a galvanized steel interior. *Sunken Pool* was sunken because Miss set it in a hole three feet deep and 20 feet across. As with the large site work of Alice Aycock and Robert Smithson, the spectator was invited to explore Miss's *Sunken Pool* physically, either by stepping into the water, or by climbing up the outer part of the wooden structure and looking over the top. Like Aycock's underground caverns, Miss's *Sunken Pool* was secretive, hiding away in a dense wood, with tall wooden sides. It seemed to speak, like Aycock's works, of childhood memories and half-remembered spaces.

Mary Miss's 1978 work *Perimeters/ Pavilion/ Decoys* was constructed in Roslyn, New York, in a field that was part of the Nassau County Museum's grounds. *Perimeters/ Pavillion/ Decoys* consists of three wooden towers, which look like tree houses with four platforms on stilts, two mounds of earth, and an underground space which's accessed by a ladder. The wooden towers are not for climbing on, but for viewing. The tallest is 18 by 10 by 10 feet. The subterranean atrium was for exploring. It was a 16 ft² pit with a seven foot hole acting as an entrance; visitors climbed down a ladder to explore the different underground spaces, some with wooden, others with soil walls.

Perimeters/ Pavillion/ Decoys was related to Pueblo Indian structures, Pompeiian and Mexican courtyards, and Mesopotamian brick complexes. The site explored the physical and psychological aspects of 'inside/ outside, above/ below, light/ dark, open/ closed, nature/ artifice'.[1] Miss's works are often large, spreading over a wide area of ground. In Illinois she created a 5-acre scale work.[2]

15

Michael Heizer

My work is closely tied up with my own experiences; for instance, my personal associations with dirt are very real. I really like it, I really like to lie in the dirt.

Michael Heizer[1]

Land artworks have proved to be, from a second wave feminist point-of-view, some of the most phallic and patriarchal of contemporary productions in contemporary art.[2] Christo works on a gigantic scale, for instance, wrapping buildings or stretching curtains across valleys or surrounding islands. Some of the most domineering works of land art are by Michael Heizer (b. 1944).[3] In his *Double Negative* (1969-70), his most well-known piece, and one of the most famous examples of land art, his team took two chunks out of the earth, a gigantic 'violation' of the planet, in ecological/ green terms.[4] Heizer claimed *Double Negative* is 'the smallest piece I've done in relation to the size of the site'.[5] Heizer directed the gouging out 240,000 tons of earth from the site at Mormon Mesa in Nevada with bulldozers. The cuts are ramps, going down 50 feet through the cliff of the canyon. The spectator can walk down them. The overall dimensions of *Double Negative* are 1,500 x 42 feet.

Michael Heizer is very much concerned with *scale*, as well as other formal characteristics of a work. Heizer said he liked working outside because of the scale; he could work large. He also said that '[m]an will never really create anything large in relation to the world.'[6]

Michael Heizer's *Double Negative* is a widely celebrated example of land art. The photographs of it have been reproduced in many art history books. *Double Negative* appeals to trendy 1960s notions of Zen Buddhism, Existentialism, negativity and emptiness. The point about *Double Negative* was its sense of symmetry and relationship, the one cut reflecting the other across the Nevada canyon.

Some viewers saw Michael Heizer's enterprise as combining the subliminity and grandeur of Abstract Expressionism with the emblematic forms of Minimalism. American earthworks art rejuvenated the myth of the sublime West.[7] Mary Miss was not convinced. When she looks at the work of Heizer or Robert Smithson: 'there's always been an aspect which impedes my relating to it... It's like a mark on the earth'.[8]

Michael Heizer went on archaeological digs as a child with his father. He started out with the ambition to be a painter, which he studied in San Francisco. He made his first earthwork in 1967, and accompanied Robert Smithson on geological expeditions. In 1968, Heizer collaborated with Smithson and Nancy Holt on a Super-8 film, *Mono-Lake*. (Heizer had invited Holt and Smithson to his parents' house at Lake Tahoe). Heizer's motorbike earthwork was entitled *Circular Surface Displacement*; it was made at Mono Lake.

Michael Heizer's other works include gouging huge holes in the ground and putting great chunks of rock in them. *Nine Nevada Depressions* (1968) comprised five cuts in the Blackrock desert, each one twelve feet long in an area 50 by 50 feet. *Munich Depression* (1969) was another cut, a line 15 feet deep. Heizer's *Complex One* (1972) was a huge bunker-like mass of earth built with the aid of two assistants in Nevada. It was 23.5 feet high and 140 feet long. Each end of the hill had a cut-off triangle of reinforced concrete like giant book-ends. Over the work were cantilevered concrete beams. '*Complex One* is a magnificent spectacle. Even its minatory look, suggesting a bunker, seems proper to the site – the edge of the Nevada nuclear proving-ground', remarked Robert Hughes.[9]

If you make the trip up to the DIA gallery in upstate New York, which I recommend highly, you'll see an enormous Heizer installation from 1967, re-done at Beacon in 2002, of giant holes in the ground (entitled *North, East, South, West*).

16

Walter de Maria

Walter de Maria (b. 1935) made a dramatic land art gesture when he cut a 4.5 mile-long 6 foot-wide scar in the desert in Nevada with a bulldozer (*Las Vegas Piece*, 1969). Commentators have criticized this cut as a 'wound' or 'scar' on the Earth. The ultimate in ithyphallic, male land art must be de Maria's *Vertical Earth Kilometer*. At a cost of $500,000, de Maria and his team sunk a one kilometre brass rod into the planet. Nothing can be seen of it except a 2 inch brass disc on the ground.

The making of Walter de Maria's work is perhaps far more interesting than the artwork itself. It must be the ultimate art statement/ non-statement. De Maria's *Vertical Earth Kilometer* remains practically invisible. It neatly melds two 1960s æsthetic movements: Conceptualism (wow, what an idea, sticking a kilometer of solid brass into the Earth!), and Minimal art (there's nothing to see of it except... a two inch brass disc!). Yeah, that's *real art*, a kilometer-long piece of metal stuck into the ground with nothing of it showing except a tiny disc. This is, in Richard Long's words, 'true capitalist art', an art of excessive cost, and maybe excessive waste (it took 79 days to bore the shaft).[1]

Shown at Kassel Dokumenta 6 in 1977, Walter de Maria's *Vertical Earth Kilometer* upset British artist Stuart Brisley so much he made *Survival in Alien Circumstances*. This was a hole in the earth dug with his bare hands, which Brisley lived in for 2 weeks, intending to mock de Maria's overblown American earthwork. But then, art has been full of idiotic amounts of money and out-size projects for ages. In 1979 de Maria exhibited *The Broken Kilometer*: 500 brass rods each two metres long arranged in rows on the floor of a New York gallery.

Walter de Maria started out as a musician rather than, like many land artists, as a painter or sculptor. He played drums with the art rockers Velvet Underground. One of his early ideas (in 1962) for an earthwork was a mile-long pair of walls that would be 12 feet high and 12 feet apart. De Maria said that 'when you walk between, you can look up and see the sky'.[2] After the four and a half mile bulldozer square cut in the Earth, de Maria made a chalk drawing in the desert.

Walter de Maria's *Earth Room* was a gallery full of dark earth made in 1968 in Munich and later in New York (*The New York Earth Room*, SoHo Gallery, 1977). It consisted of 125 tons of soil, taking up 3,600 square feet, 22 inches deep. This was a vivid (and aromatic) example of bringing the Outside inside, one of land art's key projects. The contrasts were immediate, between the flat, clean, white, controlled gallery space and the 1,600 cubic feet of uneven, 'dirty', dark, organic soil. Roberta Smith said it was a 'shock' to see the soil taking up the interior space usually reserved for things such as furniture and people. 'The dirt carried its own absence, was somehow a living substance'.[3] A related work, *5 Continents Sculpture* (1987-88), comprised white rocks filling an area 42 by 77 feet in a Stuttgart gallery.

You can see a recreation of the *Earth Room*, and also the *Broken Kilometer*, in downtown New York City, at the DIA centres, for free. If you haven't seen them, you must go: these are very large artworks in the heart of Gotham, classic Minimal and Sixties and Seventies artworks. You don't walk around them, but view them from a single vantage point. The *Earth Room* is very impressive: it takes up the whole floor of a building.

Walter de Maria's *Bed of Spikes* (1969) was called 'a

piece of Dadaist Sadism' by Harold Rosenberg.[4] *Bed of Spikes*, an installation at the Dwan Gallery, was 153 metal spikes set in five planks on the floor. Spectators were asked to sign a release that exempted the gallery for being responsible for any accidents on viewing the installation. *Bed of Spikes* looked forward to *Lightning Field*.

Critic Kenneth Baker called Walter de Maria's most famous work, the *Lightning Field,* the 'grandest Minimalist work of the 1970s' and 'the closest thing to a masterpiece to come out of Minimalism'.[5] De Maria's first *Lightning Field* was sited 40 miles from Flagstaff in Arizona, consisting of 2 inch diameter steel poles, 18 feet tall, 30 feet apart, in five rows of seven.

The second, larger *Lightning Field* is a grid of 400 stainless steel poles, 16 along the width, 25 along the length, each about 20 feet high, situated in the New Mexico desert.[6] The poles were set in concrete, one foot below land, able to withstand winds of 110 mph. The site was chosen for its flatness, isolation and lightning activity. The most lightning occurs during May-September; there are about 60 days when thunder and lightning can be seen from *Lightning Field*.[7]

Lightning Field is about a mile by 0.6 mile in size. The poles in *Lightning Field* stand alone, about 220 feet apart. Nothing remains on the ground of the work needed to set them there. The tips of the poles define a plane in space parallel to sea level: the length of each pole varies according to the contours of the landscape. The *Lightning Field* is an exact, mathematically-precise human site laid onto nature, where the poles are tiny mirrors which mark out and calibrate the landscape. The site looks like a scientific or industrial project – like a radio telescope site, say, or a military communications centre. *Lightning Field* is spectacular, with masculine and phallic connotations (lightning is related in symbolism to male creativity, sperm, fire, power and shamanism).

Lightning Field is ambiguously associated with the DIA

Art Foundation, which financed its construction. The site recalls technological experiments, while the poles themselves evoke Constantin Brancusi's *Birds in Space*, and his *Endless Column*.

Walter de Maria's *Lightning Field* attracts lightning, and a storm, as anyone knows, can be about one of the most erotic and spectacular phenomenon in nature.[8] May to September is the season of the great storms in the area, sometimes 'two or three a week cross this field of poles'.[9]

Joseph Beuys produced a striking piece entitled *Lightning* (1982-85): a gigantic chunk of bronze, narrow at the top, splaying out towards the bottom, as if he was trying to make manifest the bolt of energy leaping down to the Earth. Justin Holland too used lightning in artworks; he collaborated with Westinghouse Electric, making humanmade lightning, and 'seeded' clouds to produce storms. Peter Hutchinson and Alice Aycock also created cloud works.

17

Other Land Artists In the U.S.A.

Some other artists living and working in North America include:

JAMES PIERCE

James Pierce created a series of earthworks at Pratt Farm in central Maine in the 1970s: there was a triangular turf maze; a small earth *Observatory*; a *Serpent* made from large rocks; a *Stone Ship*; a *Burial Mound*; a stone *Altar* (in the shape of male genitals); and figures built out of grass and soil: *Earthwoman* and *Suntreeman*. Pierce's *Earthwoman* (1976-77) was a recumbent female shape, with prominent buttocks, evoking the erotic gardens of the 18th century, and the links between prehistoric earth mounds, fertility and femininity.

HERBERT BAYER

Herbert Bayer (1900-85) created earthworks which directly evoked prehistoric structures: Bayer's *Earth Mound* (1955) in Aspen, Colorado, contained the familiar motifs of ancient religions and cultures: a circular rampart enclosing a small mound; a standing stone and a hollow were placed beside the mound. In Kent, Washington, Bayer built a series of earthworks (*Mill Creek Canyon Earthworks*, 1979-82), which featured circular ramparts, circular moats, mounds surmounted by walkways, and circular bulwarks split by a path. At a quarry in upstate New York, William Bennett fashioned a *Wedge (Stone Boat)* (1976), an 80 foot-long smooth-sided channel in the limestone.

PATRICIA JOHANSON's (b. 1940) most well-known work is probably the large water park she fashioned in Dallas, Texas, between 1981 and 1986. *Fair Park Lagoon* comprised a series of interlacing walkways above the pool in an 'organic', Gaudiesque manner, and cost over $2 million. Christine Oatman lit a fire on a frozen lake in the centre of a circle of tall icicles in *Icicle Circle and Fire* (1973).

GORDON MATTA-CLARK

Gordon Matta-Clark (1943-78) transformed buildings by knocking enormous holes in them (*Conical Intersect*, 1975), or cutting a house in New Jersey in half (*Splitting*, 1974). But these were not sculpted spaces or physical gestures so much as Conceptual reorganizations of a structure. It's easy to discern the influence of Matta-Clark's interventions in houses and buildings (which he called 'unbuilding') on Andy Goldsworthy's holes and Rachel Whiteread's works (such as her impressions of rooms and houses).

Gordon Matta-Clark bought up pieces of land in the borough of Queens (in 1973), in another Conceptual piece; none of them were big enough for housing or for much else (some were only 2 by 3 feet, tiny strips of land). *Reality Positions, Fake Estates* explored the notion of land ownership. Matta-Clark explained:

> One or two of the prize ones were a foot strip down somebody's driveway and a square foot of sidewalk. And the others were kerbstone and gutterspace. What I basically wanted to do was to designate spaces that wouldn't be seen and certainly not occupied. Buying them was my own take on the strangeness of existing property demarcation lines. Property is so all-pervasive.[1]

ANA MENDIETA

Ana Mendieta (1948-85) covered herself in mud (while nude, of course) and stood against a tree (for *The Tree of Life* series, 1977, made in Old Man's Creek, Iowa), a combination of Goddess art, performance art and environmental art. In *The Tree of Life* series, Mendieta left the outline of her body in leaves on a tree trunk. In the *Silueta* series (1979), Mendieta imprinted her body in the snow in Amana, Iowa, and in mud on a riverbank, set the form on fire in the earth, and made a silhouette from flowers.

These pieces echo Andy Goldsworthy's rain and snow 'body prints' (however, Ana Mendieta's art has an undisguised ideological, spiritual and ecological agenda; some of Mendieta's works are explicit performance explorations of rapes, and Mendieta was also delved into her Cuban and Latin American heritage).

In some pieces Ana Mendieta remodelled the entrance of a cave and a ravine into her Goddess shape. She also buried herself under turf – a literal Earth-Goddess mound, and had herself photographed in an ancient Mexican stone grave.[2] Mendieta also lit fires in sculptures (such as *Volcano*, 1979), like Chris Drury and David Nash, and lit candles and fireworks in the shape of a woman. Teresa Murak, in a Mendietan gesture, covered her naked body with cress seeds, while lying in a bath (in *Seed*, 1989). 'They sprout, swell and begin after a few hours to grow right on my body'.[3]

DONNA DENNIS

Donna Dennis (b. 1942) took the vernacular architecture of New York City as her starting-point in her 1970s works: *Tunnel Tower* was based on the entrance building to the Holland Tunnel. Later, nostalgic works, such as *Deep Station* (1981-85), recreated the shadowy recesses of subway stations (in full-scale, something like a movie set or an installation). Elyn Zimmerman created large-scale ecological land art, such as her *Keystone Island* (1989), a 50-foot wide artificial island built on a lagoon in a mangrove swamp. Jackie Ferrara's works include *Garden Courtyard* (1989), a large piece of landscape art involving steps, grass, trees, seating, platforms and walkways at the Fulton County Government Center in Atlanta.

CHARLES ROSS

Charles Ross (b. 1937) constructed a large observatory, *Star Axis* (1989), which recalled the celestial viewing spaces of James Turrell, Nancy Holt and Robert Morris. It was designed for viewing the North Star (the North Star was undoubtedly the land artists' favourite star – apart from the sun – appearing in works by Turrell, among others). Charles Simonds made an *Abandoned Observatory* (1976), in model form. Juan Geuer has also worked with the sky: he mounted four pairs of large mirrors in the National Gallery of Canada in order to reflect the sky in the glass cupola above (*Karonhia*, 1989).

DOUGLAS HOLLIS

Douglas Hollis (b. 1948) constructed 'sound gardens' – a series of wind organ pipes mounted on towers beside the shore in Seattle, WA (1980). Hollis's *Field of Vision* (1980) comprised 900 wind vanes at Lake Placid, NY, to 'explore the choreography between windscape and landscape'.[4] In the Seventies Hollis experimented with sending up kites that emitted sound (*Sky Soundings*, 1975).

18

Chris Drury

Chris Drury was born in 1948 (in Sri Lanka) and educated at Camberwell School of Art in London in the late Sixties. Drury is a British artist who has made works with numerous links with those of Andy Goldsworthy. Drury is 8 years older than Goldsworthy and belongs to the generation of Alan Sonfist, Michael Heizer, Alice Aycock, Mary Miss, David Nash and Richard Long (all born between 1944 and 1946). Drury had begun with figurative sculpture. Among the artists that Drury admired were Roger Ackling and Constantin Brancusi (Drury said he found Joseph Beuys 'immensely irritating' and 'too self-obsessed').[1] Drury has exhibited in many solo shows, including the Henry Moore Centre in Leeds, Royal Botanic Gardens in Edinburgh, and London's Serpentine Gallery). (Many of the quotes from Drury come from *Silent Spaces*, 1998, and an interview in *Song of the Earth*, edited by M. Gooding and W. Furlong, 2002).

The art of Chris Drury and Andy Goldsworthy share so many elements: they are both British land artists, both emphasize spirituality, both use similar forms (cairns, shelters, globes, spirals, circles), use similar materials (boulders, grass, willowherb stalks, wood, snow, clay), and both have worked and exhibited in similar territories: Japan, the U.S.A. and Scotland (Drury has created works, though, in places Goldsworthy has not been associated with, such as Ireland, Italy, Denmark and Spain, and Drury has produced many works near his home in Lewes, Sussex). They also share the same book publishers (Thames & Hudson and Cameron Books), the same art critics who've written about their work (Paul Nesbitt and Terry Friedman), and have worked with the same institutions (such as the British Council, Common Ground, the Henry Moore Foundation, Sustrans, the Scottish Arts Council and the Arts Council).

One of Chris Drury's concerns was human history, the relation between people and the land: his artworks re-use dewponds and stone walls, draw attention to prehistoric tumuli by building domes over them, and altering maps, one of the most elegant manifestations of human history. *A Dense History of Place* (1996) was one of Drury's map works which combined maps with written text (a common motif in land and Conceptual art). Dense lines of text spread outwards in a circular pattern from an area near the coast in Sussex depicted in an Ordnance Survey map, a region which has many personal associations for Drury.

Another form of Chris Drury's is the globe set on the ground. Drury has created spheres from pine cones (1984), deer bones and deer scats (*Four Spheres,* 1984), and bamboo, ginkgo, vines, moss and seeds (*Shimanto River Spheres,* 1997, Japan). In *Bound Oak* (1990), made in Sherwood Forest, Drury wrapped a rope of grass around an old oak tree.

Chris Drury's art departs from Andy Goldsworthy's art at many points, however: the use of materials such as animal bones, antlers, horns, and feathers, the basket weaving, the spherical 'baskets' like pots, the kayaks, and the cloud chambers. Drury is much more inclined than many land artists to use in his sculpture material from animals, such as whale bones, or reindeer antlers, or ram's horns, or elk bones, or gull's feathers, or cow dung. In the *Adharc* pieces (1991-92), Drury took the form of a ram's horn and multiplied it in peat and bronze. Drury affirms the community aspect of his art more than some land artists, and the spiritual dimension (he speaks of meditation and the Buddhist void, for instance).

A key sculpture in Chris Drury's œuvre was his *Medicine*

Wheel (made in 1983), a calendar work which collected 365 found objects strung on bamboo stalks mounted around the edge of plant papers and a mushroom spore at the centre. Drury wrote his diary in lines spreading outwards from the centre (a recurring motif in his work). Among the objects were hen feathers, wheat, runner beans, snail shells, pebbles, twigs, bark, berries, acorns, flowers, seeds, fish bones, grass, grapefruit, cherry blossom, hawthorn, crab, mussels, sheep bone, mistletoe, seaweed, cork, walnuts, quinces, rabbit skin, figs, and a cat's skull. The *Medicine Wheel* inspired many new forms in Drury's art:

> out of that came different categories of work. It started me off on making shelters and baskets, and then the shelters led to cloud chambers, and the baskets and the large, woven works I've made outside led me to the dewpond works. I've made woven maps, weaving ideas of landscape. And then there are the found objects.[2]

Like many land artists and sculptors, Chris Drury has created many works near his home in Lewes, Sussex (like Andy Goldsworthy in Penpont, David Nash in Blaenau-Ffestiniog and Richard Long in Bristol and the South-West). Drury's works in Sussex include *Vortex* (Lewes Castle), *Cuckoo Dome*, *Beehive Shelter* (Goodwood), *Holding Light* (Brighton), *Guardian Shelter* (Sheffield Forest), *Chalk Chamber* (a barn in Sussex), *Rhythms of the Heart* (Hastings), *Heart of Reeds* (Lewes), Towner Art Gallery, Eastbourne, *Seven Sisters Bundles* (near Eastbourne), and the dewponds.

Chris Drury stated that his work was not self-referential, that it referred to things outside of itself. (One of Drury's criticisms of Joseph Beuys was that his work was too self-obsessed). However, there was plenty of self-referentiality in Drury's art: the *Medicine Wheels*, for example, comprised diary entries for every day of the year. Another work also heavy with thousands of closely written words, *A Dense History of Place*, was full of autobiographical associations. The emphasis on cataloguing also had a biographical element, as did the penchant for works linked to Drury's homeground of Lewes in Sussex. Then there's the emphasis on community projects, where the artist interacts with a local community. Those personal interactions, which Drury cherishes, also contain a strong biographical element.

Basket weaving is one of Chris Drury's passions, and he has created many forms using weaving, including a large open dome from hazel branches (*Cuckoo Dome*, 1992), kayak forms (*Kayak Bundles,* 1994), globular forms (*Basket For the Forest Deer*, 1987), and small vessels (*Basket For the Trees*, 1988, *Hollow Vessel*, 1989). Many of Drury's baskets are recognisable traditional baskets: *Five Sisters* (1994), *Basket For the Moment Between Life and Death* (1985) and *Dream Basket* (1985). In *Basket For the Crows* (1986), the distinctive black crow feathers are employed to weave a basket, placed on the floor, with a long row of feathers suspended above it.

Linked with the basket woven pieces are the small bundles of found objects (such as *Cholla Bundles* [1993], *Beaver Sticks* [1991], and *Stick Bundle* [1992]). *Seven Sisters Bundles* (1994), for instance, comprises objects found at the famous Sussex cliffs (driftwood, flint, chalk and fishing twine). The bundles, for Drury, were 'talismans of time and place, souvenirs, made simply at a campsite, or alternatively made at a later date as an act of remembering' (1998, 58).

An off-shoot of Chris Drury's penchant for weaving is the interlacing of maps (maps being one of the key components of land art). Thus, Drury has interwoven a map of Manhattan with one of the Hebrides (1996), and West Cork with New Mexico (1995). Like Tony Cragg, Drury has collated found objects into patterns (such as *Tidelines*, 1985, made from pieces of plastic, metal, rubber, driftwood and feathers).

Some of Chris Drury's vessels have been woven from willow (1994), or bamboo (1997), some have been covered with cow dung (1992), and some have been created with turf (1991). Some of Drury's wall drawings, fashioned with river mud (*River Vortex*, 1998), recall Richard Long's mud wall drawings.

Chris Drury's art tended to be interconnected: the baskets and woven vessels were linked to the woven maps, and the woven globes, and also some of the larger shelters. The dewponds were patterned after baskets.

> On occasion I have taken a basket weave, enlarged it, and turned it upside down to act as a shelter or as valve between inner and outer... basket to shelter, shelter to basket... A web of interconnections links all these works. (1998, 22-23)

One of Chris Drury's most striking sculptures was *Stone Whirlpool* (1996), built from river stones arranged into a spiral in a Japanese river (in Okawa-mura), near a waterfall. It was one of a number of Drury's works which explored vortexes and spirals. An associated work which took on currents of energy was *Edge of Chaos* (2000), a large paper work covered with handwritten texts describing the world's ocean currents and winds. One of Drury's largest vortex works was *Heart of Reeds* (2000).

Chris Drury has reclaimed and reworked dewponds, mainly in Sussex (*Basket Dewpond*, 1997 and 1999), some of which are quite ancient. In these shallow dips in the landscape Drury has fashioned his favourite motifs of spirals and vortexes from grass and snow. *Snow Vortex* (1999) was a labyrinth with paths dug out of snow on Firle Downs in Sussex. Drury has also made a dry stone vortex maze and a 'wave garden'. (Drury has his favourite motifs: the mushroom gill form, the dome, and the spiral or vortex, which recur in so many sculptures.)

Boats, kayaks and 'vessels' are another recurring form in Chris Drury's art. Some of the vessels are enormous cannibalized stone walls (such as *Long Vessel*, 1995), or heaps of stones willow and reeds woven on top of them (such as *Shelter Vessel*, 1988, made in County Galway). Some of the vessels are basket woven (such as *Connemara Vessels*,

1988). *Air Vessel* (1994), woven from willow, is one of Drury's most intriguing sculptures: in the form of a kayak, a skeletal form of woven twigs, it was exhibited hanging in space in the gallery, evoking all sorts of associations (with boats as flying transports, or the rich symbolism of flight, or shamanic flight). For Drury, *Air Vessel* was about journeying, the 'moments of exhilaration on mountains where I have experienced a feeling akin to flying' (1998, 12). Some of the shelters, Drury said, were 'like overturned boats and denote journey, movement' (ib., 20).

Chris Drury has treated his cairns in different ways: many of the stone cairns have had fires lit inside them, such as *Midsummer Fire Cairn* (1989), *Falling Water Fire Cairn* (1997, Norway), *Fire Cairn* (1993, Ireland), *Fire Mountain Cairn* (1996, Japan), and *Fire Cairn* (1989, Colorado). Some cairns have been enclosed with basket weaving, such as *Basket Cairn* (1991) and *Covered Cairn* (1993, Denmark).

Like Richard Long's stone rows or Andy Goldsworthy's cairns, Chris Drury's stone cairns are usually erected in wilderness or spectacular scenery: Norway (1988), New Mexico (1993), De Lank River, Cornwall (1990), Lappland (1988), Webster Ross, Scotland (1992), Kintail, Scotland (1994), Ladakh (1997) and Colorado (1989). For Drury, the cairns are about commemorating a particular moment in a special place: 'they're just saying, 'this is an extraordinary place. Grab a few rocks, put them up before the moment's gone and photograph it'' (2002, 79). If the shelters were the stopping-places on a journey, the cairns were the 'markers of highpoints/ moments of exhilaration along the way' (1998, 58).

Another favourite Chris Drury motif is the shelter: low, squat structures, some like teepees or witches' hats, some like prehistoric beehive huts. The shelters were often made from stone (but also in chalk, turf, ice, wood, plants and coal. Some of these materials, such as turf, coal and chalk, are unexpected, and give Drury's shelters a very particular quality). The shelters are usually (but not always) constructed at human scale. That is, in the correct scale for someone to enter them bodily. *Beara Shelter* (1995), in West Cork, Ireland, was a squat, square, stone structure, with views of the sea and Bulls Rock. 'The intention was to provide a space for being and contemplation' (1998, 20). Some of the shelters, such as *Shelter For the Winds That Blow From Siberia*, made near Drury's home in Lewes in 1986, have a distinctly Goldsworthyan flavour: blocks of ice mounted on a hazel frame, looking like an igloo. *Shelter For the Northern Glaciers* (188) was constructed in the spectacular coastal setting of Seiland island, in Norway, surrounded by snow-capped mountains. Geoffrey Harris has also constructed wooden shelters in forests (*Hollow Spruce*, 1988).

Some of the shelters, as with the cairns, have had fires lit inside them (*Shelter For Dreaming*, 1985). Some of the shelters are open structures, without a covering (rather like a frame tent before the canvas is pulled on top). Others are a frame which's wrapped with ice, or turf, or reeds (such as *Shelter For Herbs and Healing*, 1986). *Tree Mountain Shelter* (1994, Italy) was a stone cairn enclosed with a cone of hazel branches. *Turf Chamber* (1992) comprised sections of turf laid on top of a hazel branch frame. The *Wave Chamber* (1996) was constructed beside a flooded valley in Northumberland, and contained a mirror and lens in a steel periscope mounted atop the structure so that the image of the waves could be projected inside, onto the floor.

Chris Drury's shelters have all sorts of connotations, stretching back thousands of years (shelters must have been one of the first structures that humans ever built – shelter being one of the primal human needs). 'Shelter is a basic human need and a manifestation of human presence', remarked Drury (1998, 20). Drury's shelters have obvious affinities (with Celtic and Bronze Age huts and houses in Britain, for example), but they are also about 'organic' forms, forms which repeat endlessly, and geometrically, like crystals.

They are stopping and resting places, and also enclosing spaces. 'I like the way this interior space draws you inside yourself, enclosing, protecting, just as mountains pull you outside yourself, pushing mind and body beyond their usual confines', said Drury (ibid.).

The shelters are also about the landscapes in which they are constructed, like land art in general. They tend to be built in rural or wilderness zones, and are the only structures of that kind in the area (they stand out as artworks, not as part of the agricultural machinery, for instance). The shelters are thus also free-standing sculptures, artworks which draw attention to themselves. The shelters are also about land art concerns, such as the tensions between what's inside and what's outside, between the human-made structure and a 'natural' context (the landscape), about the relation between form and function, æsthetics and use. The shelters draw attention to the landscape around them.

One of Chris Drury's shelters, *Covered Tumulus* (1997), took on the theme of human history directly, and the sense of revealing what's there: Drury built a dome of hazel branches over a prehistoric mound on the South Downs in Sussex. The *Hut of the Shadow* (1997) was sited in North Uist in the Scottish Western Isles with the local community in mind. In *Covered Cairn* (1993), made at TICKON in Denmark, Drury placed a hazel and willow twig frame dome over a stone cairn, an approach that combined the Druryan motif of the open, woven frame with the stone cairn created by balancing rocks atop each other. 'The woven dome is a division between outside and in,' commented Drury, 'which nevertheless allows a transition from one to the other, a free flow of inner to outer. The experience inside it is different from the experience outside' (1998, 80).

One of Chris Drury's more unusual shelters was *Mind Wave* (1996), made in the Botanic Gardens in Copenhagen: Drury combined a couple of his favourite forms: the mushroom-shaped text drawing, and the dome. In *Mind*

Wave, Drury opted to adapt a geodesic dome greenhouse, which he painted in blue and scratched the words 'mind' and 'wave' in the paint, spreading outwards from the centre of the dome, in the pattern of the gills of a mushroom.

Some of Chris Drury's most appealing sculptures are 'cloud chambers', developments of his shelter form: these are basically circular stone or wooden shelters with holes and mirrors in the roof which act as lenses and reflectors. In these *camera obscuras*, the spectator can observe the sky above projected onto the floor below. The cloud chambers (constructed in many areas) articulate classic land art concerns: the dialectic between inner and outer, indoor and outdoor, stillness and movement, nature and culture. Drury's cloud chambers include *Coppice Cloud Chamber* (1998, Kent), *Cloud Chamber* (Piccadilly, London, 1993), *Cloud Chamber* (1994, Aberdeen), *Eden Cloud Chamber* (2002, Cornwall), *Reed Chamber* (2002, Arundel), *Cedar Log Sky Chamber* (1996, Japan), *Hut of the Shadow* (1997, Western Isles), *Clohan Cloud Chamber* (1992, Dublin), *Cloud Chamber* (1990, Belgium), *Cloud Chamber For the Trees and Sky* (2003, North Carolina) and *Wicklow Cloud Chamber* (1990, Glencree, Ireland). The cloud chambers are 'still, silent, meditative and mysterious places', Drury wrote on his website.

Chris Drury's cloud chambers are linked with historical structures, such as the Roman Pantheon, which contains a hemispherical dome 142 feet above the floor (built in the 2nd century AD). At the apex of the dome is the *oculus* (eye), which lets in light: it was associated with the 'eye of Heaven'. Even though they are much smaller in scale than the beautiful Pantheon in Rome, then, Drury's meditative cloud and wave chambers have symbolic and religious connotations.

Some of Chris Drury's larger works, such as *Vortex* (an enormous hollow cone of woven hazel and willow made at Lewes Castle in 1994), have aspects in common with artists such as Tony Cragg or Richard Deacon. Another large work, *Heart of Reeds* (2000), was a proposal for a spiral vortex on five acres of reclaimed land in Lewes, Sussex (completed in 2004).

A later development of Chris Drury's art was to see the (human) body as 'landscape', to explore the processes of the body, and the relationships between the body and the Earth. Manifestations of this development in Drury's interests were the Lewes *Heart of Reeds* project (which was based on the human heart), *Heart River* (1999), a pattern on paper from a cross-section of the heart, and the several works Drury has made in conjunction with hospitals (such as *Rhythms of the Heart*, 2000, made at Hastings). In these works, Drury has explored the flow of blood and water in the body, wave patterns from echocardiograms, and the formations in rocks, trees and the landscape.

For Chris Drury, there wasn't a separation between humans and nature, no 'us and them' (or, rather, 'us and it'): nature was all around, inside as well as outside: '[w]e ourselves are nature... We're a part of nature' (2002, 79.) Drury was interested in exploring the relation between inside and outside, nature and culture, and how 'nature is really culture' (ib., 76). For Drury, the natural world could never be 'natural', on its own, completely distinct from humanity – at least as far as humans were concerned. The natural world was always totally enculturated. In other words, if humans were looking at nature, they could only ever see nature in human terms.

> When you're out in the countryside, culture, or our view of nature, determines how you see what's in front of you. So you never see a thing as it is, you always see it in the way that you've been programmed to see it. And you can't get away from that, ever... We *are* nature, we have to touch nature, we touch it every single second of the day, we breathe it.[3]

Chris Drury said he went out into the countryside (into the 'natural' world) to make art because it was inspirational, it was away from telephones, people, cars, etc, and it was different from human-made environments (like cities). Also, work made outside tended to be less self-conscious (2002, 72).

A work being 'site-specific' was important for Chris Drury: it was about the place, the uses of the place, the history of the place, and the people who lived in the place.

> It's made there, it's made out of the material that's there and it's made by people who live there. All those elements come into it and it has to find its place with the landscape but also within the culture relative to what those people are. (2002, 73)

Chris Drury saw the spaces he made that people entered as 'meditative spaces'. They were direct experiences. The cloud chambers, for example, were 'very still, meditative places' where visitors would not sit and think but sit and experience the place directly. The effect the cloud chambers had depended upon the person. They worked best when they encouraged the viewer to sit still for a moment and reflect (2002, 76). The idea of the *Beara Shelter* was 'a space for being and contemplation' (1998, 20).

One of the developments of 1960s land art was to put the artist *inside* the art. In the traditional manner of painting the landscape, the artist was viewing the landscape from a distance, standing back; but 'since the 1960s artists have been putting themselves into it', Drury observed (2002, 76). For Drury, the photograph is a poor substitute for the work itself. Drury said he had taken photographs of ephemeral works (such as the cairns), but was more interested in working 'with people in the real world' (2002, 81).

Unlike some of his British contemporaries (Andy Goldsworthy, Richard Long, Hamish Fulton), Chris Drury encouraged people to visit the sites of his works. He published a website and postcards with instructions on how to find them. 'In no way could that work communicate itself through a photograph because it's an experience, and nothing you could bring to a gallery would get anywhere near what the thing is about' (2002, 81). In this respect, Drury has more in common with American earth artists, such as Dennis Oppenheim or Robert Smithson, who exalted site and location.

Going out and walking or making work from time to time is important for Chris Drury – especially if he hasn't done any travelling or walking for a while. 'I'm really fortunate to be invited to extraordinary places to go and make work' (2002, 79). However, it wasn't the object itself that was the really valuable aspect of travelling or working on commissions for Drury, but the process and experience of making it, interacting with people, living in particular environments. 'The main thing you bring back is how the experience has changed you inside' (ibid.). So some of the pieces Drury makes are not about specific places or times, but 'the whole activity of being out there in those places'.

> In a sense you can't not be a conceptual artist these days, because you have to think about the world and if you don't you're not contributing to the debate in any useful way. But at the same time, in order to make art that's really interesting you have to stop thinking.[4]

Chris Drury said he didn't think of himself as really fitting into the land art or art and nature genre. 'As soon as you say 'art and nature', it makes people think of fiddling about with sticks, which is really not what I'm interested in' (2002, 90). Although labelled as a land artist, Drury preferred to see himself as an artist who 'explores nature and culture, inner and outer'.[5] There was no division between art, nature and humanity, for Drury: the artist – and art – was always part of nature ('there is no division between man, art and nature').[6]

Chris Drury did not think of himself, either, as the kind of artist who had something to express, who wished to make statements about issues or the world.

> Personally I have nothing to communicate, consciously or unconsciously; the work simply reflects the moving from

> moment to moment in the world as it is, and so it is
> nature itself that communicates. (ibid.)

In this view, Chris Drury saw himself as a shamanic translator of nature and the world, a creative interface between the world and the viewer. As well as shamanism, critics have also linked Drury's art to Buddhism. Rather than an 'creator' of art, or an 'expresser' of emotions or statements or views, then, Drury would be seen as a 'reflector' of nature and the world, someone who does not 'create' art but reflects what is already in the world and in nature (and in himself and in other people). In this view, Drury's output is a manifestation of his being-in-the-world, so to speak. It's an art of ontology, of beingness, of being in the moment, of reflecting the moment (or the passing of moments), rather than the traditional (Western) view of art as being about personal expression, about crises of subjectivity, about angst and suffering, about visionary creativity, and all the rest of the Freudian, Nietzschean, psychological baggage. It's not an art of putting a personal stamp on the world (such as making the big earthworks gestures in the American desert), or promoting ego and self (and celebrity and fame), or advertizing a set of philosophical or ideological views. 'Making art, for me, is never the means of finding insight. It is rather the reflection of a growing consciousness'. Drury spoke in Zen Buddhist terms of his artistic process: 'I go to 'outer nature', which is thoughtless, void, in order to see the whole. From the void comes insight, which makes art'.[7]

19

David Nash

One of the most intriguing and sensual of land artists working in Britain is David Nash (born in the same year as Richard Long – 1945), with whom Andy Goldsworthy worked. Nash's æsthetics chime with those of Long, Chris Drury and Goldsworthy among British artists.[1] Hugh Adams saw Nash as a kind of 'fixed abode Richard Long', working from one place (North Wales), while Long travels the globe, regarding the whole world as his studio, as material for making art.

David Nash built a number of 'stoves' and 'hearths', out of natural materials – snow, slate, wood. These structures burn away – fire as 'living' sculpture (like Chris Drury's cairns or Ana Mendieta's *Volcano*). *Snow Stove*, made in Japan in 1982, burnt beautifully – a snow pyramid, fusing those two eternal mysteries – fire and snow, fire and ice. Nash also made a *Wood Stove* (1979), a *Slate Stove* (1981) and also a *Sea Hearth*.[2] Anyone who's lit a fire right next to the ocean will know what a magical experience it can be, and Nash's *Sea Hearth* is certainly rich in magic (there is something fascinating about fire next to water). Nash set his fire built of large stones inches from the waves, to accentuate the contrast between the two elements. Nash's stoves and hearths are thick with alchemical and elemental allusions: they are a poetry of elements, the basic elements out of which everything is made. (William Jackson Maxwell has created burnt tree stumps, like Nash).[3]

David Nash loved working with wood: his *Wooden*

Boulder (1978) was exactly that – a huge, near-spherical chunk of oak. Nash tipped the boulder into a stream near his studio at Blaenau Ffestiniog, North Wales. His idea was for the sculpture to make its way to the ocean. Instead, it stayed put in a pool, and now it interacts continually with the environment (Nash later recorded that the boulder moved about seven times in 22 years, and looked 'more and more like a stone').

Welsh streams, with their chilly, clear water, mossy boulders and constant noise, are one of the most poetic environments Britain possesses. Ramblers are aware of brooks and rivers, not only because they have to cross them somehow, but also because they are crucial sources of drinking water. Nash's art, like Robert Smithson's, is respectful of water and the landscape. His art is gentle and based firmly in a reverence for nature.

In the Forest of Dean, David Nash made a circular mound of larch poles charred at the end. He spent two weeks charring nine hundred pieces of wood, which were then stuck together in a 'wide circular hole in the ground'.[4] Nash wanted to have his *Black Dome* as a mound of nothing but charcoal, but realized it would not last long enough for the public to see it. He wanted to use charcoal because it was a part of the industry of the forest. It was important too that Nash's large sculpture would decay away and become integrated into the forest again. Nash envisaged his *Black Dome* 'gradually reintegrating with its environment, rotting down gradually – fungus, leaf-mould, plants adding to its process of 'return'' (ib., 66).

David Nash constructs fascinating pieces, works which are instantly appealing, partly because of the materials, the natural materials which urban-based cultures are so thirsty for: wood, stone, water, fire. These are the elements not found in cities. Well, one sees trees, stones, skies and wood in cities, but it's not the same somehow: land artists wake the viewer, making them aware, again, of nature, of natural materials. One of Herman de Vries's aims was to 'make visible that which people don't see anymore', to draw attention to things happening in the 'primary reality' (nature) that people have forgotten about.[5]

It's refreshing, after being encased in grey concrete and a maze of straight lines in the city, to imbibe these works of artists such as David Nash, Chris Drury and Nicholas Pope. For instance, Nash's marvellous *Fletched Over Ash Dome*.[6] This is a circular group of trees in Wales which Nash planted in 1977: it is a 'living' sculpture, which, over thirty years, will be trained into a dome. It will be not only a circle of trees, but a dome of trees. Nash wrote:

> A circle of young ash trees fletched and woven into a
> thirty foot dome fletched three times at ten year intervals
> then left alone. A silver sculpture in winter, a green
> canopy space in summer, a volcano of growing energy.
> (1978)

While Robert Morris and Hans Haacke used steam, and Nancy Holt assembled stone, David Nash's deployment of living trees (such as in his *Fire Engine Sweep*, planted in 1980) created a new form of sculpture, a sculpture which is alive, which changes over decades, rather than seconds. Morris's and Haacke's steam and fog works last mere moments, while Nash's, Jackie Winsor's and Chris Drury's fires last a few hours. *Fletched Over Ash Trees*, though, is a sculpture that will endure for decades, and will change year in year out. Nash's trees will grow and develop for a long time before they decay, which will make them a particularly exciting type of sculpture.

David Nash explained:

> Earlier, I used sawmill wood, regular standard units;
> later, greenwood, fresh from the tree; now the tree itself.
> The more I look at the tree, the more I see the tree; it's
> space and location, its volume and structure, its engin-
> eering and balance. More than that, I see the uniqueness
> of each simple tree, and beyond that still I see it as a

> great emblem of life. A potent vibrant tower, a whirling prayer wheel of natural energy.[7]

David Nash spoke of 'observing trees: how they enter and survive in the particular space of their location. Their form being the balance of continual change in the elements and the seasons'.[8]

Other vertical or tower-like works of David Nash's include *Oak Spoon* (1988, collection: the artist), and *Red Throne* (1989, collection: the artist). *Started Beech* (1989, collection: Eric Franck, Switzerland) was a tree trunk split into a series of thin planks, still connected at one end to the end of the beech tree trunk. The ends of the planks fanned outward slightly, creating the 'skirt effect'.

At Grizedale David Nash's *Horned Tripod* (1977) was a tall tripod made from straight trees, a large scale work. *Crack and Warp Column* (1989, collection: the artist) was a tower made from thin squares of wood, piled on top of each other. *Crack and Warp Column* was irregular; each slab of wood bends slightly. In *Crack and Warp Column*, the warped slabs were more severely bent, but the size and shape of each slab was still controlled. The now-destroyed column of 1970 was one of the most Brancusi-like of Nash's sculptures: it was fashioned in sections, one tapering into the next. The tall, vertical Nash sculptures recall not only Constantin Brancusi's *Endless Column* but also Barnett Newman's *Broken Obelisk* (1963, MOMA, New York) and notions of growing upwards, skywards, verticality, and are related to Nash's idea of a tree as a fountain of energy.

Some more of David Nash's works include: *Vessel and Volume II* (1988, General Mills), a hollow boat form in black, next to a similarly-shaped boat, as if one could fit inside the other. *Serpentine Vessels* were also boat shapes (1989, collection: the artist), but their prows and sterns were tilted up, away from the floor. These were large objects, basically two slabs of wood fixed together. *Three Longboats* (1986, in oak) were hollow boat-forms, set on pieces of wood (Chris

Drury has also made groups of boat forms). These are not boats that will float; they are bottomless. *Descending Vessel* (1988, collection: the artist) was another boat-form, again hollow, set upright on top of a wooden plinth-wall, more a tower. The end of the vessel was slid into a crack in the top of the tower.

Quite a few of David Nash's sculptures consisted of two objects seen in tandem, one above the other. Like *Descending Vessel*, *Comet Ball* (1989, Trans Art, Cologne) was one object above the other – a tall curving piece of wood was stuck into a near-spherical globe of wood. Like *Descending Vessel*, *Comet Ball* recalled Constantin Brancusi – *Descending Vessel* was particularly reminiscent of *Birds in Space*. To emphasize the inspiration for the 1990 *Comet Ball*, Nash built a fire under it. Nash has also made waterfalls and streams from hollowed-out tree trunks, entitled *Wooden Waterways* (1978, Grizedale, and 1982, Japan), in which water from a stream was diverted along the trunks of a fallen oak tree, an ash, a sycamore, and onto more troughs.

David Nash has produced giant-size versions of common, domestic forms, such as *Ancient Table*, *Table with Cubes*, *Oak Spoon*, *Branch Chair* and *Bowl and Platter*. *Ancient Table* (1983, collection: Capel Rhiw), which has huge weathered trunks for the table's legs; *Table with Cubes* (1971, National Museum of Wales, Cardiff) has a variety of sizes of cubes on it; *Elm Bowl* (1988, collection: the artist) was a large, thin bowl, irregular, the outside smooth, the inside showing the marks of a chisel on top of a chunky wooden pedestal; *Bowl and Platter* (1988, collection: the artist) set the oversize objects on a large, thick table. Other large scale versions of everyday objects included *Big Ladder* (1984, Japan), *Branch Chair* (1976) and *Standing Frame* (1987, Walker Arts Center).

David Nash took the common form, put it into wood, roughed up the outlines and textures, and enlarged the forms. Some of his most intriguing works were spindly, expanded versions of household items. *Branch Chair*, for example, was a recognisable chair, but with twigs and branches poking out of it; *Branch Cube* (1982, private collection) was a recognisable cube, but with branches and sticks sprouting out of it, making it a much larger sculpture than it would be if it was just a cube.

Some of David Nash's sculptures were slotted together, extended forms, one form expanding outwards to produce a series of forms, as in *Extended Cube* (1986, collection: the artist), where the cube spilled out over the floor, in ever-decreasing sizes. *Slot Table* (1979, collection: the artist) was a tree trunk with a large slot cut in it, and displaced slightly. *Extended Length* (1980, Rijksmuseum Kroller Muller) was a large oblong which was dissected, so that the inner part slides out, showing its internal perspectives. *Nature to Nature* (1987, Walker Arts Center) took three simple forms – a globe, cube and pyramid – and made them out of solid wood. Nash put the three solids together in a row and built a fire under them. The blackened solids were shown in a gallery, with charcoal drawings of them on the wall behind.

In *Sod Swap* (1983), David Nash took sods of grass from Caen-y-Coed in North Wales to Kensington Gardens (and vice versa), planting the grass in a circle. Later Nash works included charred wooden sculptures based on the yew hedge 'twmps' which Nash had seen at Powis Castle garden in mid-Wales (such as *Beak Twmp*, 2000).

20

Richard Long

The central fact and act and experience of Richard Long's art is walking. Long's work is founded on the art of walking, the act of walking. On walking as art, as act, as experience. His walks become 'artwalks', art-walks which become artworks. For Richard Long, (art)walking is (art)working. Art-walking and art-working become interchangeable. 'I have met with but one or two persons in the course of my life who understood the art of Walking, that is, of taking walks – who had a genius, so to speak, for *sauntering*', wrote Henry David Thoreau.[1]

Born in 1945, Richard Long studied at the West of England College of Art (Bristol) and St Martin's (1966-68). In 1967 Long created his first important walk-work, *A Line Made By Walking*. Like most land artists, Long creates indoor (gallery) works and outdoor works (not intended for public consumption). He also produces art books, which are not typical exhibition catalogues, but artworks in their own right, usually with text works, photo-works, and sometimes map works. Long has had one-man shows in most of the major Western galleries, including the Whitechapel (1971), MOMA, New York (1972), Venice Biennale (1976), Arnolfini (1983), Fogg Art Museum (1980), Stedelijk, Amsterdam (1973), Guggenheim, New York (1986), Hayward Gallery, London (1991), and many one-man shows at Anthony d'Offay Gallery in London, which have produced art books (*Mountains and Waters*, 1992, *Sixteen Works*, 1984, *Five, Six, Pick Up Sticks*, 1980, *Old World New World*, 1988, *Kicking Stones*, 1990,

River Avon Book, 1979).

Richard Long is associated with the American land, Minimal, Process, Conceptual and postmodern artists (such as Lawrence Weiner, Michael Heizer,Dennis Oppenheim, Nancy Holt, Mary Miss, Alice Aycock, Donald Judd, Robert Smithson, Eva Hesse, Sol LeWitt, and especially Carl Andre), and with European Arte Povera and Minimal/ Conceptual artists (Hans Haacke, Christo, Jannis Kounellis, Lucio Fontana, Piero Manzoni, and Mario Merz). Other key names one might link with Richard Long include Joseph Beuys, Yves Klein, Constantin Brancusi, Isamu Noguchi, Bruce Nauman, Barnett Newman, Anthony Caro and Henry Moore.

Fellow students of Richard Long's at St Martin's included Gilbert & George, Bruce McLean and Barry Flanagan. Long is also associated, at different times, by several critics, with other British sculptors such as Tony Cragg, David Nash, Richard Deacon, Michael Craig-Martin, Nicholas Pope, Peter Randall-Page, Stephen Cox, Bill Woodrow, Anish Kapoor, Hamish Fulton, Alison Wilding, and the Art & Language group. These sculptors are sometimes grouped together as the 'New British Sculptors' or 'the New Sculpture'. Long still lives in Bristol, and is very active, travelling the world, making art, and having exhibitions.

Richard Long appears as a late British Romantic landscape artist, someone who fuses Sixties Conceptualism with 1800s pantheism; he's something of a High Modernist and a postmodernist Conceptualist. He has been described a 'traveller, explorer, pilgrim, shaman, magician, peripatetic poet, hill-walker' as well as an artist.[2] He says it is not enough for him to have an idea or concept: he has to make it.[3] His stone circles espouse the sensuality and beauty of the post-Romantic and modernist art object (as in sculpture by Auguste Rodin, Pablo Picasso, Aristide Maillol, Henry Moore, Käthe Kollwitz), while his photographs and text works exhibit the cool, philosophic distantiation and ideations of Process, Serial, ABC, Conceptual and Minimal art. Long's mud and stone and terracotta works are real, sensual objects, which satisfy the modernist critics who exalt the art object. The text and photographic pieces, however, 'feed the imagination', as Long told me.[4] They are only understandable, like television shows or traffic signals, by a heavily enculturated imagination. The text pieces are lingual structures, dependent for their effect on what the viewer brings to them.

Like Hamish Fulton and Andy Goldsworthy, Richard Long has travelled to some wild places in pursuit of interesting spaces: Lappland, Africa, Australia, Peru, Alaska and the Himalayas. It's easy to see Long's and Goldsworthy's art as simply pure Romanticism, a 'back to the land' art that utterly ignores political, societal, ideological, racial, economic and gender issues. True. Their art does not seem to be concerned with the urban 'real world' at all. And it looks odd to see their work in galleries in cities, to see the stones and stalks in a setting quite different from the wilderness. Rather, the art of Goldsworthy, Long, Chris Drury and David Nash comes across as deeply poetic, personal, subjective and romantic. It is *all* about a response to nature, about getting into connection with nature.

Richard Long's art mixes contemporary, (post)modernist and Romantic (traditional) æsthetics. For Anne Seymour, Long

> has not only penetrated more deeply into the world of natural landscape than anyone since J.M.W. Turner, he has taken abstract art with him, creating a new art which allows all parties to retain their full identities.[5]

Mary Rose Beaumont also placed Long within a British Romantic tradition. This was a tendency of art criticism of the 1980s, as espoused by fine art gurus such as Peter Fuller and Robert Rosenblum. There was much talk in the 1980s of New Romantics/ Neo-Romantics/ New Ruralists, and so on. Whether High Modernism or postmodernism, Long's art is certainly a romance with nature, but always in an ecologically-friendly fashion. Long lives in Bristol. Certainly, the pagan/ New Age/ hippy influence is very prominent in Bristol, and in all points South and West of Bristol, in Britain's West Country.

Like Andy Goldsworthy, Chris Drury and Hamish Fulton, Richard Long uses his hands and feet to make his art, and not an array of machines and tools. The aim is to be unobtrusive, 'invisible', in tune with the Earth. So Long acts like many walkers and hikers: he covers his tracks, does not leave behind trash, does not harm nature. So fierce is the 'right on', politically correct, eco-friendly tendency of some walkers and campers, they worry about leaving even a footprint in the grass as they pass by. Fulton declines to make any mark on the world as he moves through it, except footprints. 'The natural environment was not built by man and for this reason it is to me deeply mysterious and religious', remarked Fulton.[6]

For Richard Long, walking itself is the primary act of his art. Walking is mainly what he does, as an artist. His talent, he said, is to be able to walk. Walking clears the mind, it is a process and experience of simplification and purification. It purges the soul, Long remarked, it forces the self to concentrate on simple things such as air, sky, earth, rock.

> Like art itself, it [walking] is like a focus. It gets rid of a lot of things and you can actually concentrate. So getting myself into these solitary days of repetitive walking or in empty landscapes is just a certain way of emptying out or simplifying my life, just for those few days or weeks, into a fairly simple but concentrated activity which, as you say, is really quite different from the way that people normally live their lives, which is very complicated. So my art is a simplification.[7]

For Richard Long, as for many people, walking is a way of simplifying life, of cutting through the clutter. When walking, one moves into a different space, a space set quite apart from the rest of life. The time of walking is not the everyday, day-in-day-out time of the working world. It is not the profane, boring time of working at a check-out in a supermarket, or slaving away in some hideous South American factory. Walking takes one right away from that sort of everyday time. Walking takes one into a non-profane time and space. Walking in fact sacralizes space and time. As the walk takes places, sacred time is re-instated. Walking therefore has a religious or philosophical dimension, which sounds odd only if terms such as religion or art sound odd to the ear. In walking, in travelling, in vacations or other escapes and escapades, people put themselves back together. Walking in wildernesses, people say, is invigorating and refreshing: walking returns people to themselves, and of course renews their contact with nature. These things can sound stupid – 'renewing one's contact with nature'. Wow, maaan, it sounds hippy-dippy, doesn't it? But one can't avoid nature in the wilderness anywhere – it surrounds the self entirely; it *is* the self. Long says:

> I do the things that have a deep meaning for me. I have the most sublime or profound feelings when I am walking, or touching materials in natural places. That is what I've decided to do and that is what I am showing you in my art.[8]

Perhaps Richard Long should move into multi-media, interactive and technological presentations. Perhaps he ought to have the sound of recorded atmospherics and wind from his walks in the gallery. Perhaps Long ought to try bringing more of the multi-sensory experience of a walk into the gallery space. Perhaps he ought to encourage someone to spend a proportion of the next exhibition budget on employing some museum designers and curators to create a multi-media *Walk Show*. Sounds crappy? But isn't having a framed Ordnance Survey map on a wall relating to a walk and calling it an artwork crappy? One knows it doesn't cost much to produce a map work (eight bucks for the map, $199.99 for the frame, a few cents for the pen to mark on the map). The stone circles 'cost' nothing, it seems, like the River Avon mud.

Long's main 'materials' for his sculpture seem to be 'free' – the walk itself is 'free'. Seen in one way, Long's works can strike the viewer as low-rent, cheesy and pretentious. Mr Joe, the (non-existent) Mr Average, might wander into a Richard Long show and exclaim, *it's just a few stones on the floor, innit? Jeez, anyone could do that!* This was the furore that Carl Andre's bricks generated. Bricks on the floor? Six thousand $$$$$? So Richard Long's works can appear extremely trashy, 'cheap' and pretentious. But Long doesn't 'risk' everything on the socio-cultural context of a gallery. As his sculptures relate to walks, they always have a solid, straightforward, no-nonsense element. No one can argue with the importance of walking. Walking is not namby-pambying around with a paintbrush and canvas like a Sunday afternoon amateur painter. No, walking is good, solid, dependable work. It's only when walking is portrayed as 'art' that the problems occur.

Art possesses nature and yet does not possess nature: something always remains elusive. What's there, in nature, is no longer there in the artwork. As David Reason noted of Hamish Fulton's work (in "Echo and Reflections"), and this applies to Richard Long's text pieces: '[i]n the work, everything derives from what cannot be shown and shared – walking and camping in close relationship to a specific patch of the natural world.'[9] The viewer does not experience the real subject of the work, which is the walk. Instead, the viewer has to place her/ himself into the role played by the artist, as s/he walks in the landscape. Land art text pieces can be seen as sophisticated forms of vacation photos, those little coloured slips of plastic, pixels and photochemicals which record two weeks' escape from labour.

Richard Long's text works do not 'describe' the landscape, in the usual manner. Short phrases, and sometimes (as in Hamish Fulton's work), single words stand in for (a description of) the landscape. Long's text works do not claim 'this is the world', but record tiny parts of the world seen from a particular subjective perspective on a particular day in a particular season and frame of mind. The particularity of each work is emphasized in the work of Long (and Andy Goldsworthy) by the artists' placing of the time and place in the final sentence of each text piece. Sometimes, as in the art of Long, Hamish Fulton and Goldsworthy, a distinct date is mentioned; at other times, just the year. The duration of each of Long's walk is also critical: thus the viewer can get an idea of when and where the walk took place, and how much mileage was covered in a certain amount of time.

Instead of trying to depict or describe nature, then, Richard Long's art (like Hamish Fulton's) may be about the impossibility of representing landscape in art. At the same time (here's the paradox again), both Long and Fulton (and David Nash, Walter de Maria, Michael Heizer *et al*) are consciously making art in or about the landscape. Even though the impossibility of the project is stressed, they are still making art. That is, still indulging in a particular kind of Western, bourgeois, intellectual, creative activity.

Whether presented as a map (*Low Water Circle Walk*, 1980) or text (*A Circle of Middays*, 1997), Richard Long's circular walks are designed as fascinating artworks. While some people might organize a circular route in a town (bank to post office, then to the grocery store then home), Long makes the circular walk a matter of Conceptual art and geometry. The casual circular walk of everyday life (once along the boardwalk and back through the town, or once round the power plant), becomes in Long's art a living sculpture founded on 'universal and common' principles. 'My work has become a simple metaphor of life... I am content with the vocabulary of universal and common means,' writes Long, 'walking, placing, stones, sticks, water, circles, lines, days, nights, roads'.[10]

Richard Long, who is not a poet of the stature or talent of John Cowper Powys or Arthur Rimbaud, is not adept at communicating the experience of a walk in words. Why, then, is Long's work so popular? It must be that before he made the text pieces he made very sensual works to which people could relate instantly. Long's (relative) fame or popularity must stem (partly) from his stone and slate circles, which people can see and touch and walk on and discuss. If Long had never created a stone circle, would he be as popular as he is today? That is, has a painter or sculptor become successful simply by sending words to a typesetter to be printed and framed and put on gallery walls? It's an interesting question (Andy Warhol has done it). Of course, Long was making the text works *as well as* the slate rings. Even Conceptual artists such as Gilbert & George had actual objects people could see. They might have been 'living sculptures', but they also made colourful works. There are few artists, it seems, who have become famous merely by manipulating and exhibiting words in frames.

The other factor explaining Richard Long's success is his use of the Great Outdoors, the wilderness landscape which is so dear to Anglo-American-European art audiences (the photos depict gorgeous wild zones in Bolivia, Iceland, Scotland, the Sahara, Nepal). In the stinking, sweltering/ freezing, grey and drab cities of the West, Long's works suggest wide open spaces, vast cloudscapes, cycles of growth and decay which have been long obliterated from the Western city.

One knows about Richard Long's walks from the maps, text and photos. So, as he walks, Long is making art. It is not quite the same with Joseph Beuys or Gilbert & George, who were performing, who were 'living sculptures'. Long's absence from his photos and texts is part of his ecologically-friendly, non-destructive stance. Long's walks, though, are not a 'performance'.[11] The walk is not 'performing' something, a performance *of* something, a representation. It is about movement in space, a lived experience.[12] The walk is the walk. To call it art is also to call it life, in Long's view. The two things are continuous. The central thing to grasp with Long's art, as also with other land artists, such as Michael Heizer, Walter de

Maria, David Nash, Fulton, Aycock and Nancy Holt, is the essence of their work, the mythic centre, which may be an idea, an essence, a structure or an experience.[14]

Richard Long, though, does polarize critics and art consumers. People seem to love him or loathe him. For fans, Long's a New Age, eco-friendly mystic, making cool, Conceptual art that doesn't harm the environment. For sceptical critics, Long's pretentious, shallow, repetitive and unoriginal. Modernist critics moan that there's no object to grasp in Long's art – for them it's a series of empty Conceptual gestures. Postmodernist fans can admire how Long plays the art market, trouncing conventional views of the art object. For Long, a sculpture can be two hundred and thirty miles long if he wishes. If a sculptor wants to make a 'real', physical object 230 miles long, s/he has to have a lot of money (like Christo with his *Running Fence*). Long, however, retorts that his 230 mile-long sculpture really is a physical thing: he walked those 230 miles, physically. He might record sensual aspects of the walk: wind direction, incidents along the way, weather, and so on. So, 'conceptual' though it seems, Long's sculptures are 'real', physical objects. A walk, after all, is one of the most physical, and fundamental, activities for humans.

Denying it or hinting at it, Richard Long's sculpture is definitely 'religious'/ 'mystical'/ 'spiritual'. Walking itself is sacred; making art is sacred; the allusions to stone circles are religious; circles themselves are religious; the awe with which viewers regard the sculpture has a religious aspect, and so on.

Not all of Long's works are circles – there are always the lines. Long continued to make lines in the shape of a cross from time to time, such as in *Two Places* (Bolivia, 1972), where a small cross is created on marshland in a pile of stalks. Another cross was produced in Iceland from some stones (*Stopping Place Stones*, 1974). The crosses are very much like geometric marks 'drawn' onto the landscape, as if to mark a place. Most of the single straight lines are short, like the crosses, such as *Walking Without Travelling* (Sahara, 1988).

Occasionally, Richard Long fashions a square zigzag line: short right angles are marked upon bare soil, as in *Campfire Ash* (Bolivia, 1972 – all these works are from *Mountains and Waters*). Another zigzag line sculpture, in Antwerp in 1973, extends outwards to take over the gallery: each Long sculpture is made for a particular space, and expands to consume the gallery floor. The zigzag lines recall the Peruvian Nazca animals and symbols drawn on the lava plain (Long had walked along one of the desert lines in 1972: he also made sculptures which employed symbols such as the puma, condor, falcon, moon, sun and rain.) Like most artists, Long has his visual motifs which he returns to time and again (circles, lines, rows, and, lately, ellipses and arcs).

Richard Long spoke warmly of Carl Andre and Lawrence Weiner, important Sixties Minimal and Conceptual artists.[14] It is significant, too, that Long felt he was working on his own in Britain, that there was nobody else doing his kind of art. When he stepped out of Britain he realized there was 'a whole new world of ideas going on'. Long noted, perhaps wryly, that '[t]here was an immediate interest and understanding of my work as soon as I stepped outside England'.[15] Long himself declined being described as a Conceptual artist ('[m]y work is real, not illusory or conceptual. It's about real stones, real time, real actions').[16] He spoke sympathetically of Arte Povera, the use of 'simple, modest means and procedures'.[17]

Some commentators have negated the tendency to view Richard Long in Romantic terms. 'Richard Long's landscape is... as modern (in feeling) as the city of Bristol from which he sets out for a walk', claimed R.H. Fuchs in *Richard Long* (43). Long, Fuchs opined, tries to play down 'as much as he can the romantic/ Romantic, poetic connotations' of his locations (ib.). Yet, surely wildernesses such as Dartmoor, Mexico, Ecuador, Nepal, Canada and Lappland, where Long makes his art, have been inscribed with connotations of Romanticism. They are places now described in terms of 'spirit' and 'soul', spaces that in contemporary romantic, nostalgic culture imbue one with a sense of infinity, solitude, pantheism, awe, eternity and all the rest of the Romantic æsthetic baggage. 'A walk is also the means of discovering places in which to make sculpture in 'remote' areas, places of nature, places of great power and contemplation', remarked Long, speaking in Romantic terms of his walks.[18]

In a walk such as *Straight Miles and Meandering Miles* (1985), Richard Long walks some 'straight miles' along the way, between Land's End and Bristol. As expected, these 'straight miles' are walked in wilderness or countryside or 'Romantic' locations, such as Bodmin Moor, Exmoor and the Mendip Hills. The starting points and the end points of the *Four Walks* (1977) sound like a list of destinations a landscape painter might make for a 1790s Grand Tour of Britain: the source of the River Severn, Snowdon, Chesil Beach, Sherwood Forest and Carantouhil peak.

Although he may downplay the Romantic associations with the art made in or about landscape, Richard Long described landscape in romantic, emotional terms. He reacted to landscape directly, facing it straight on, as is apparent in all his interviews and writings. He spoke of the need for transcribing landscapes purely and clearly. So, for instance, his photographs are simply taken, without too much trickery, and they are printed in a straightforward manner.[19] At the same time, Long described 'places of great power and contemplation', terms which William Wordsworth might have used a hundred and fifty years before Long, or Henry Vaughan, the Metaphysical poet born on the Welsh borders, before that.

Stressing the Romantic heritage/ tradition of Richard Long's art though, only makes up part of the picture. Like other artists of the Sixties (whether Pop, Conceptual, Minimal, Process, ABC, Cool, Arte Povera, body, performance or other art), Long suppressed notions of poetry and Romanticism. 'My art is not urban, nor is it romantic', Long said.[20] Looking at *A Line in Iceland* (1982), a line of boulders in a wilderness space, shot against a brooding sky and a backdrop of snowbound mountains, one can see the affinities with the High Romanticism of William Wordsworth's poeticizing of the Lake District, J.M.W. Turner and his watercolours of Snowdonia or the Alps, or John Ruskin and his evocation of the Sublime. 'Working out there in nature, then, Long is a performer in the open-air theatre of the sublime', wrote David Sylvester. True, *Red Slate Circle* (1980) in the Fogg Art Museum in Cambridge (MA), or *Sandstone Spiral* (1983) in the National Gallery of Canada, or the *Puget Sound Driftwood Circle* (1996) in Houston, or *Forte de Vinadio Circle* (Italy, 2001), are set on museum floors, in the clean, sparse gallery environment, and look Minimal. What concerns Richard Long is that '[e]ach work is appropriate to its place and context', and the wilderness works and the museum pieces are 'equal and complementary'. What counts, Long asserted, is the feelings that the work, whether inside or outside, aroused: 'my ambition is basically with the emotional power of the work, in both idea and image.'[21] Walking, nature and the landscape are at the heart of Long's work,[22] but Long knows, as any professional artist must know, that the art world conducts its business indoors (and chiefly in cities).

Richard Long's slate, stick and wood circles look like late 20th century artworks, not 'Romantic', but Minimal, Conceptual and Arte Povera, like Carl Andre's copper and zinc plates. They have a coolness and clarity that one associates with Dan Flavin, Robert Morris, Tony Smith and Sol LeWitt. Long's stone circles make sense partly because of the viewer's grounding in the discourses of contemporary art. Without a knowledge of the myriad discourses, analyses and signs that flow around contemporary art, one might not know how to make full sense of Long's circles. True, the circle as a shape has been around for eons, but only in the contemporary era have circles been made out of bits of the landscape, in galleries and in landscape settings in this particular way.

The *Tarahumara Circle* (Mexico, 1987) is what seems at first to be a simple shape. But it's not 'simple'. It's a 'negative circle', a circle made into a circle by the ring of rocks around it. The line of rocks marks out the circle, but not evenly. Some of the rocks are piled deeper on one side of the circle. Hardly anyone will have seen this circle intact, in its situation, so one knows it only from a photograph. The seemingly straightforward approach of Richard Long's photography has made a few æsthetic decisions, which shape spectators' perception of this artwork. For instance, one sees the stone circle in the centre of the frame, in the lower third, in the sort of classical composition that was taught in the fine art academies of yore. Behind the circle one sees the trees and hills of Mexico. Long's photograph thus 'captures' the stone ring amidst the Mexican landscape, placing it firmly within a wilderness landscape. The setting is impressive and it is meant to be. With its wooded slopes and hills receding into the blue haze, the photograph is worthy of the ærial effects described by Leonardo da Vinci in his treatise of Renaissance painting. The composition of *Tarahumara Circle*, the more one studies it, becomes increasingly 'classical': there are even two small trees either side of the stone circle, in the foreground, framing the circle, a compositional device favoured by J.M.W. Turner, Thomas Girtin, John Sell Cotman and other late 18th century landscapists.

Richard Long's *Brough of Birsay Circle* (Orkney, 1994) is a large open circle which relies on plants and their blooming in summer to make it work. Like his late 1960s lines made by walking, Long has walked in a large circle on a field of flowers. The flowers have been pressed flat, leaving a circular mark. The largest of Long's circles are of course the circular walks he creates, which could be many miles in diameter. Some of these are on maps, some are suggested through words. These are 'imaginary' circles but no less significant than the tactile stone circles.

One or two of Richard Long's stone circles are small – *Circle of Standing Stones* (1983), which is 26 stones arranged in a circle of a half yard in diameter, *Cornwall Slate Circle* (1982), 34 stones in a 2 yard circle, and *Standing Stone Circle* (1982), 36 stones in a similar size circle. The small prehistoric stone circles are often made of standing stones, and many of the outdoor circles are of this type (*Evening Camp Stones*, 1995, for instance). Long's use of standing stones, rather than ones laid flat, echoes prehistoric stone circles – for instance, the Scottish stone circle *Stones and Stac Pollaidh* (1981), or *Sincholagua Summit Shadow Stones* (1998). Long's small stone circles are intimate works compared to the broad, large pieces. In Britain there are a number of small stone circles which produce similar atmospheres of human-scale and intimacy (such as the small circles on the ridges of hills in Dorset). 'I like simple, emotional, quiet, vigorous art', remarked Long.[23] While the large circles in the galleries of Western cities spoke of polished, upmarket art, the small, 1.5 yard stone circles evoked small wayside shrines. The large gallery circles are planned and organized months in advance, but still look spontaneous. Long's small outdoor stone circles, though, are direct and spontaneous responses to a landscape.

Some of Richard Long's techniques echo Andy Goldsworthy's: Long sprinkles snow in a circle, or smears mud, often from the River Avon near his home in England, in huge circles or lines or arcs on walls, or he makes marks on grass using his feet. The use of hands, feet, the body, mud, soil, stones, snow and sand chime with many of the standard practical methods of land art.

> I like the idea that I can make a show anywhere [said Long] by just going down to the river taking a few handfuls of mud... and literally get on a plane and go anywhere and make a big show with the mud from my bag.[24]

Richard Long's art ethic – *have mud, will travel* – fits in with the notion of a pared-down, simplified, 'essential' æsthetic that was current in the 1960s and 1970s (how does Long get thru airport security and customs?: 'What's in the bag, sir?' 'Err, mud.' 'Mud?' 'Yeah').

The great thing is not so much that Long can splatter mud on a wall and call it art (he does the former, but not the latter), but that people around the world accept mud splattered on wall as art. Long – one of the success stories of the British art school system (along with David Hockney, Patrick Caulfield, Peter Blake, Barry Flanagan and Shirazeh Houshiary) – knows only too well from his days as an art student at St Martin's College of Art that he is lucky to be able to travel the world with a bit of Avon River mud in his bag, and have gallery audiences lap it up, because for every major (successful) artist there are thousands of students pouring out of the art schools each year. These art students are often producing work just as rich and challenging as that of David Inshaw, Anish Kapoor, Anthony Gormley, Jean-Luc Vilmouth, Tony Cragg, and Bill Woodrow.

21

Andy Goldsworthy

Andrew Charles Goldsworthy was born in Sale Moor, Cheshire, in 1956. Goldsworthy grew up in Cheshire, and on a housing estate on the edge of Leeds (in Alwoodley). Goldsworthy worked on a farm part-time (Grove House Farm, Alwoodley) from age thirteen. Goldsworthy later said (in 2000) that working on the farm had been as important as attending art college. Goldsworthy failed the 11-plus exam, for the grammar school system, and went to Harrogate High School instead. Goldsworthy would subsequently fail to gain entrance to his chosen foundation and degree colleges.

As a young art student, Andy Goldsworthy spent much of his time outside college, working on the beaches at Morecambe and Heysham. Goldsworthy preferred to learn by direct experience, finding out about leaves, mud, stone, rivers and tides by living amongst them. Goldsworthy would go into college for one or two days a week, for the art history classes. This was not enough for the lecturers, who suggested that he spend more time in school, including attending life drawing classes. Little did Goldsworthy's lecturers know – that their errant student, who spent hours clambering around the muddy reaches of Heysham Head and Morecambe Bay instead of dutifully attending college classes, would one day become an artist of international renown, with exhibitions and commissions around the world.

At the time (*circa* late-1970s), Andy Goldsworthy must have seemed just another crazy art student in jeans and long hair, pursuing his own wacky ideas (British art schools contain plenty of kooky folk – not all of them students). Hearing of his beach-mud-stone-tide antics, Goldsworthy's tutors must have sighed heavily and put another stroke through the 'absent' column on his attendance record. Amazing to think that this artist-in-the-making would one day be exhibiting at the one of the most prestigious museums in the world (the British Museum), designing Royal Mail stamps, and making a Holocaust memorial in New York. For Goldsworthy, the time spent working at Grove House Farm and the Lancashire beaches was as critical as his art education: '[t]he energy and unpredictability of art outside the studio and gallery were important to me. Going outside art college felt so much more raw, and that's what interested me' (*Time*, 180).

There's not a lot of anger, or angst, or suffering, or self-doubt, or lust, or violence, or propaganda, or neurosis, or disturbance in Andy Goldsworthy's art (many land artists are similarly laid-back). A guy who goes out into the countryside to build cairns with stones or pin leaves together is definitely not a haunted, tormented artist like Vincent van Gogh, or an aggressive, flamboyant self-publicist like Salvador Dali or Andy Warhol, or an ironic, fey commentator on the postmodern condition, like Jeff Koons or Robert Rauschenberg, or a stridently ideological combatant like Ana Mendieta or Karen Finley, or a crazy performance artist like Stuart Brisley or Annie Sprinkle, or a darling of the *avant garde* scene, like Yoko Ono or Matthew Barney.

'My art', Andy Goldsworthy noted in *Time*, 'is rooted in the British landscape, and this is the source to which I must return' (*Time*, 7). In 1986 Goldsworthy moved from Yorkshire and Cumbria, where he'd spent most of his life, to Penpont in Dumfriesshire, where he has remained ever since. This's where Goldsworthy produces most of his work. A nearby 2 1/2 acre piece of land (dubbed Stone Wood by the artist) was leased from the Bucclech estate in the late 1980s. The River Scaur, one of Goldsworthy's most beloved spots, is on one side. Goldsworthy's first *Wall*, and many other works, were made at Stone Wood.

Many of Andy Goldsworthy's site-specific works and commissions have been in (and about) the North of Britain: the giant maze and *Lambton Earthwork* (at County Durham, 1988-89), the Grizedale Forest site works (1984 onwards), residencies at Yorkshire Sculpture Park (1987-88), the Lake District National Park (1988), and St Louis Arts Festival (1986), *Sheepfolds* (1996-), and so on. Large Northern commissions included *Sidewinder* (1985) and *Seven Spires* (1984), *The Wall That Went For a Walk* (1991) at Grizedale, Cumbria, *Lambton Earthwork* and *Maze* in Durham (1988), *Stone Gathering* at Northumberland (1993), and *Enclosure* in Edinburgh (1990). It's Goldsworthy's contemporary, though, Anthony Gormley, who has made the sculpture in Northern Britain that has bedded itself in the public consciousness since the late Nineties: the *Angel of the North,* a 65 foot tall steel figure at Gateshead (1998). Goldsworthy has made a work at Gateshead, a steel cone (1991) constructed on the site of a foundry (this was part of a proposal to build a group of cones, which was unrealized).

Andy Goldsworthy has created land art in Grise Fiord, the North Pole, in Japan, upstate New York, California, Castres, Digne, La Rochelle and Sidobre in France, the Australian Outback, and in Haarlem, Holland. The first work that Andy Goldsworthy sold was a bunch of photographs to the Arts Council (via Andrew Causey at North West Arts). He has had one-man shows in France, Japan, Holland, the U.S.A. and Great Britain, and participated in groups shows in Italy, Germany, and the U.S.A.. A major retrospective, *Hand to Earth: Andy Goldsworthy: Sculpture: 1976-1990*, was held at the Henry Moore Centre for the Study of Sculpture, Leeds City Art Gallery: the show also travelled to the Royal Botanic Gardens in Edinburgh, Stedelijke Musea, Gouda and Centre Regional d'Art Contemporain Midi-Pyrénées in Toulouse. This show also produced the most useful and detailed publication to date on Goldsworthy's art (*Hand to Earth*, later reprinted – see bibliography, with 2000's *Time* as a handy update).

In the 1990s, Andy Goldsworthy's art began to rise in popularity: the glossy coffee table book *Stone* became a bestseller (bear in mind it was priced at 35 British pounds or about 55 dollars). In 1994 Goldsworthy took over some West End galleries with a large one-man show, *Stone* (this included *Herd of Arches*, also made for the Hathill Sculpture Foundation at Goodwood in Sussex, and ultimately finding a permanent home in Cornwall).[1] In 1995 he took part in an intriguing group show, *Time Machine: Ancient Egypt and Contemporary Art*, at the British Museum in London and Museo Egizio, Turin, creating sculptures, along with Richard Deacon, Peter Randall-Page and others, in amongst the monumental statuary of the famous Egyptian Hall. Also in 1995, Goldsworthy designed a set of Royal Mail stamps. As well as commissions, installations, TV and radio programmes, and books, Goldsworthy has also produced limited edition prints (the pictures of cairns were made with Eyestorm, in editions of 500, priced at $720 each).

Other Goldsworthy shows and projects of the 1990s and after included *Mid Winter Muster* in Australia (1991), sand and mulga branchworks; *Seven Holes* (for Greenpeace, 1991); *Black Spring* in Adelaide (1992); a large gateway at Hooke Park in Dorset (1987); wall commissions (such as in New York, 1993, 1996 and 1997); several *Cones* (New York and Oxford, 1995); *Four Corner Stones* (Nice, 1993); *Rockfold* (Northumberland, 1993); *Fieldgate* (New York, 1993); clay holes and throws at Runnymede Sculpture Farm, California (1992); *Two Autumns* in Japan (1994); *Breath of Earth* at San Jose Museum of Art (1995); a clay installation (a hole) in L.A. (at the Getty Center for the Arts, 1997, later destroyed by a burst pipe); 'ice houses' and stick lines made in Alaska (1995); a slate cone and chamber for British Airways at their West Drayton HQ in 1998; cairns and 'refuges' at Digne les Bains in 1998; new groups of work at the National Museum of

Scotland in Edinburgh (1998); the new *Wall* at Storm King (1998); another wall at Storm King (*Folded Wall,* 1999); a large stone arch in Montréal (1998); *Snowballs in Summer* in London (2000); *Garden of Stone*, a memorial for victims and survivors of the Holocaust, sited in Manhattan (2003); *Stone Houses* (New York, 2004); *Passage* (London, 2005); *Roof* (National Gallery of Art, Washington, DC, 2005); Yorkshire Sculpture Park in 2007; a Provence art trail in 2009; and a *Clay Dome* in Rio de Janiero in 2012.

Andy Goldsworthy continues to work in countries such as Japan, Australia, Canada, North America and France, but his home ground of Dumfriesshire in Scotland remains (at) the heart of his work. (From the mid-Nineties, Goldsworthy increasingly frequented Digne in South France; it became one of the most valuable places for the sculptor outside of his home in Scotland, and was the site of a major commission, *Réfuges d'Art*).[2]

Andy Goldsworthy has not created art everywhere. There are plenty of places Goldsworthy has not visited for making art. Even in the British Isles, Goldsworthy has not made much art in Cornwall or Devon or the South-West, or the East (Norfolk, Suffolk, the Fens), not much in the English Midlands, only a few works in Wales, and hardly any in Ireland. If Goldsworthy makes work in Great Britain, it's usually Scotland, Northern Britain (Cumbria and Yorkshire, but not so much the North-East), or London.

Around the world, Andy Goldsworthy has concentrated on Westernized territories: on America, of course (it's the centre of land art), Western Europe, Australia and Japan (with the odd excursion to exotic spots, such as the North Pole). Goldsworthy has not made much art in Eastern Europe, in Russia, in mainland China, in India, in Africa or South America. (Goldsworthy did visit Russia in 1991, but 'administration difficulties' prevented the intended work in Siberia).[3] Visits to India, Africa, China and so on will probably come.

It's significant, I think, that Andy Goldsworthy had a job

as a gardener for the first half of the Eighties. Goldsworthy's art parallels development and trends in gardening in Britain and elsewhere. For instance, the use of stones and pebbles in the gardens as ornaments or sculptures. The popularity of Goldsworthy's art, I would argue, is in tune with events such as the rise in gardening shows on TV (and those shows' links with house, food and interior design programmes), the spread of DIY stores and gardening centres, more gardens open to the public (including many more private gardens), the interest in ecological and environmental politics, anti-pollution and recycling drives, and the increase of New Age and mind/ body/ spirit pursuits (such as *feng shui*). One of the things that fuels this revived (or new) interest in gardens, art and the environment, of course, is an increase in leisure time (and money for entertainment), an ageing population (which also lives longer), new technologies, and new distribution and consumption networks.

Andy Goldsworthy works with the natural world, and within nature. He uses natural materials in (apparently) natural shapes and forms set in natural contexts. Goldsworthy takes his cue from nature: as Jan Dibbets put it in 1969: 'I realized that if you want to use nature, you have to derive the appropriate structure from nature too'.[4]

Andy Goldsworthy seems to be a particularly gentle and sensitive artist, compared to many sculptors and land artists: he stitches together leaves to forms lines (which're often placed in water, or over branches), or makes circular slabs of snow, or entwines twigs in an arc. He creates a delicate spiral of chestnut leaves, called *Autumn Horn* (1986); he pins bright yellow dandelions on willowherb stalks in a circle, on bluebells (1987); he makes lines and cairns of pebbles; a horizontal line of red sumach leaves was pinned to a willow (at Storm King in 1998); he rubs red stones to stain rockpools; he pins leaves to tree trunks; he makes hollow, circular structures, recalling igloos, from slate, leaves, driftwood and bracken; he fashioned long wavy ridges in Arizonan and

Australian desert sand; he throws sand and sticks in the air and photographs the moment; he builds arches, globes, hollow spheres, slabs, spires, spirals and star-shapes out of snow and ice. Very impressive it all is. The sculptures crafted from sticks, for instance, stuck together in an arch, or a line, reflected in the mirror-like water of Derwent Water in Cumbria in 1988, are indeed wonderful. The sculptures exude tranquillity, an early morning calm (quite the opposite of another water work, Klaus Rinke's *Water Sculpture*, where a water canon blasted water over visitors as they approached a gallery, or Jim Sanborn's 1995 *Coastline*, which employs a wave generator to simulate waves in a Maryland garden).

Then there's the globe made from oak leaves in different states of Autumnal decay, superb (Dumfriesshire, 1985). Or the globe of sticks made in Fairfax, California (1995), set next to a sheltering tree. Or the sand serpent in the British Museum (1994). Or the globe made out of snow, and perched amidst some young trees (1980), or the slabs of snow, set up in a line with slits cut in them (1988).

Andy Goldsworthy said: 'I want an intimate physical involvement with the earth. I must touch'.[5] Touching is 'deeply important' for Goldsworthy.[6] Only touching gives the artist the deep understanding of his materials and nature, he asserted.[7] Goldsworthy's *Forked branch and twig* is exactly that: a forked branch with a twig suspended between the two parts of the branch. The photograph of this 1978 work shows a space enclosed by the twig and branch, a rough circle of air and sky enclosed by the twig and branch. Goldsworthy rarely uses animals in his art; stones and vegetation are his usual materials. Some sculptures refer to animals (such as sheep and cows). One or two pieces were made from feathers (*Goose feathers*, 1983, *Wood pigeon wing feathers*, 1977, *Feathers plucked from a dead heron*, 1982, and *Wet feathers wrapped around a stone*, 1999). And some from wool (*Wool line*, 1995).

The eroticism of Andy Goldsworthy's sculpture is readily apparent, but the sensuality of Goldsworthy's art is non-human; there are no 'human' figures in his work, though there are vaginal openings, phallic rocks, mounds like breasts or pregnant bellies, and stalks that bend gracefully like ballet dancers: if one wants to anthropomorphize and sexualize Goldsworthy's art, it's easy. Goldsworthy himself anthropomorphizes his work. He says the cones on a hillside are like sentinels or a group of people.[8] Goldsworthy spoke of stones and seeds in terms of phallic tumescence and orgasmic release: 'I found an energy in stone that can best be described as a seed that becomes taut as it ripens – often needing only the slightest of touch to make it explode and scatter its parts' (*Wood*, 23).

Andy Goldsworthy has made more traditional forms of art in galleries: his bracken, fern and horse chestnut stalk works, for instance, were created by pinning the materials onto white gallery walls. These works – *Bracken fronds* (Ecology Centre, London, 1985), *Reeds, bracken and horse chestnut stalks* (Centre d'Art Contemporain, Castres, and Galerie Aline Vidal, Paris, 1989) and *Reed line drawing* (Paris, 1990) – were essentially free, open wall drawings, often employing basic motifs such as the circle and open curve. Hanging screens of plants that Goldsworthy made in galleries include the *Susuki grass* and *Horse chestnut leaf stalks* (both made in Japan in 1993), *Horse chestnut leaf stalks* (1994, Japan), *Yucca blades* (New Mexico, 2000), and *Rushes thorns* (1992, San Francisco). *Rosebay willowherb* (1990) was crafted in Goldsworthy's studio.

Although he has carved stone from time to time, in the traditional sculptural manner, and also modelled clay, he disliked both processes. Although both methods have been central to sculpture for centuries, Andy Goldsworthy rarely used them. 'I dislike the malleability of modelling and the imposition of carving as processes. Carving is a process that relies upon the integral strength of the block of stone'.[9] Instead, Goldsworthy preferred to employ drawings or shaping with his hands, or weaving stalks or plants or leaves, or rubbing stone to make powder, or splitting stone to make walls or cairns, or piling up snow, or throwing stalks in the air, or balancing rocks.

Andy Goldsworthy's æsthetics are those of a neo-pagan, shamanic, Native American, Maori, pantheistic, nature worshipping kind, the sort of beliefs that some people call Goddess worship, and others kinda pagan or 'New Age'. Goldsworthy evokes the earth's energies and atmospheres. His talk of 'earth energies' recalls ley lines, the so-called 'dragon lines' or *feng shui* of Chinese geomancy. Goldsworthy has emphasized his notions of 'energy' in nature by 'drawing' around stones.

Andy Goldsworthy's main visual motif is the circle, whether as a globe made of leaves, slate or snow, or a cone or cairn (often made of slate or snow), or circles made of leaves half-frosted or stone rubbed with red powder, or circles cut into snow or leaves. The circle is 'such a fundamental form, one can never get away from it altogether', says Goldsworthy,[43] though his circles are usually deliberately slightly irregular — he avoids the connotations of traditional symbolism.[44] There are many 'negative' circles, made by the surrounding material.

The 'feminine' quality of this primary circular symbol has already been mentioned. It sounds too obvious to say that Andy Goldsworthy's circles, globes, cones and rings should have 'feminine', maternal connotations, but it is precisely in this sort of simple world of equivalents and responses that Goldsworthy operates. The simplicity of the structures, such as a circle, cannot be improved upon, but no matter how 'natural' the circle is as a shape, it always looks humanmade in Goldsworthy's art. His circles of white leaves in amongst dark leaves (1981, Yorkshire) always stand out from the surroundings. The viewer is always aware that a human has made those marks, or arranged the leaves in that way.

The globe made from oak leaves (1985), for instance, is typical of Andy Goldsworthy's melding of the 'natural' and the human. Yes, the viewer has perhaps seen oak leaves many times, or any sort of leaves. Yes, the viewer has probably admired the multicoloured leaves of Fall. But Goldsworthy's sphere of leaves in the forest is not an object the viewer might expect to come across on a walk. The oak leaf globe asserts itself instantly as *art*, as a humanmade artifact. Yet how right these globes of ice, snow, slate and leaves can appear. The simplicity of the structure (the circle) makes these sculptures seem curiously 'obvious' and 'natural'. Like a really good pop song or movie, one wonders: *why haven't they been made before?*

Andy Goldsworthy always speaks of the significance of the surrounding environment in his works. His sculptures are as much about the surroundings in which they are situated, as about the 'sculptures' themselves. An exhibition inside, in a gallery, is always going to be a problem, then. The contemporary gallery, with its sparse settings, white-washed walls and trendy magazines and postcards, is a powerfully *cultural* environment. The contemporary gallery is not 'natural' at all, it is not 'nature', it is not a place of mist, wind, skies and soil. No wonder, then, that earth artists such as Walter de Maria wanted to fill a whole gallery with dark soil, to bring nature into the contemporary gallery in a big way.

Andy Goldsworthy's shows are something of a disappointment, in one view, because the works have to breathe without their usual natural surroundings. Goldsworthy did emulate Walter de Maria in a direct manner: in November, 1992, he covered the interior of the London gallery of his agent with clay (*Hard earth – Dorset clay smoothed out, left to dry*). The exhibit began as a smooth creamy-white expanse of wet clay/ earth. It looked as if the gallery was empty, said Goldsworthy (*Stone*, 64), recalling Yves Klein's empty gallery show, *Le Vide*, of 1958. *Hard earth* directly re-echoed Walter de Maria's *New York Earth Room* (1977): the natural world was present in the gallery in both works in force: in de Maria's *New York Earth Room* the dark soil had a solemn, weighty, fecund presence; in Goldsworthy's *Hard earth* time and transformation played a part: gradually, the clay dried and cracked, allowing the Goldsworthyan vision of the dark energies of nature to well up: nature was erupting into the gallery space.

Andy Goldsworthy's writings are sometimes simple, matter-of-fact, and sometimes blunt – in a stubborn, Northern fashion. Goldsworthy comes across a rugged man of the wild, a 'whole earth man', ecologically sensitive, someone 'in touch' with nature, working with his bare hands, in boots, hat and an anorak, often in Winter. There is a macho posturing to this (no doubt unintentional), in which the relationship with nature is 'fundamental', 'raw', 'violent', 'intense'. Goldsworthy sees working in the hard conditions of Winter a challenge, a 'test of my commitment to the landscape'.10 Goldsworthy has spoken about being 'shocked' by small-scale natural events, about work suddenly becoming 'intense', about the 'raw energy' of colours. Goldsworthy's writings are marked by words such as 'powerful', 'wildness', 'deeper', 'rooted', 'flesh and bone', 'feeling', 'essential', 'sense', 'energy', 'touching' and 'essence' (these words are taken from one page of Goldsworthyan philosophy, in *Stone*, 6).

Of a cairn made out of scrap steel which was placed next to an old foundry, Andy Goldsworthy said that the cairn 'touches the nature of an urban environment' (*Stone*, 35). Does it 'touch the nature' of the place? What is the nature of the place? How can a human 'touch the nature' of the place? What is the quality of this touching? What kind of touching is it? And what is the nature of 'the nature of an urban environment'? How does the artist know he's touched it? Simple: he believes wholeheartedly in his subjective, intuitive feelings. Of steel, for example, the artist stated: 'I can feel its source' (ibid.). What does this 'source' 'feel' like? And what is the 'source' of steel? The Earth? The energies that formed it? The people that dug the source material out of the ground and shaped it? How, too, does the viewer know about this feeling for the source of a material? Is it expressed in the work? How can the audience test the authenticity of the artist's feelings? These are questions which one can (and should) fire at any artist. Goldsworthy's art is often unsure about the answers. It knows it is about nature, ecology, place, organic form, and so on, but its views on these matters, and its relation to them is often confused, ambiguous, banal or simplistic.

A dandelion work such as *Dandelions* (1993)[11] highlights the recurring problems with Andy Goldsworthy's sculpture: it has instant appeal: brilliant yellow dandelions are set in a mossy, pitted rock next to a stream. The work seems to emphasize the relative beauty of both the flowers and the setting: the 'organic', individual shape of the rock pool, the contrasts in brightness and colour in nature (grey and green rock, yellow dandelions), the transience of nature (the dandelions' colour will fade; the flowers will be pummelled by the next rain, or swept away when the river rises). Yet the sceptical viewer might also say, well *anyone* could make that work (or many other Goldsworthy sculptures). There is little 'technique' or skill involved: one simply places dandelions in a pool (or rocks on top of each other, or wraps boulders in clay, or rubs the bark off twigs, or cracks open pebbles, and so on).

Dandelions seems so simple, so easy, like so many of Andy Goldsworthy's sculptures (*Beech leaves, Balanced stone, Balanced rocks, Two Scaur Water snowballs, Red river rock pools, River rock, Peat, Clay-covered rocks, Torn stones, Red sand thrown into a blue sky, Orange stones* and *Yellow elm leaves*, to cite some works from the book *Stone*). Hang on, the sceptic might claim, the charlatan has simply stuck some flowers in a pool! That can't be 'art'! Easy to see how Goldsworthy's art can seem a sham, like Carl Andre's bricks, or Yves Klein's leap, or Andy Warhol's six hour film of someone sleeping. *Come on*, the sceptic'll say, this can't be *serious*.

Andy Goldsworthy sculptures such as *Yellow elm leaves, Red maple leaves, Beech leaves, Red river rock pools* and other riverside works seem so simple, so easily put together. But Constantin Brancusi's eggs and fish and heads are also very 'simple' shapes and forms: he reduced and rationalized natural forms until he reduced them to an 'essence' (the 'essence' of a fish, of a head, of a bird in flight). Yet Brancusi does not get accusations of superficially and banality thrown at him. Indeed, his sculpture is really powerful precisely because he radically simplified it. (What the viewer doesn't see in the gallery, of course, are the hundreds of failed attempts, the mistakes, and the years of research and refinement to get to that stage).

With Andy Goldsworthy, though, the simplicity is of a different order: is the confusion and criticism of Goldsworthy's work because he is using the *actual* material of nature? An actual leaf, rock, petal, ice sheet, not an imitation or image of them? Is it that anti-Goldsworthy critics see a rock covered with real leaves, not a mock-up made in an artist's studio, or a bronze or marble interpretation? Is it that Goldsworthy is getting so 'close' to nature that he is using the very materials of nature themselves, without altering them much at all? Goldsworthy doesn't seem to *do* much with his materials: he wraps them round a rock, sticks them in a pool, builds a mini tower out of 'em, takes a photo, and then it's 'art'. Is it that his art does not do anything more than this?

This is how the art of contemporary (postmodern) artists such as Andy Goldsworthy, Yves Klein, Andy Warhol, Joseph Beuys and Carl Andre differs from traditional Western art. They use the *actual object*, a process begun by Marcel Duchamp with his *Urinal* and developed by Kurt Schwitters. Schwitters' reasoning was along the lines of: why not stick on some real objects? Jasper Johns said the same thing: he preferred the real object itself to a representation of it. Instead of using a replica or imitation or image of a rock or icicle, Goldsworthy uses the rock and icicle themselves. The confusions of this relationship between reality and illusion, object and image, life and art in Goldsworthy's art are compounded by his use of photography, which instantly renders everything an image, a mode of representation, a simulation, a copy, subject to all the strictures and structures of art and representation. Goldsworthy's photographs are plainly *not* the object in itself, but a representation of it, which is very different, and much more complicated.

Andy Goldsworthy has to face up to the fact that most people know about his art (and love his art) from photographs. Most people who know of Goldsworthy have *not* seen a Goldsworthy exhibition; have *not* seen his art in its outdoor environment; have *not* seen Goldsworthy making a work. They have bought the book *Time*, or seen photos of his art in magazines and books. For the punter who consumes art in books and printed material (or on TV or radio or the internet), the 'real' art object doesn't need to exist: what counts is the media representation of it. But this would upset a realist/sensualist (modernist) like Goldsworthy, who so passionately needs 'to touch' ('I must touch', as he puts it). A world of computerized virtual reality would be abhorrent to him. Yet that is how his art is mainly consumed. Punters have bought the books, seen the photos in magazines and that, for them, is Andy Goldsworthy art. Thus, the *photographs* of Goldsworthy's sculptures are *already* 'so real' that they have, for the consumer, replaced his art. Goldsworthy has said that it is important for the viewer of his art to fill in the gap between the photograph of the sculpture and the real sculpture that he made someplace else. The photographs are incomplete on their own, as artworks: they require the spectator to create the rest of the artwork by using their imagination and memory, by remembering what it was like to be cold or wet or in a wood. To recall what it was like to be a child, touching leaves or snow or ice.[12]

The viewer, then, supplies the 'reality', the 'real' experience, the effect, which the photographs suggest but cannot complete. (This could be another reason for Goldsworthy's popularity: that his art leaves some part of the sculptures incomplete, and the viewer can supply the rest from their many memories of the real world. A kind of art of interactivity, fed by nature photography). It's also a not insignificant fact that by the time the photographs are published or exhibited in a gallery, most of Goldsworthy's sculptures have already ceased to exist (they're been blown away, collapsed, eroded, dissolved, etc).

Of course, art consumers would probably like to know that the stones *really were* balanced on top of each other on the Welsh coast, or the icicles *really were* stuck to a wall in Dumfriesshire. It's probably essential, in fact, for many spectators to think that Andy Goldsworthy really made those works. But Yves Klein faked his *Leap*, and invited people to see an empty gallery. In the age of art impresarios and art 'terrorists' (such as Andy Warhol, Claes Oldenburg, Jeff Koons, Bruce Nauman, Piero Manzoni, Gilbert & George, and the KLF), when artworks are only known through radio, TV, the web and the press, Goldsworthy could have faked everything. (There are numerous techniques to fake images – not just with modern computers, digital manipulation and Photoshop, but older methods such as montage, airbrushing and printing separate negatives. Consider masters of photographic superimposition such as Oscar Rejlander, Henry Peach Robinson, Alexander Rodchenko, Max Ernst or John Heartfield).

Richard Long told me he regarded Andy Goldsworthy as a 'second generation' artist, who was 'decorative (!)'.[13] Most critics, though, have been extremely praiseworthy of Goldsworthy. Neil Hedges wrote: '[t]he artist always achieves his goal, establishing and stimulating our own senses to view or touch conversant shapes and materials with much delight' (73). Goldsworthy uses 'feminine' modes of art-making: *weaving* stalks or *stitching* leaves together. Weaving, sewing and stitching are regarded as 'feminine' means of production, linked with art and craft, and denigrated by masculinist criticism.

A suspended leaf shield turned out to be 'one of the best

pieces I have ever made', as Andy Goldsworthy put it. The hanging leafworks enable light to become a key element in the sculpture: the translucence of the leaves was highlighted. The sun completed the sculpture, making the leafwork as 'extraordinary as going to the Arctic'.[14]

Light is one of the key formal elements that Andy Goldsworthy explores in his sculpture. Critics have spoken of Goldsworthy's 'stunning effects of light and atmosphere'.[15] The two leafworks of October, 1997, at Storm King (orange and yellow leaves stuck onto a rock), were created specifically to catch the morning sunlight.[16] Another shield, *Horse chestnut leaves* (Yorkshire, 1987), was deliberately created for darkness, hanging in amongst some rhododendron bushes. The Getty Institute clay hole was positioned so that the sun would shine on it once a year, at Midsummer. Some of Goldsworthy's *Réfuges d'Art* were constructed to take advantage of certain lighting effects (such as the rising sun at certain times of the year).[17]

Because place is so important,[18] light (and colour) becomes a primary tool. Some of Andy Goldsworthy's works pivot very much on luminosity and opacity, not just the leaf shields, but some of the snow walls, the holes in sand, and so on, so that without the right sort of lighting, they do not work properly. Some sculptures are created in response to certain lighting conditions – the stick sculpture in the Lake District (1988), made in the pale, liquid light of dawn, for example. 'When I work with the land I work with the sky. When I work with water I am working with the clouds', Goldsworthy stated.[19] The branches from a mulga tree in Australia (in 1991) were edged with red sand in order to catch the light of the setting sun: set end to end, the red-edged branches looked like a snake (appropriate for the Australian Outback). Some of Goldsworthy's weakest works were made in Australia in 1991: *Mulga branches* had the branches laid on the red sand in two directions; they changed colour as the light changed. Other sculptures are seen in a variety of lighting conditions – stormlight, snowlight, misty skies (the snow wall at Blencathra in Cumbria is an obvious instance). Some of the brightest of Goldsworthy's leafworks were made in Japan, where the maple leaves are dazzling in October and November (in, for example, *Maple patch*, November 22, 1987, or *Japanese maple*, November 21-22, 1987).

Andy Goldsworthy's flower pieces are inevitably 'pretty'. It's difficult to use flowers, in poetry, sculpture, painting or performance, without appearing 'pretty' (Goldsworthy realizes this).[20] Think of Rainer Maria Rilke's many flower poems (to roses, irises, lilies), or the beautiful, sonorous flower watercolours of the German Expressionist Emil Nolde. Like Nolde's radiant flower-pieces, like the flowerpieces of Flemish and Dutch art, Goldsworthy's flower sculptures are luminous. The dandelion piece (April 28, 1987), which is a spread of flowers making a hole in the middle, is striking not because of the shape the artist's made, but because of the vibrant yellow of the flowers.

It is the *colour* of Andy Goldsworthy's 'red splashes' or 'throws' that contributes much in making them powerful. Goldsworthy has spoken of the significance of using the colour red: in Japan, he remarked, he learnt about a 'deeply disturbing' red (*Wood*, 15), a 'heightened awareness of red. A bright red maple tree in the middle of a green forest, like an open wound' (in ib.). Goldsworthy often uses red in his art – in the boulders covered in red maple leaves (1991) or the poppy-leaved covered stones (1989), or poppy petal-covered branches (1992), or the ridged holes made on the beach at the Isle of Wight with red edges (1987, AG). Red maple leaves climb up rocks or are layered on top of little rockpools (1993). Goldsworthy relates red to the iron in human blood.

Andy Goldsworthy's photographs present an idealized world, veritably the pastoral world of ancient times. Goldsworthy's Arcadia, though, is definitely a Northern European pastoral realm, not the Southern, Mediterranean paradise of satyrs, shepherdesses, gods and wild animals. Goldsworthy's 'pastoral sublime', to use the phrase applied to a category of J.M.W. Turner's works, is a Northern European realm, very much in the tradition of Turner's paintings of the Alps, with lowering, gloomy skies, raging wind, snow-capped mountains and mossy riverbanks. John Martin, Thomas Girtin, John Sell Cotman, John Constable and Turner made many paintings of the landscapes Goldsworthy works in. Apart from Australia and Japan, Goldsworthy's art centres around cold, rain-sodden, Northern landscapes. True, there is much sunlight in his photographs of Australia, photographs that evoke the colonial view of the Outback as a rugged, inhospitable place where the white people sit around camp fires. Goldsworthy's Japan is a more sublime, rarefied place, though it is still rough and distinctly non-human.

Andy Goldsworthy photographs his sculptures often looking down on them, so the surrounding landscape is not seen. He edits out unsightly buildings or roads, but art has always involved much more editing than many artists would admit. Goldsworthy knows that what one leaves out of a work is as important as what one puts in. Goldsworthy said that photographs were 'very important to me as a working record', and that he had a record of nearly everything he'd made, which he could look on and use.[21] 'A good work is the result of being in the right place at the right time with the right material', said Goldsworthy.[22]

Some of Andy Goldsworthy's earliest works were tidal, beachbound sculptures which relied very much on the power and majesty of the sea to make them work. Some were works which required the action of the tide to complete them. They were fabricated specifically so that the sea would cover them up.

At Morecambe Bay in Lancashire, U.K. in October, 1976, Andy Goldsworthy buried a serpentine line of stones and photographed them as the tide came in. Another work, at Heysham Head, comprised the now-familiar Goldsworthy motif: a series of rocks on a tidal pedestal: as the water rose, the sculpture altered. Goldsworthy's later sea sculptures of balanced rocks are essentially no different from these early Lancashire works. The early works, like the latest sea pieces, employ the formal elements of the littoral environment: the presence of the sea, the changing levels in water, the reflectivity of the water, the colour of the sea, and sky, the movement of the water, and so on. These elements are incorporated into Goldsworthy's sea sculptures.

Many (land) artists have worked with the tide: Barry Flanagan, Christo, Dennis Oppenheim, Michael McCafferty, Michelle Oka Doner, Chris Drury and Jan Dibbets. Dibbets had a tractor plough the sand on a beach which would then be covered by the tide, in a film made for television (in 1969), for a *Land Art* exhibition.

Much of Andy Goldsworthy's art is about and made from ice and snow. Other artists who have worked with snow include Dennis Oppenheim, Joseph Beuys and Hans Haacke. Goldsworthy is distinctly a 'Northern' artist, who makes work in landscapes that come out of the 'Celtic fringe', out of the sort of landscapes that Celtic culture exalts: misty, rocky hillscapes; sodden Autumnal forest floors knee-deep with leaves; wild snowscapes; cold, clear streams banked with large mossy boulders; and still lakes at dawn. Goldsworthy's landscapes could have mythical figures such as the Lady of Shallot, Lancelot or King Arthur riding through them without altering anything. They are the landscapes of Merlin, Taleissin and Morgan Le Fay, of Welsh legends such as *The Mabinogion*, of historical events shrouded in mists, of historical figures such as Robert the Bruce, Owen Glendower, King Edward and Boadiccea. The places associated with Goldsworthy – his studio at Penpont, Scaur Water in Dumfriesshire, Carlisle, Yorkshire Sculpture Park, Grizedale in Cumbria, Leeds, Leadgate in Durham – are all Northern British sites. And the stereotypes of Britain's North – grimy towns, rain, bleak moors, gloomy skies, grim humour, down to earth and no-nonsense attitudes – all chime with Goldsworthy's sculpture.

One wonders whether Andy Goldsworthy would like to work in snow and ice more than in any other medium. His notes and titles record many frustrations stemming from working with snow. In temperate snowlands, though, one feels Goldsworthy is very much at home. Snow has the right sort of qualities Goldsworthy looks for in a material: it is malleable, it melts and changes, its whiteness makes for good, contrasty imagery, and it seasonally alters the landscape, and later dissolves into it. And it's free, and there's plenty of it. In Goldsworthy's snowworks one senses also the sheer fun of working with snow. For people in most of Britain, snow is not a definite occurrence each year, as it is in, say, Northern Russia or Alaska. For children, snow can be an exciting event (while British adults usually gripe about it). Snow was a perennial delight and 'shock' for Goldsworthy. In *Midsummer Snowballs* he wrote that '[e]ven in winter each snowfall is a shock, unpredictable and unexpected'.[23] Goldsworthy retained the child-like enjoyment of snow falling in Britain throughout his life. While much of Great Britain grinds to a halt at the sight of a snowflake, Goldsworthy has the child's joy when it snows (school's cancelled, snowball fights, ice skating, sledging, and making snowmen and snowballs).

Andy Goldsworthy speaks in wonder and awe of 'the effect, the excitement' of the first snowfall.[24] Some of this excitement comes across in Goldsworthy's snowworks. He has made, for example, patterns in the snow by rolling a snowball around a field, exactly as kids do when it snows (*Snowball trail*, Brough, Cumbria, 1982 and Yorkshire Sculpture Park, 1987). Linked to the snowball trail was a rectangular wall of snow built on the hills in Penpont in March, 1998. Some of Goldsworthy's earliest works with snow were large snowballs. In some of these early snow works, Goldsworthy placed snowballs in areas such as woods or fields which didn't have any snow, so the snowballs stood out against the trees and grass (as in Ilkley, Yorkshire, 1981). Into some snowballs Goldsworthy inserted branches and other material (as Clapham, Yorkshire, 1979, Bentham, 1980, and London, 1985).

The biting cold maybe gives Andy Goldsworthy a sense of heroism, for suffering invariably enhances a work (as in, 'this work was difficult, made under adverse conditions'). After all, Goldsworthy is not an artist who makes work in the 'comfort' of a home or studio (working indoors doesn't feel 'real' to him). No: he goes out into the wilderness, where it can be uncomfortable and challenging. He claims to know the landscape around his studio in Penpont, Scotland, very well, so that the snow does not hide the world: 'I know what lies under the snow – I know the earth beneath' (HE). Always Goldsworthy stresses the intimate relationship he has with nature. Part of this intimacy comes from returning to the same patch of land again and again. Through successive visits, layers of touch and meaning in the landscape are uncovered by the artist. The artist returning to the same space always works in time as well as space, for s/he creates a personal history of that place. S/he works with her former selves, as well as in the present – with the artist and ideas she had two years ago, ten years ago, twenty years ago. 'Some places I return to over and over again, going deeper – a relationship, made in layers over a long time'.[25]

Sceptics can claim that many of Andy Goldsworthy's sculptures gain much of their fire from their situation in wilderness landscapes. They would be right. Although Goldsworthy states that many of his sculptures are made in built-up areas, areas of dense population and human activity, a glance through any Goldsworthy book or a visit to a Goldsworthy show will reveal the large proportion of wilderness or rural landscapes in his art. He expunges all the trash, houses, telephone poles, billboards, cables, signs, aerials, apartment blocks, cars and roads from his photographs, and presents lush streams, moorland, forests and hillsides. There are no people at all in his art, except Goldsworthy himself, who is sometimes seen, with his beard, sweater and jeans, making a piece of art. In this sense, Goldsworthy's work is not at all figurative – but neither is it 'abstract', in the Mark Rothko or Piet Mondrian sense, for real, recognisable objects appear in his work. This is one of the reasons for the growing popularity of his work: apart from the Eighties ecological/ Green movement, and the accessible, decorative quality of his work, it is thoroughly countrified and rural, quite in keeping with primæval desires for escape into the country, that nostalgia for nature that lies behind the pastoral and landscape tradition in the West.

Andy Goldsworthy's skill is not just to 'touch nature' (whatever that means), but to touch the chords of desire for nature in people. Goldsworthy's art is popular partly because of this powerful desire among Western audiences for contact with the natural world, an appetite which is manifested in natural history programmes on television, in jaunts to zoos, gardens, windswept hillside car lots, in Edward Hopper, John Constable, Vincent van Gogh and Claude Monet posters and prints, in gardening magazines and gardening centres and plants in the house, and in the popularity of English rural novels by George Eliot, Thomas Hardy and Emily Brontë. The eco/ green movement (and its associated movements in pagan/ New Age/ anti-road, anti-capitalist, anarchist and animal activism), taps into this nostalgic love of an urban-centric culture for all things 'natural'.[26] The natural world seems to be green and life-giving and untarnished by the complexities of modern life. The natural world, which is Goldsworthy's preferred world, is a place of leaves, rivers, animals and stones, a place seemingly devoid of people, the ones who mess things up, who complicate things, who introduce the concepts and realities of neurosis, confusion, waste, violence, consumption and politics into the 'pure' natural world.[27]

It's not like that at all, but these eco/ Green/ pastoral feelings are powerful. Andy Goldsworthy's art, like the pastoral novels of George Eliot and Thomas Hardy, like Green politics or the money-spinning popularity of Vincent van Gogh and Claude Monet, trades on the desires for an earlier, ancient Paradise, a time when things were simpler, richer, deeper. This is the 'green world' of childhood, a time of playfulness and living close to the Earth, enjoying the seasons passionately but also freely, in a relaxed manner. In mythology, it is the 'Golden Age', *il illo tempore, ab origine*, in the Creation era, at the origin of the world, before the Fall of Adam and Eve into sin, a time before œdipal anxiety and patriarchal psychosis, a Gaia time, a whole earth time, all 'natural' and recycled and vegetarian, a holistic time, a time of social unity, when everyone felt as one in communities and loved each other, a time of maternal bliss, when women were nurturing Mother Goddesses and men could be sweetly dreaming babies without feeling embarrassed. Goldsworthy's art books, commissions and shows trade on this pastoral imagery and desire: they allow stressed, confused, overworked and neurotic city dwellers time out from staring at the control screens (TV, computers, cell phones) of the megavisual world, encouraging a little day-dreaming into the soft greens and greys of wild moorlands. Goldsworthy's art may be increasingly successful because it reminds people that, yes, one does love nature after all: one came from it, one'll go back into it, in the end, in death.

Andy Goldsworthy's art may hit home because it does *not* bombard people with telephones, computers, cars, factories, radios, TVs, microwaves, washing machines, hoovers, irons, faxes, all those machines that connote *labour*, that are the symbols and mechanisms of working life. In Goldsworthy's green world, all is natural, untechnological, with artifacts that connote a return to basics: stone, wood, leaves, ice.

Snowballs In Summer (a.k.a. *Midsummer Snowballs*, 2000) was one of Andy Goldsworthy's larger, more complex installations. Fourteen snowballs were gathered from the snowfields of Dumfriesshire and Perthshire in 1999 and 2000, kept in storage, transported to London and exhibited on the streets of the City of London. This, coupled with the show *Time*, at the Barbican Centre (in August-October), made 2000 the most prominent display of Goldsworthyania for some years in the U.K.. Goldsworthy liked the idea of the snowballs appearing in the middle of Summer in an urban setting. The snowballs were not 'made for people. They are about people'.[28]

One of the problems Andy Goldsworthy's art addresses head on is the age-old tension between the 'real world' and art, between objects as they are in the everyday world, and objects as they are represented in art. Goldsworthy encourages the viewer to look again at the natural world: not just at the beauty of it, but at the multitudinous variety of forms in nature. The snowball in the *Snowballs* installations (1989 and 2000) is not plastic or concrete masquerading as a snowball, but a real snowball. Similarly, the twigs and stalks and needles and pebbles folded into the snowballs are real. What's amazing is the actuality of nature: the variety of forms (the way the branches twist, for instance).

Andy Goldsworthy's sculptures used all the tricks and devices of post-Renaissance illusion and representation, including figure-ground relationships, negative space, perspective, selective viewpoint, *chiaroscuro*, silhouettes, outlines, and so on. A good example of the strong pictorial element in Goldsworthy's art are the sculptures that use negative space to create the illusion of continuous form: these sculptures typically have loops of ice or sand on two sides of a rock or a tree. In, for instance, *Reconstructed refrozen icicles* (1999).[29]

Andy Goldsworthy's ethics are those of Chris Drury, Hamish Fulton, Richard Long, David Nash (he has worked at Nash's Blaenau-Ffestiniog studio) and other British land artists: a mystical feeling for the landscape, expressed by an exquisite sensitivity of *touch*, that all-important component in the eroticism of sculpture:

> Movement, change, light, growth and decay are the life-blood of nature, the energies that I try to tap through my work [wrote Goldsworthy], I need the shock of touch, the resistance of place, materials and weather, the earth as my source.[30]

As Andy Goldsworthy affirmed, he *must* touch. A world in which he would not be allowed to touch would be hateful. A world in which the trees had 'DO NOT TOUCH' signs on them would be horrendous. Significantly, Goldsworthy works mainly in areas in which the ownership of the land is not contested. He operates in landscapes where he has been given permission to work. No 'DO NOT TOUCH' signs for him.

Land artists such as Andy Goldsworthy use their hands, primarily, as their means of making art. Goldsworthy does not go out into the landscape with anything, except a knife.[31] Perhaps he should, to be really purist, make do without even a knife? Anyway, he *does* really go out into the landscape with 'tools' – the camera not least among them (also spare film too, maybe an extra lens filter or two, and a tripod). Without that camera, the viewer wouldn't know about many of his works. Ditto with all land artists. Without the camera, their work is 'lost'. That is, not really 'lost', but the camera means the viewer too can share in the work. Without the camera, the viewer would have to rely on written texts, perhaps, as a means of 'recording' artworks. Photography is also 'a way of communicating', Goldsworthy told an interviewer, 'and we wouldn't be sitting here if I didn't take the photographs.'[32] Here Goldsworthy admits that without the photographs there would be not much communicating going on with his art: it needs photography to work. But, as one can see, Goldsworthy and other land artists are not writers. Indeed, their writings are, well, often in note form, designed as a 'record' for themselves, or as notes towards some artwork. While there have been any number of painters and sculptors who were also good writers who provided many insights – Leonardo da Vinci, Ad Reinhardt, Vincent van Gogh, Donald Judd – Goldsworthy is not among them. So, relying on photographs, the viewer gets to find out about many works of land art that might otherwise have never known. The camera is thus an essential 'tool' for the land artist.

Andy Goldsworthy also goes out with many other invisible tools of his craft – his awareness of land art, his education, his knowledge of other sculptors and art history, his memory of previous works, and so on. No artist works alone, culturally. Goldsworthy's art, like all land art, like all art, works within a culture and tradition and history of contemporary art. Tracing the links with Minimalism, Arte Povera and Conceptualism, for instance, is only one way of looking at Goldsworthy's art.

Andy Goldsworthy's sculptures are marked by a number of elements familiar in land art: transience, domination, penetration, circular forms (globes, circles, spirals, snakes, cones) and nature mysticism. The ephemerality of the pieces, for instance, is a key component. Snow and ice will melt away, leaves will disintegrate, stones will be blown over.

Each Andy Goldsworthy sculpture has a date printed with its title. Not just a year, as in the usual artwork, but a specific day. Thus, one of his best pieces, the delicious poppy covered boulder, has the title: *Poppy petals wrapped around a boulder held with water*, with the time and place inscribed as: Sibobre, France, June 6, 1989. The petal-covered rock, with its brilliant red colour, nestled in some mossy boulders, looking very much like one of Constantin Brancusi's 'cosmic eggs' (egg-shaped sculptures which Brancusi titled *The Beginning of the World*). The red colour revealed the rock's shape, size and form, its position amongst and relation to other rocks. Not wishing to disturb or move the rock (it's not that small really), Goldsworthy's act of covering it in wet poppy petals drew attention to this particular egg-shaped rock, *this* one and *not* the others (although the surrounding boulders also became the subject of the sculpture: attention was drawn to them as well as to the red rock). In *Poppy petals wrapped around a boulder held with water,* then, the place becomes as crucial as the centrepiece, the red rock.

In 1994's *Herd of Arches* in London, Andy Goldsworthy had fitted together masses of small slabs of stone, with tiny pebbles and wafer-thin stones wedged in, to hold the arch tightly together. Roger Partridge has made an arch out of stone (1983, private collection) which recalls Goldsworthy's *Herd of Arches.* Alan Sonfist's *Rock Monument of Rocky Mountains,* very much an ancestor of Goldsworthy's arches, was made in 1971.

The largest section of Andy Goldsworthy's book *Wood* (1996) is devoted to the *Capenoch Tree* series of works, made between 1994 and 1996 in Dumfriesshire in Great Britain. The 'Capenoch tree' was an old oak tree standing slightly apart from other trees on private land. Goldsworthy concentrated not on the whole tree, its trunk or its branches (as he often did), but on one particular branch that grew sideways out from the tree, horizontally, a few feet above the grass. As Goldsworthy explained, '[t]he long branch that has grown horizontal to the ground has taught me that the tree is the land. The branch is like the landscape' (*Time,* 195). So Goldsworthy treated the branch as a landscape in miniature, a small-scale setting for a range of sculptures which represent all of Goldsworthy's work in microcosm.

In a way, the *Capenoch Tree* series offered a summary of all of Andy Goldsworthy's land art techniques: there were leaves pinned along the branch; wood and snow cairns and globes placed next to the tree; snowballs set in the tree; arches made out of ice and stone on the branch; screens of willowherb and rosebay; walls of snow (some serpentine, some holed); lines of dandelions; and holes in the ground.

Andy Goldsworthy, like James Turrell, Alice Aycock and Robert Smithson, has made some huge pieces, such as the long 'snake' and the 'pool' or maze, in Country Durham,

England, large works which take up a lot of space, and certainly *dominate* the surrounding landscape. Goldsworthy's large-scale outdoor works often use the serpent coil as a fundamental form. Goldsworthy maintained, however, that his 'snake-like' or serpent-shaped sculptures does not refer directly to snakes.[33] Instead, he preferred to call one of his favourite motifs a 'river of earth', or a tree root, or a river.[34]

Whatever the artistic intention, however, it is impossible to limit readings of sculptures such as *Sidewinder, Lambton Earthwork* or the serpentine shapes in the British Museum's Egyptian Hall to responses to the environment. The serpent as symbol connotes time, change, seasons, birth-and-death-and-rebirth, eternity, sexuality, evil, the cosmos, and so on. Andy Goldsworthy might wish to determine how viewers read his serpent-shaped forms, and emphasize the response he makes to the natural environment, but consumers of art will make any interpretation they like, and some they might wish to suppress (snakes also connote dirt – they slide on the dust; and excrement; the alimentary canal; eating and defecating; poison; reptile life, and so on). In 1998, Goldsworthy confessed:

> after working for many years, I have to admit that I have a fascination for the snake. For me it is perfect sculpture. It's so simple. The way it moves on the ground or in the water, it draws the place. It's so expressive of the place it moves through. It's not like any other animal. It actually moves with the surface of the land.[35]

While Andy Goldsworthy insisted that he wasn't interested in the symbolic associations of the snake, or in the snake as an animal, he did link his use of the snake to Constantin Brancusi's birds and fish (Brancusi sculpted radically simplified, abstract versions of birds and fish). For Goldsworthy, the serpent wasn't a totemic or symbolic creature, but a form that expressed 'the energy of movement' (ib, 113).

Andy Goldsworthy's large-scale works, like James Turrell's, Nancy Holt's or Herbert Bayer's, are monumental works, which sprawl across the landscape. *Sidewinder* and *Seven Spires*, at Grizedale, U.K. (a Forestry Commission site between Windermere and Coniston Water), are trunks of trees stripped of their branches, and pinned together. In *Sidewinder*, the curved trunks were placed on the ground, to form a long snake-like sculpture: the form rests on the ground then curves into the air. The impression was of sliding, arching kinetic energy. In other words: a huge serpent slithering along the forest floor.

In *Seven Spires* the trees were pined together to form tall spires. The result was a series of enormous edifices made of wood in amongst other trees. Goldsworthy wanted to harness the sense of the 'almost desperate growth and energy driving upward' in the pine wood, and to evoke a cathedral-like atmosphere, with the spires stretching skyward with the brown gloom underneath.[36] It is, at first, not clear which is a tree and which is sculpture. Both, of course, are made of wood: Goldsworthy has simply drawn together the surrounding trees, it seems, but in doing so, he re-defines the surrounding forest. *Seven Spires* looks at first to be a gentle sculpture, blending in with the surrounding forest. 'In avoiding monumentality, however, Goldsworthy's sculptures do not forego grandeur', wrote Andrew Causey.[37] Yet they do stand out, really, they are distinctly works of art, existing in a paradoxical relationship with the environment. A 'collaboration' is a polite way of saying what Goldsworthy's *Seven Spires* is about: a 'collaboration with nature', a phrase used about much of his art. Other spires, made at the same time, include *Bracken Spires* (1983) and *Stone Spire* (1983). Goldsworthy later reworked the spire form in 2008 in San Francisco, in the Presidio Park (it's well worth visiting).

Commissioned by Sustrans and Northern Arts, *Lambton Earthwork* (1988) was a quarter-mile long bank which coiled along the ground near Chester-le-Street in County Durham. The site was associated with railroads and industry, but Andy Goldsworthy turned it into something wholly concerned with æsthetic and religious themes. The long spiralling banks of earth clearly derived from the earthwork sculptures of Robert Smithson and American earth art (Goldsworthy said he is wary of using the 'overblown spiral', the too-obvious spiral as a shape).[38] Goldsworthy spoke of the serpentine shape as being like a river winding through a valley, or the root of a tree.[39]

The other Durham earthwork (*Maze*, 1989, at Leadgate) also used ancient mythology and symbolism, this time the labyrinth. Like *Lambton Earthwork* (but unlike most of Andy Goldsworthy's works), *Maze* was intended to be used by the general public. Both *Maze* and *Lambton Earthwork* were about responses to the energies in nature – thus the public was invited to explore similar things as they physically walked around the earthworks. The usual experiences of the maze were apparent in Goldsworthy's *Maze* – not being able to see the whole plan from above; being enclosed by high banks; a bewildering series of turns and paths. The interwoven series of embankments also recalled Iron Age forts (of which there are many in Britain), such as the complex (and enormous) array of defences at Maiden Castle in Dorset.

Other large-scale Andy Goldsworthy works include installations *Slate Wall* and *Clay Wall* (1998, Edinburgh), *Clay Wall* (1996, San Francisco) and *Clay Wall* (2000, London). The *Fall Creek* installation, at the Herbert F. Johnson Museum of Art at Cornell University (in 2000), comprised a group of low holed mounds fashioned from hundreds of branches on the floor. Goldsworthy has worked at Cornell a number of times: the university has a long history of land art links: one of the important land exhibitions, *Earth Art*, took place in 1969 (it featured Richard Long, Oppenheim, Robert Smithson, Robert Morris and Michael Heizer).

One of the most important of Andy Goldsworthy's later commissions was the installation *Garden of Stone* (2003) at the Museum of Jewish Heritage in Lower Manhattan. *Garden of Stone: A Living Memorial* was a group of 18 hollowed

Vermont granite glacial boulders, with an oak tree inside (dwarf oaks, which only grow very slowly). The largest boulders weighed 13 tons. *Garden of Stone* was situated on the second floor garden, and cost a million dollars (the Public Art fund collaborated with the museum), making it easily Goldsworthy's most expensive commission to date.

Garden of Stone was made as a memorial for the victims and survivors of the Holocaust. Andy Goldsworthy was an unusual choice, perhaps, for an artist to tackle such a massive political and ideological issue. Goldsworthy has not been known for addressing issues such as the Holocaust in his art. Certainly he could not be described as a high profile political artist. He has also not had much of a connection with Jewish culture or history.

In 1994-95 a new form appeared in Andy Goldsworthy's *œuvre*, the 'stone house', usually consisting of a hollow stick cairn or cone with a round or elliptical opening. Sometimes the cairns or chambers are constructed from stones, like Goldsworthy's stone walls, but the basic structure is the same: an enclosed space, often with a hole to see in (and out), and often with an object (a boulder, a tree) sitting inside. (Chris Drury has made the shelter one of his primary forms). Inside Goldsworthy balanced a column of stones. Examples of the 'stone house' include those constructed at Digne les Bains and Mt. Kisco, New York (both 1995). Like Drury, Goldsworthy has occasionally enclosed his cairns with other materials, such as the slabs of ice surrounding a stone cairn (1996), and the stone spire inside a stick cairn (1995). A *Stone House* built in Melbourne (Australia) in 1997 took the form of a rectangular wall with a circular opening and a boulder placed inside.

One of Andy Goldsworthy's favourite structures is the stone wall. The wall he made (his first) between his land and a neighbouring farmer's at Stone Wood, Penpont, in Scotland, was a snake-like sculpture (*The Wall*, 1989). *The Wall* was a 'monument to walls',[40] a neat way of creating, on Goldsworthy's side of the wall, a sculpture, and on the farmer's side, a sheepfold. Goldsworthy's walls have a dual purpose: practical, and æsthetic. The walls are boundaries or sheepfolds as well as artistic objects. Their æsthetic derives from their practical applications (*Stone,* 106). While later walls (such as *Room* or *The wall that went for a walk* or the *Storm King Wall*) did not have a 'practical' or agricultural function, Goldsworthy still related them to the practicalities of stonewalling. Goldsworthy spoke proudly and sentimentally of the practice of stonewalling: he talked in terms of 'tradition', 'history', and 'years of experience' (*Stone,* 106).

The wall that went for a walk (1990, Grizedale) was a 150-yard long wall that literally snaked through the forest. The serpentine form of *The wall that went for a walk* related to *Lambton Earthwork* and *Sidewinder* (another Grizedale sculpture). *The wall that went for a walk* has no 'proper' function – i.e., no 'practical' function. It weaves between the trees and follows the lay of the land. Instead of ploughing through trees or rocks, Goldsworthy's curving wall assiduously avoids them. 'The wall itself is an expression of movement; a line moving through the landscape'.[41] However, the wall doesn't need to be there in the first place (a notion that Goldsworthy cannot quite resolve: in the book *Stone* he related *The wall that went for a walk* to the old fields that were at Grizedale before the forest, but it's not a convincing argument).

At 2,278 feet long, another wall, 1998's *Storm King Wall,* was not only Andy Goldsworthy's biggest wall, it was one of Goldsworthy's most significant works. Other artists who had work at the Storm King Art Center included Richard Serra, Louise Nevelson, David Smith, Mark di Suvero, Isamu Noguchi, Alice Aycock and Alexander Calder.

In the mid-1990s, Andy Goldsworthy developed the *Sheepfolds* project: building or renewing a hundred sheepfolds in the North of England. The *100 Sheepfolds* project was funded by public money from the National Lottery (who contributed a grant of £340,000 or about $545,000). The project included exhibitions in Cumbria, St Albans and

London, TV documentaries, and books by Goldsworthy (*Sheepfolds* and *Arch*). 1996, the Year of the Visual Arts, was the launch of *Sheepfolds*; the completion date was later extended to 2003 and beyond. Initially, the *Sheepfolds* proposal was presented to local councils, environmental agencies, countryside agencies, educational institutions, land owners and arts development boards.

The *Sheepfolds* project – Goldsworthy's largest undertaking to date – revolved around sheep farming, the herding, washing, cleaning, branding, breeding, rearing, and shearing of sheep. Goldsworthy saw the *Sheepfolds* project as a 'monument to agriculture' (Sh, 16). There were six different variants of sheepfolds in the project; cairn folds (pinfolds), boulder folds, drove arch folds (folds restored for the *Arch* project), restored folds, touchstone folds, which have works built into the walls, and the ephemeral pieces made on the Samuel Taylor Coleridge walk route. The sheepfolds containing cairns were built near the Nine Standards in Cumbria, rock formations which have long fascinated Goldsworthy.

Andy Goldsworthy has continued to build arches: it has become one of his most distinctive motifs. No other land artist has employed the arch so often as a key structure in their *œuvre*. Goldsworthy's arch sculptures include the offshoot of the *Sheepfolds* project, the *Arch* project of 1996-97; a number of 'herds' of stone arches (such as *Herd of Arches* and *A Clearing of Arches*); arches exhibited in Montréal (1998); a private commission made near the Storm King Art Center, *Eleven Arches* (1997); and some large commissioned arches: a stone arch sited in Montréal (1999) and Rainscombe Park, Oare, Wiltshire (2000), both constructed from red Scottish sandstone. Of the *Montréal Arch*, commissioned by Cirque du Soleil for its HQ, Goldsworthy remarked: '[t]he arch is heavy and strong, expressing permanence, but it is in fact about change, movement and journey' (*Time*, 60).

In July, 1995, Andy Goldsworthy constructed a multi-layered cairn within sight of Mont St Vincent (in the river Bès valley). The cairn was built in South France, at Digne les Bains, which became one of Goldsworthy's favourite spots (which he has returned to nearly every year since). The rocky, wooded hills and icy, rushing rivers of this beautiful area of South France became a kind of Mediterranean version of Goldsworthy's homeground of Dumfriesshire in Scotland: it had the rivers, the valleys, the forests and the hills which Goldsworthy loved, but lit by a Mediterranean light (and quite a bit warmer than Scotland, too – in fact, Goldsworthy found the heat a little uncomfortable, and took to working early in the morning and late in the afternoon. Keeping Mediterranean hours, in other words). And Digne offered a Southern, Mediterranean culture to Goldsworthy's usual stamping ground of Northern European culture.

Andy Goldsworthy was pleased to have cracked creating sculptures under the harsh, bright sun of South France. One of his methods was to submerge stones in the River Bès (which he had tried once or twice before). 'I like the way that the water confuses the form of the stones, so you forget the stone and all you see is the colour', Goldsworthy commented.[42]

Andy Goldsworthy said that he is really working with time. 'If I had to describe in one word what I do, I'd say I work with *time*'.[45] Although it seems, at first glance, to be all about space, about particular spaces and how materials react with certain locations, time is an important element in Goldsworthy's art. The mystery of time, and the relentless, unstoppable, implacable, unforgiving force of it.

Time was central to Andy Goldsworthy's collaboration with a dance troupe. In 1995 the Ballet Atlantique-Régine Chopinot company put on a dance-based performance called *Végétal* at La Rochelle in France. *Végétal* consisted of five sections: earth, seed, root, branch and leaf. For the backdrop Goldsworthy made a wall drawing from ferns and bracken stuck on with rabbit skin glue in serpentine patterns. The ballet featured Goldsworthy's installations, which included sculptures (using stones, sticks, leaves and earth) that were built and taken down by the dancers.

Andy Goldsworthy explained in *Wood* that collaborating on a dance work was quite natural for him, because the body plays such a large part in making sculpture: 'the body as the sculpture. I've always seen myself as an object in the work; that I'm nature too' (*Wood*, 7). Goldsworthy had already used the body directly in many works – the 'throws', for example, or the 'prints' and 'shadows' made by lying on the ground during rain or snow. Another performance by the ballet group, *La Danse du Temps*, took place at La Rochelle in France in November, 1999, and the Barbican Centre in London in September, 2000.

Andy Goldsworthy can be expected to explore more collaborations, such as live performance, dance, maybe video or installations and the like. But the core, the spiritual heart, the essence of his art, will continue to be his work within the landscape – and mainly on his own, and mainly in South-West Scotland.

22

Land Artists In Europe

CHRISTO

Christo is perhaps the most well-known land artist working today. He makes huge, very public gestures: tarpaulin and plastic shrouded buildings, the wrapped Pont Neuf and Reichstag, and curtains hanging across Colorado valleys. His art is not 'invisible' like Walter de Maria's kilometre-long brass rod which only reveals a brass disc on the ground, or Hamish Fulton's walks, which are now only memories or text pieces.

Born in 1935 in Bulgaria, Christo (Christo Javacheff) attended the Fine Arts Academy in Sofia. One of his early activities as a student involved tidying up the Orient Express railroad route through Bulgaria by covering old farm machinery and haystacks with tarpaulin. At Prague Christo studied set design, and one of his mid-1960s works in New York involved making replicas of storefronts, like a stage set, but the windows were covered with cloth or paper. In his early works, Christo wrapped up items such as books, bottles, tins and boxes. Other Assemblages or *empaquetages* (Assemblages as packages) included nude models, cars, chairs and motorbikes.

Christo's most famous Assemblage, though, was on a larger scale, the *Wall of Oil Barrels – Iron Curtain* (1962). This was a pile of barrels stacked across and blocking one of Paris's oldest streets, Rue Visconti. *Wall of Oil Barrels – Iron*

Curtain parodied the Berlin Wall, which had recently been constructed. The sculpture annoyed the locals, and Christo's large-scale works have been upsetting neighbours, councils, politicians and pressure groups ever since.

Christo's first major wrapping was to cover the Museum of Contemporary Art in Chicago with 10,000 square feet of brown tarpaulin. Christo's wrapping of the museum made it the focus of attention in the neighbourhood – some people hadn't realized the museum was there until it had been wrapped. The museum's director reckoned Christo had parodied 'all the associations a museum evokes: a mausoleum, a repository for precious contents, an intent to wrap up all of art history'.[1] Inside the museum was the *Wrapped Floor*, consisting of 2,000 square feet of rented drop cloths.

In 1969 Christo wrapped a mile-long section of the Australian coastline. The use of open weave cloth (1 million square feet) meant that wildlife would not be affected. *Wrapped Coast*, at Little Bay near Sydney, stayed in place for 4 weeks. It was a dramatic land art gesture, difficult to ignore.

Valley Curtain (1972), at Rifle Pass in Colorado, did not last so long. It was blown down. The huge bright orange curtain hung across the valley, providing a passageway as well as a visual block to what was beyond.

> When I was doing *Valley Curtain* [Christo said] everybody knew that this is a huge curtain crossing a valley. Now everybody knew what it is that is behind the valley. The thing that is behind is not so important... only that motion, the passing through.[2]

The use of orange, as with the pink in *Surrounded Islands*, gave *Valley Curtain* a new æsthetic, more attuned to Henri Matisse and Claude Monet, quite different from the dull brown tarpaulin of the *Wrapped Museum*. Christo would continue to use such colours throughout his career on his major wrappings.

Many of Christo's large-scale wrapped works were

situated next to water: *Running Fence* plunged into the sea; *Wrapped Coast* was submerged by the tides; *Surrounded Islands* floated on the ocean; *Pont-Neuf* stretched over the River Seine. *Surrounded Islands* (1980-83) was one of Christo's largest works. Not a wrapping this time, but still involving masses of fabric (6 million ft^2 of it). With a budget of $3.5 million, 4 engineers, 2 ornithologists, a marine biologist, 2 attorneys and 430 helpers, Christo surrounded 11 little islands for 2 weeks in May, 1983. The choice of brilliant pink meant the enclosed islands stood out vividly against the green sea at Biscayne Bay in Florida. The pink-enclosed islands looked like flowers floating on the sea, recalling the Japanese Buddhist ceremony of setting flowers afloat. Or, more in tune with Western art history, evoking Claude Monet's waterlilies.

Running Fence (1972-76) comprised 2,050 18-foot panels of white nylon attached to steel poles, running across Marin and Sonoma counties and 12 roads in California. As with Christo's other mammoth projects, there was much opposition to *Running Fence*. A committee designed to 'stop Running Fence' brought the subject to the Superior Court of the State of California 3 times. The subsequent report on the environmental impact of the *Running Fence* project found that there were no endangered species in the region, except for the Brown Pelican, and virtually no wildlife would be affected by it. *Running Fence* went ahead, and stayed up for two weeks in September, 1976.[3] When it was taken down, nothing remained of it in the area: the holes were filled in, and bare parts of soil were reseeded. As with other Christo projects, when it was taken away some locals were dismayed, the work had helped them realize the beauty of the area. Christo says his art is

> about displacement. Basically even today I am a displaced person. And this is why I make art that does not last. Of course, it will stay for ever in the minds of people.[4]

Christo here espouses the fundamental Romanticism in land art: that it will live on in the memories of people. Christo's large-scale projects – *Running Fence, Surrounded Islands, Wrapped Coast* – were spectacular works, part of the land art tradition which moved towards the sublime in landscape art (which has affinities with the Abstract Expressionism of Mark Rothko, Barnett Newman and Robert Motherwell). The ocean end of *Running Fence* was particularly impressive: at Bodega Bay the *Fence* extended gracefully into the Pacific, 558 feet, descending from a height of 18 feet on land to 2 feet at the section which was anchored to the bottom of the sea. Also in California (and Japan), the *Umbrellas* were exactly that, a groups of umbrellas which stretched over 12 miles in Japan and 18 miles in California.

Christo's large-scale works are expensive: *Running Fence* cost over $3 million, *Surrounded Islands* cost $3.5 million, and *The Umbrellas* in Japan and California cost $26,000,000. Denigrators of Christo's work have noted the expense of the projects, but Christo pays for them himself, by selling photos, drawings, collages, models, lithographs and plans and other works, and by collaborating with industry.

HANS HAACKE

The German artist Hans Haacke (b. 1936) has produced some of the most intriguing land artworks (although Haacke is more usually linked with Arte Povera, Conceptual and Process art, than land art). Many of Haacke's early works explored natural or organic systems. Later, Haacke moved on to social, economic and political systems (what Haacke called 'real-time systems'). Haacke's 1965 artistic statements included: 'make something that lives in time and makes the "spectator" experience time... articulate something natural'.[1] One of Haacke's tenets was 'the simpler the better'.

Grass Grows (1966 and 1969) was a mound of soil with grass growing out of it. Hans Haacke later fashioned a row of beans growing along string suspended at an angle, in soil mounted on glass on the gallery floor (*Directed Growth*, 1972), and in tropical plants growing on a circular area of soil, *Rye in the Tropics* (1972). *Condensation Cube* (1963-65) was a Plexiglas cube (a yard on each side) with water inside which condensed on the clear sides of the box, an exploration of process. 'It is changing freely, bound only by statistical limits', remarked Haacke of his 'Weather Box'.

In *Sky Line* (1967), Hans Haacke released white helium balloons over Central Park. Haacke commented that

> in spite of my environmental and monumental thinking I am still fascinated by the nearly magic, self-contained quality of objects. My water levels, waves and condensation boxes are unthinkable without this physical separation from their surroundings.[2]

Many of Hans Haacke's most compelling artworks were made to explore the ephemeral qualities of ice, snow, fog, steam, smoke and water. *Fog, Flooding, Erosion* (1969) employed a sprinkler system to turn a lawn in Seattle (WA) into mud. *Fog Dripping From or Freezing On Exposed Surfaces* (Boston, 1971) and *Spray of Ithaca: Falls Freezing and Melting On Rope* (1969) explored water and fog freezing on waterfalls and trees.

One of Hans Haacke's air and wind constructions comprised a fan blowing a seven by seven foot chiffon sail hung parallel to the gallery floor. Another air sculpture was a balloon balanced above an air jet (a favourite with science and natural history museums). He had proposals for monumental-sized windmills and sails, all naturally powered by the winds. Haacke preferred to use unmechanical sources of energy.

In *Rhine-Water Purification Plant* (1972), the process of purifying polluted river water was examined. Via a series of acrylic containers, filters, hoses and pools, the spectator could follow the process of the purification of the contaminated Krefeld sewage water. The final destination of the water flow was a square pool containing goldfish. *Rhine-Water Purification Plant* recalled the 3-D displays in public museums that explained the processes of nature and science.

In Hans Haacke's piece *Ten Turtles Set Free* (1970), the animals were released in a forest near St Paul-de-Vence (France), a symbolic gesture about humanity's relationship with the natural world and its inhabitants. Haacke photographed seagulls feeding on bread scattered on a lake in *Live Airborne System* (1965/68).

Hans Haacke later considered economic systems in works such as *Shapolsky et al, Manhattan Real Estate Holdings, a Real-Time Social System* (1971). For the *Information* show at Gotham's MOMA (in 1971), Haacke exhibited a poll about Governor Rockerfeller running for election, inviting visitors to vote. Haacke took on cultural institutions such as museums, landlords, and politicians such as President Reagan and British PM, Margaret Thatcher. On a few occasions Haacke's proposals were negated by the authorities of the Guggenheim, Wallraf-Richartz and Metropolitan museums, with works and shows being cancelled as a result. Other artists (such as Daniel Buren) protested in support of Haacke.

HAMISH FULTON

For Hamish Fulton (b. 1946), the walk is central to – *is* – the artwork. If there is no walk, there is no work: 'no walk, no work', as Fulton put it. Most of his walks have been made alone, Fulton said. But not every walk needed to be be made into a work of art. They were sufficient unto themselves.[1] On the other hand, Fulton commented that he had to walk to be able to make a work of art. The artwork came out of the work, and if he didn't walk, there couldn't be any art.

Among Hamish Fulton's influences were artists such as Marina Abramovic, Nancy Wilson, Roger Ackling and Richard Long, Tibetan religious art, Native American culture, mountaineers, *haiku* poetry from Japan, and 'the walking peoples of the world from all periods of history', Fulton noted in "Into a Walk Into Nature" (1995; many subsequent quotes are from this article).

As with Richard Long, Hamish Fulton rarely included images of people in his art, but his art 'should not be thought of as anti-people' (1995). Instead, Fulton's photographs are of wildernesses (mountains, fields and country lanes). Fulton separated the walk from the artwork. 'The artwork cannot represent the experience of a walk', Fulton affirmed (1995). Aspects of the work could remind the artist of making the work, but could not communicate the experience of the work to the viewer. 'The texts are facts for the walker and fiction for everyone else' (1995).

Hamish Fulton said he preferred to walk rather than sit in a train or plane or car. Travelling (sitting) was of 'little interest' to him (1995). And when he embarked on a walk, Fulton said he walked directly from his home, rather than use transport. The walk was the thing, always. 'I am an artist who walks, not a walker who makes art', (1995). Fulton complained that he seemed to spend more time on organizing exhibitions, on admin and paperwork, than walking (1995).

The typical Hamish Fulton artwork is a large black-and-white photograph in a frame with a short piece of text in capitals underneath (the look of Fulton's text and photo pieces recalls Richard Long's art). Fulton's work include *Rock Fall Echo Dust* (1988), recording a walk made on Baffin Island; *The Crossing Place of Two Walks at Ringdom Gompa* (1984), *Rock Path, Switzerland* (1986), *Grims Ditch* (1969-70), *Night Changing Shapes* (1991) and *Gazing At the Horizon Line, Sky Horizon Ground* (Australia, 1982). Some of Fulton's works consist only of text in capitals painted on a wall in a gallery: *No*

Talking For Seven Days (1993) and *Rock Fall Echo Dust* (1988).

Like many British land artists, Hamish Fulton didn't want to make massive and long-lasting marks on the landscape. On the contrary, it was totally the opposite. Fulton said his art was not aggressive or technological: 'I do not directly rearrange, remove, sell and not return, dig into, wrap or cut up with loud machinery any elements of the natural environment', Fulton asserted, clearly having several well-known land artists in mind (1995).

OTHER LAND ARTISTS IN EUROPE

PAUL RUSSELL COOPER

British sculptor, Paul Russell Cooper (b. 1949), has produced a distinctly Andy Goldsworthyan sculpture, *Two Circles in a Stone Bridge*. This is a large dry stone work at Portland in Dorset (1983). Two circles are made with the stones, one 'positive', the other 'negative': the 'negative' circle was a large hole like an archway. Other works by Cooper include *Quincunx*, a series of five globes in concrete set in an open space at Rufford Country Park (near Newark, 1983). The globes sit open partially to display something different in each globe: water, rocks, burning detritus from the garden and a sundial. Cooper's *Quincunx* is based on natural forms – in this case, five-petalled plants.

MICHAEL DAN ARCHER

Michael Dan Archer's *Observatory* (1994) recalled Robert Morris's *Observatory*: it was basically a low circular embankment, the kind seen in Iron Age hillforts or in some Bronze Age stone circles in the United Kingdom (Archer's *Observatory* in particular recalled Avebury stone circle in Wiltshire). A stone shaped like a post and lintel (as at Stonehenge) marked the entrance, and two broken circular stones did for benches in the centre of *Observatory*.

JULIA BARTON

Julia Barton created *A Rural Landmark: Viewing Platform* (1994) in Yorkshire stone at Kirklees Way: the circular platform was cut into a hillside, backed by a low wall and clad in stone. There were no signs to indicate what to look at, as in municipal viewing sites (the sort of tourist brass discs found on hilltops that state '25 miles to Hay Bluff'). British filmmaker Chris Welby is a kind of land artist; he explores the relation between landscape and humanity, nature and mind, in films which experiment with film speed and time-lapse photography (*Seven Days* and *Stream Line*). Patricia Leighton reworked the earth at the side of the M8 freeway, turning it into a series of *Sawtooth Ramps*.

PETER RANDALL-PAGE

Peter Randall-Page (b. 1954), one of the most appealing of contemporary sculptors in Blighty (certainly one of the most accomplished of the members of the Royal Society of British Sculptors), created an interaction between modern sculpture and mediæval architecture when he sited some of his boulders made from Finnish glacial granite at Wenlock Priory in rural Shropshire. *Boulders and Banner Boulders: Secret Life I, II, III, IV* (1994) contained sculptures that were split open like gigantic seeds. Randall-Page's sculptures were suitably monumental (and abstract) for the architectural space of the ruined Priory.

YVETTE MARTIN

In the Forest of Dean a number of interesting commissions took place in the late 1980s. Yvette Martin's *Four Seasons* was an environmental, 'land' sculpture. The first work, *Spring* (1986), was an oval-shaped pond with copper coloured water, a marshy space surrounded by webs of twigs and branches. It was a womb-like space, with a sense of being closed-in.[1] The branches on the trees growing on the bank of the small pond were bent down to add to the feeling of enclosure.

Yvette Martin's *Spring* was the sort of space novelists such as Thomas Hardy and John Cowper Powys would like, for secluded pools recur in their fictions (Rushy Pond in *The Return of the Native*, and the haunting Lenty Pond in Powys's great novel of nature mysticism, *Wolf Solent*). Like other land artists, Martin spoke in terms of 'growth cycles', the 'cycle of life from conception, emergence, growth, reproduction, maturity, decay and death' (ib., 75). The pond or pool is a recurring favourite in land (it's found in the work of Chris Drury, Patricia Johanson, Mary Miss, James Turrell, Evelyn Zimmerman, and Jim Sanborn, among many others).

CORNELIA PARKER

The most exciting sculpture at this time in the Forest of Dean was Cornelia Parker's (b. 1956) *Hanging Fire*, a large ring of iron hung 25 or so feet above the forest floor. Parker created a ring of iron flames, which were rusted overnight in salt water. They hung upside down from the ring. Parker wanted to portray the idea of a perpetual flame, a 'flame that would perpetually burn because it was cast in iron' (ib., 89). Hanging sculptures, as Alexander Calder showed time after time, are usually intriguing, and Parker's *Hanging Fire*, though made of heavy materials, floated in the trees. She also wanted to incorporate the notion of a 'circle or fairy ring', and a crown, and to use iron because iron was mined in the Forest of Dean.

Cornelia Parker's most famous work was probably *Cold Dark Matter: An Exploded View* (1991), an installation of a garden shed that Parker had blown up by Army experts, exhibiting the debris hung from wires in the gallery (it became a favourite at London's Tate Modern). Parker's installation concerned cosmological themes of opposites, inhaling and exhaling, centripetal and centrifugal motion.

PETER HUTCHINSON

Peter Hutchinson was born in England (in 1930), but spent most of his artistic career in the U.S.A. (based in Massachusetts). He collaborated with Dennis Oppenheim on a series of underwater works: fruit, vegetables and bread were packed in plastic bags and suspended from a fishing line in the West Indies (1969). Hutchinson also planted flowers in the sand underwater, and made a dam from sand bags in Tobago (*Underwater Dam,* 1969). Along the rim of a volcano (Paricutin, 1970), Hutchinson sited a 76 yard line of white bread wrapped in plastic. Hutchinson recorded the growth of mould and decomposition. Later works include *Ice Sandwich* (1994), a Brancusi-like tower of slabs of wood interlaced with blocks of ice, and 'thrown ropes' of flowers planted in the ground in the shape of a rope that Hutchinson threw (1996). Hutchinson preferred works that combined his love of horticulture, science, art and botany.[2]

NICHOLAS POPE

Nicholas Pope (b. 1949) is an artist whose works recall Barbara Hepworth's and Stephen Cox's – in particular Pope's outdoor works, such as *The Arch* (1985). Made from oak, the arch is large (18 feet long). It is the arch itself that fascinates Pope, for the arch is such an elegant structure, as anyone who has seen ancient Roman architecture (such as the Pont du Gard or Colosseum) can appreciate. Pope's *Arch* was dovetailed and pegged together, made from two young trees and one mature tree. Pope was consciously trying to create a work with oak, not just with any wood. 'I wanted to make an oakwood arch not an arch made from wood.'[3]

Like Carl Andre, Nicholas Pope has placed large stones in an urban environment. Pope's *Three Wilderness Stones* (1980, Southampton) and *Five Amorphous Shapes* are huge boulders of Forest of Dean stone in humanmade environments. Pope's stones spread out across parkland or the forecourts of modern business complexes, bringing the individual, irregular forms of nature into the angular, linear environment of the city.

Like Barbara Hepworth and Constantin Brancusi, Nicholas Pope was fascinated by stones. Hepworth loved the white granite rounded stones of West Penwith, and scattered them around her studio in St Ives. It's easy to see how some of Hepworth's sculptures took some of their inspiration from the beautiful granite boulders of Cornwall. David Nash made a large wooden boulder, while Anthony Gormley (b. 1950) emulated a large granite glacial boulder in 1981. Each of Gormley's *Two Stones* is nine feet high, one made of granite, the other of bronze. Set beside an artificial lake in Kent, the 'natural' granite stone was already contextualized as a work of art by its placement in such a setting, just as Carl Andre's boulders on the city street are made into art by their context (ditto with Andre's infamous bricks).

SJOERD BUISMAN

Sjoerd Buisman (b. 1948) constructed a floating mound of willow sticks on a wooden frame in the moat of the Old Castle at Jeemstede (Netherlands, 1995-98). In 1975 Buisman knotted a willow tree stem which the tree absorbed into itself as it grew (*Knotted Willow Branch*). In 1991 Buisman constructed an 'arch' of lime trees (at Haarlemmerhout, Netherlands), which formed a low curve along a road. Using petals and berries, some of Nils Udo's sculptures are uncannily like Andy Goldsworthy's use of the same materials. Udo has, for instance, pressed berries into the bark of an old tree.

OTHER LAND ARTISTS

Richard Harris (b. 1954) has produced a wall sculpture, *Dry Stone Passage* (1982). Harris wrote: 'I want the sculpture to become a living and working part of the existing environment'.[4] Harris made a *Willow Walk* (1990), a walk lined with willow branches. Harris's works at Grizedale, apart from

Dry Stone Passage, included *Cliff Structure* (1978), slate slabs set on split oak, and *Quarry Structure* (1977), a 'bridge' of slate and oak sticks.

At Grizedale, Helen Stylianides produced a tree sculpture that looked like a tree with the branches cut off, about five feet from the trunk. A tree with no leaves, but stumps for branches (*Tree Sculpture*, 1984). Collins made a 40 foot diameter steel ring that was set, vertically, next to a tree. The enormous ring, *Ting*, was entangled in the branches: the aim was that the circle of steel could not be seen as a whole, in one view, but only glimpsed in parts through the leaves. Alyson Brien fashioned *A Curve Around a Lime Tree* (1987) which looked like a low fence of stripped wood. Eric Geddes bent two young trees over and tied them to a central tree, so they formed a semi-circular arch, with the tree in the centre standing upright.

Nigel Lloyd's *Red Deer Wallow* (1983, Grizedale) was a horse-shoe-shaped stone wall enclosure. Also at Grizedale is a large circular enclosure made from wickerwork and larch posts, by Keir Smith (b. 1950). Smith is sensitive to the work done by people in a landscape, to the sense of labour: thus, Smith includes in the enclosure hints of human activity, such as stag antlers, which suggest human hunting, while a pair of shears allude to 'sheep-shearing and animal husbandry'.[5]

Graham Moore's works include three circles of mown grass, entitled *Herbe Garden* (1989, Christchurch Park). This work echoed Richard Long's early turf circles. Gwen Heney made a 30 yard long snake out of bricks at the Garden Festival Wales show (1992). Also at Garden Festival Wales was Mick Petts' *Mother Earth*, created out of a huge pile of slag which was required to be disguised. Valerie Pragnelli made a spiral from rocks in a stream (*Langslie Spiral*, Milepoint). Ron Haselden produced a dance of lights, called *Fete* (1992), out of strings of lights hung from a group of willow trees. One of the largest of contemporary garden and landscape design projects was Giuliano Gori's Parco di Celle.

Like Andy Goldsworthy, Giuseppe Penone (b. 1947) has created sculptures with trees, such as his *I Wove Together Three Trees* (1968), made in the Maritime Alps. Penone's *To Breathe Shade* (1997-99) was a human shape made from bronze bay leaves installed in five bay trees, and his *Skins of Leaves* (2000), a 'skin' of bronze leaves in humanoid form. In another group of tree trunks tied together, Jackie Winsor's 1971 piece *30 to 1 Bound Trees*, the binding of the trees, as in much of Winsor's work, relates to autobiographical, childhood experiences, often painful, as well as the formal aspects of density, weight and repetition.[6] Jan Dibbets produced a tree-work, *Construction of a Wood,* in 1969.

Gabriel Orozco worked with snowballs – in *Planets of the Volcano* (1992) he placed small snowballs on top of some posts near Popocatepetl volcano. Anish Kapoor's *Void Field* (1990) comprised twenty large pieces of sandstone with small holes bored in the top, which were painted black inside.

Chris Jenning's *Vault* (1992) reacted to the Museum of Installation's space by filling it with curving metal rods which connected the walls and floor together. The thin rods curved through space. Bill Viola brought a whole tree into the Newport Harbor Art Museum in California for his *Theatre of Memory* (1985), the branches were hung with bells blown by electric fans. The tinkling tree faced a giant video image of hissing static.

Recalling Wolfgang Laib's pollen floor pieces, Shelagh Wakely covered the marble floor of the British School at Rome with a layer of tumeric spice (*Curcuma sul Travertino*, 1991). Anthony Gormley covered the entire area of a gallery floor in his *Field* installation (1991) with over 35,000 small humanoid figures. Giovanni Anselmo used stone like painted canvases, mounting thin slabs of granite on a Paris gallery wall like paintings (*Meeting of Two Works*, 1990).

Some installation artists used liquid to cover the floor area: in Glen Onwin's alchemical installations in Halifax (1991), water, wax and black brine were poured into a large concrete pool. Richard Wilson's *20/50* (1987) was a steel pool of sump oil with a walkway into the middle of it. Per Barclay also used pools of oil: in *Old Boathouse* (1990) an oil pool was set in a Norwegian boat-house beside the sea; in *The Jaguar's Cage* (1991), made at Turin Zoo, a large oil pool was set behind bars. Rasheed Araeen spoofed Richard Long's art in his 1988 London installation: a Longian floor circle was made with empty wine bottles, and a Long-like row was made with bones. Eve Laramee spread a rectangular mound of cobalt glass on the gallery floor in her *Requiem For a Blue Fluid* (1991).

Nikolaj Recke (b. 1969) planted a field of clover in a gallery (1999) covering the whole floor in a carpet of green plants. Although the result recalled land art gestures such as Walter de Maria's *Earth Room*, the aim, according to Recke, was to explore the folklore of four-leaf clovers.

○

While some land artists died young (such as Robert Smithson), and others seem to have completed their best pieces, and are in their 70s and 80s, many others are still very active, and will no doubt continue to produce work in this thriving area of contemporary art.

Illustrations

Including some examples of land art, followed by influences and forerunners of land art in painting and photography, some prehistoric art, and some landscapes associated with land art.

Christo, Wrapped Reichstag, 1997

Chris Drury, Stone Whirlpool, 1996

Andy Goldsworthy, Garden of Stones, New York City, 2003

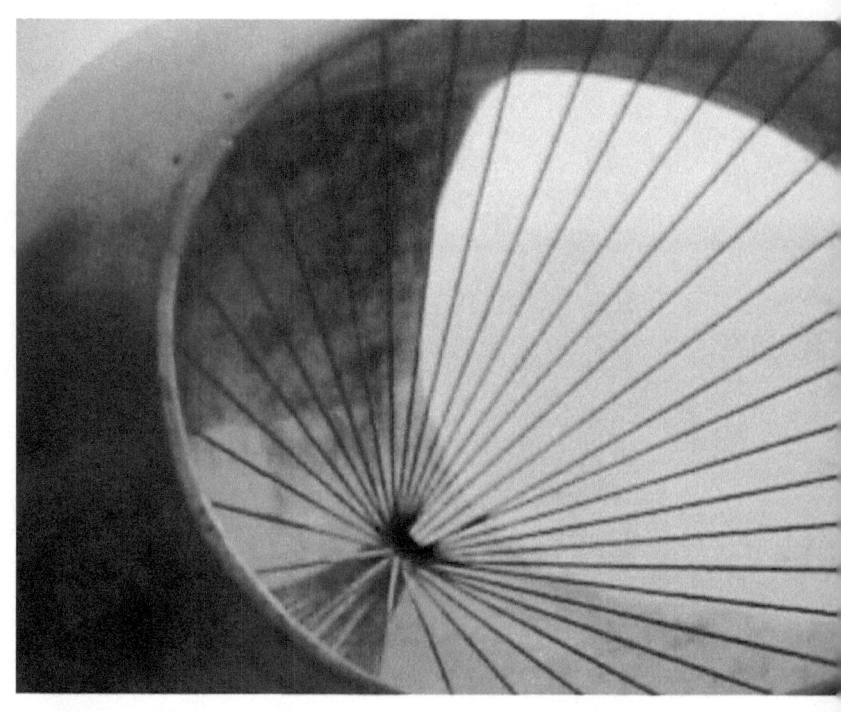

Barbara Hepworth, Sculpture with Colour and String, 1939-61

Alison Wilding, Iron Meteroite

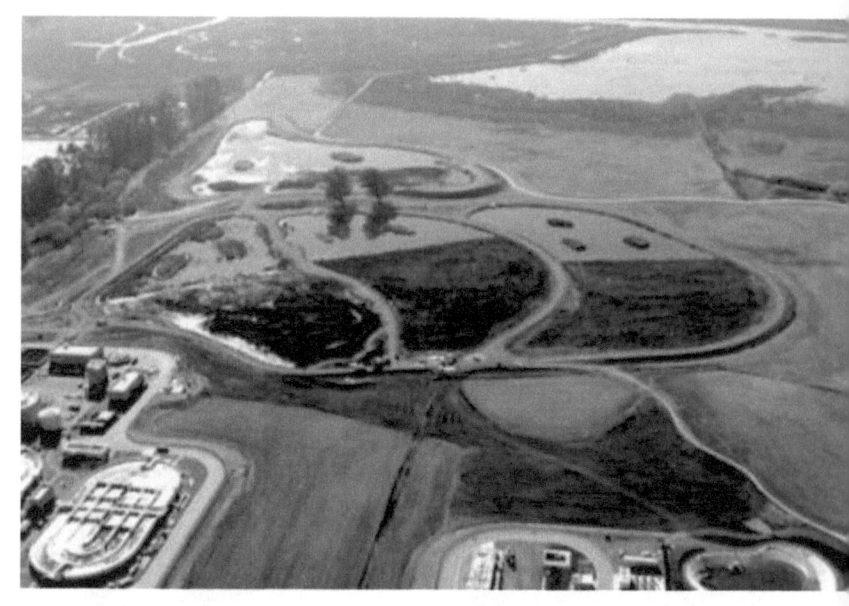

Patricia Johanson, Ellis Creek Water Recycling Facility, Petaluma, California

Mary Miss, Perimeters/ Pavilion/ Decoys. 1978

Ana Mendieta, Silueta Series, 1979

Alice Aycock, A Simple Network of Underground Walls and Tunnels, 1975

Carl Andre, Stone Field, 1977

Walter de Maria, Earth Room, 1977

Robert Morris, Observatory, 1971

Robert Smithson, The Spiral Hill, 1971

James Turrell, Roden Crater, 1974-

ONE QUART EXTERIOR GREEN INDUSTRIAL ENAMEL THROWN ON A BR

れんがのかべに まかれた 一クォートの みどりいろの おくがいとそうよう エナメ

Lawrence Weiner

Peter Hutchinson, 1970

This page and over: examples of the landscape painting tradition.
J.M.W. Turner, watercolours of Folkestone (above) and Bridport (below).

J.M.W. Turner, London (Greenwich), 1809

John Constable, Cloud Study

Albert Bierstadt, Among the Sierra Nevada, California, 1868 (above).
Thomas Cole, Indian Sacrifice, 1826 (below).

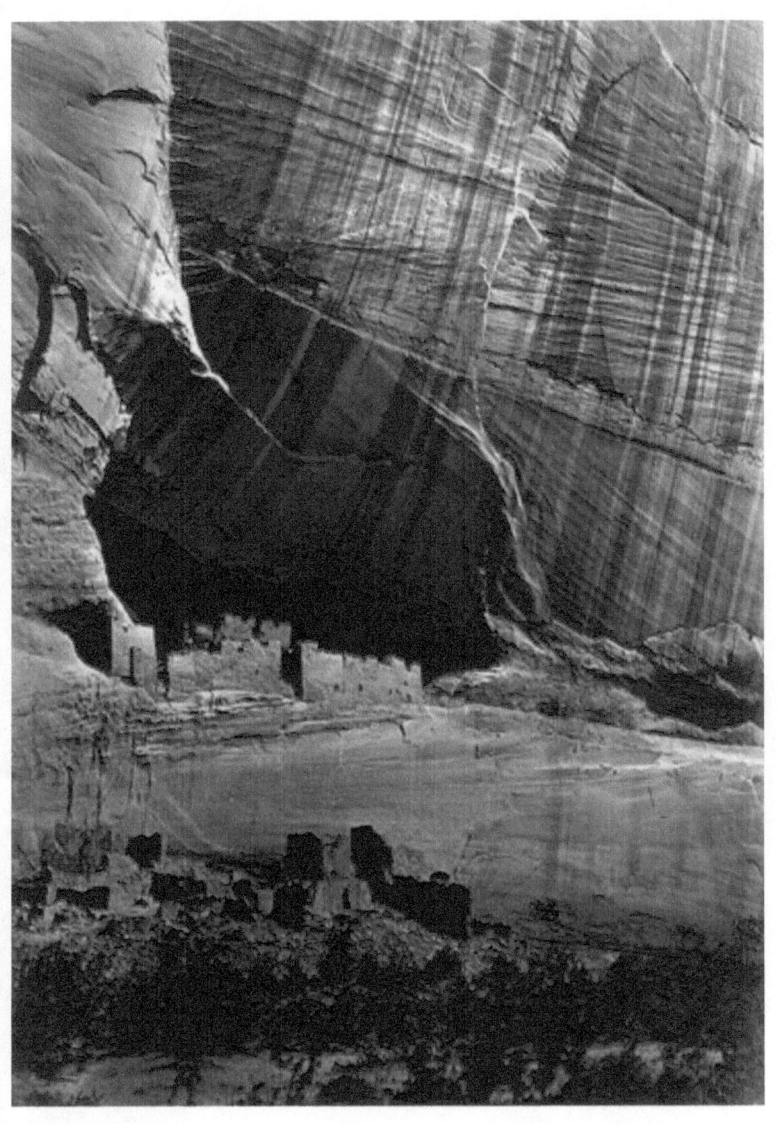

Timothy O'Sullivan, Anasazi Ruins (The White House), Canyon de Chelly, Arizona

George Barker, Niagara Falls

Avebury, Wiltshire, England

Winterbourne Abbas Stone Circle, Dorset, England

e kind of heavy industry which inspired land artists such as Robert Smithson and Dennis Oppenheim (Photos: Cassidy Hughes, London)

The view from Glastonbury Tor, Somerset, England

Stone cairn in Snowdonia, North Wales

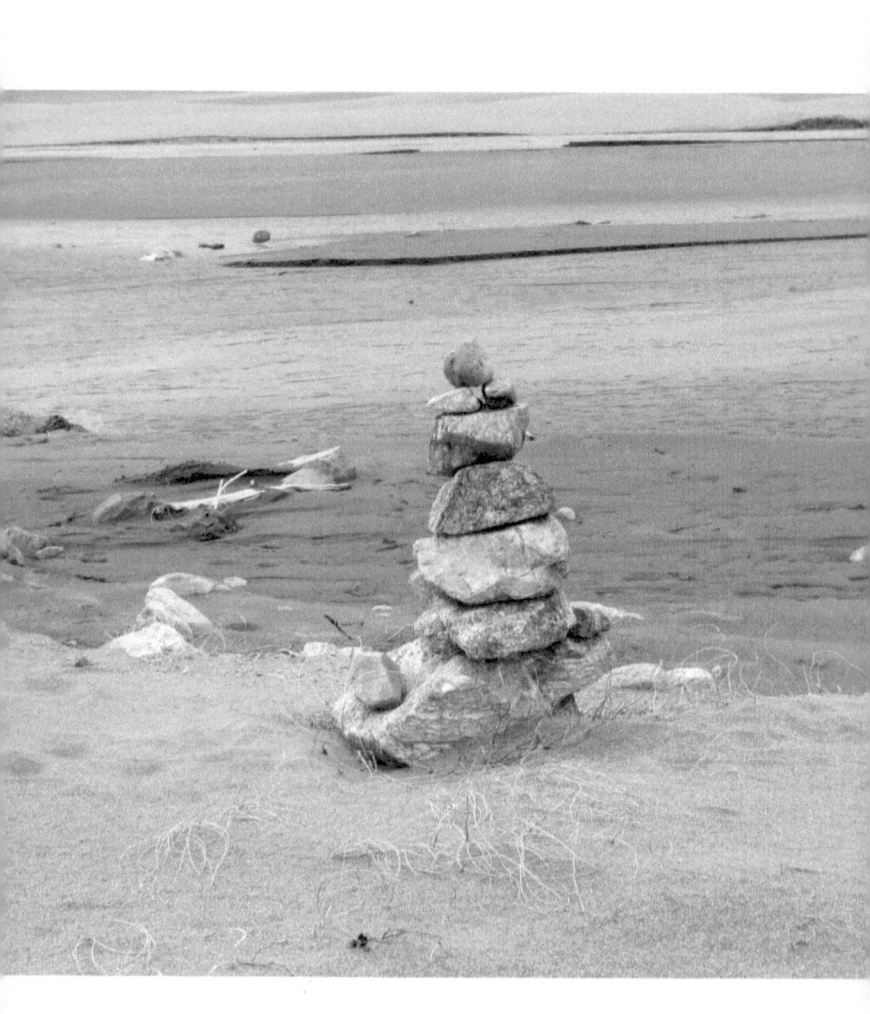

A found cairn in the Rockies, Colorado

The open road in South-west America

The Rockies, Colorado

Salt flats in Death Valley, California

Volcanic crater at Amboy, U.S.A.

Notes

1 INTRODUCTION

1. R. Krauss, 1978.

2 THE ALCHEMY OF MATTER

THE LAND ART SUBLIME: LAND ART AND ROMANTICISM

1. R. Hughes, 1991, 386.
2. There is eroticism in Tony Cragg's steel vessels, or Anne and Patrick Poirier's long, elegant *Archæological Model*, or Jannis Kounellis' *Cotton Sculpture*, a mass of cotton stuffed into a large steel container – a sculpture of contrasts between the softness of the cotton and the rigidity of the steel, or Jackie Winsor's *Burnt Piece*, a 3 ft cube made of concrete, wire and burnt wood. Cragg has spoken of having 'an erotic response to the external world', something which, it seems, all artists have, or have to have, to be truly great artists (quoted in D. Wheeler, 1991, 324). See also T. Neff, 1967; B. Jones, 1977, 16; L. Ponti, 50-51; I. Lamaitre, 1985, 7-11; G. Celant, 40-46.
3. W. Laib, in A. Benjamin, 91.

LAND ART AND GARDENS

1. S. Ross, 1993, 161.
2. S. Ross, 1998, 23.
3. R. Smithson, paraphrased by Lucy Lippard (1983).

'TRUE CAPITALIST ART'?: THE COST OF LAND ART

1. A. Henri, *Total Art*, 81-82.
2. Richard Long, quoted in S. Gablik: *Has Modernism Failed?*, Thames & Hudson, London, 1984, 44.
3. 'I make art in the capitalist system which in itself is a political statement (selling art for the next walk)', remarked Hamish Fulton (1995).
4. In A. Haden-Guest, 40.

LAND ART AND PHOTOGRAPHY

1. S. Mills: "Special Kaye [Tony Kaye]", *Sunday Times Magazine*, June 12, 1994, 55.
2. In N. Hedges, 77.
3. E. Hesse, in *Eva Hesse*, Guggenheim, New York 1972.
4. J. Dibbets, 1970.
5. R. Long, Santa Fe interview.
6. R. Long, in W. Malpas, 1995.
7. R. Long, 1985, 1, 1.
8. R. Smithson, in C. Robins, 1984, 78.

INSIDE—OUTSIDE

1. Robert Smithson reckoned that a 'work of art when placed in a gallery loses its charge and becomes a portable object or surface disengaged from the outside world.' (*Selected Writings*, 132).
2. D. Oppenheim, 1992.
3. In A. McPherson, 30.
4. In M. Heizer, 1970.
5. In ib.
6. L. Weiner, in *Avalanche*, Spring, 1972, 67.
7. A. Goldsworthy, *Time*, 11.

CHANGES, CYCLES, SEASONS

1. J. Beuys, in *Documenta 7*, 2, Documenta, Kassel, 1982.
2. R. Smithson: *Writings*, 56-57; C. Robins, 1984, 80.
3. R. Long, 1986, 1, 9.
4. R. Long, in *Words After the Fact*, in R. Fuchs, 1986, 236.
5. 'Goldsworthy's pieces dig at the roots of our relationship with nature, he is conducting an interrogative process with the fundamentals of our world – water, stone, earth, growing things and – latterly, in his work with volcanic rock and 'fired' stones – fire' (P. Whitaker, 1995, 109).
6. In B. Redhead, 19.
7. See J. Burnham, 1971.
8. Quoted in G. Baro, 1969, 122; see C. Harrison, 1968, 266-8; J. Kirshner: "Barry Flanagan", *Artforum*, 23, 10, Summer, 1985, 112.

TREES

1. Writers on the symbolic and religious aspects of trees include Mircea Eliade (*Patterns of Comparative Religion*), Robert Graves (*The White Goddess*), James G. Frazer (*The Golden Bough*), and J.R.R. Tolkien, among others.

HOLES

1. C. Koelb: "Castration Envy", in P. Burgard, 1994, 79.

STONE CIRCLES: LAND ART AND PREHISTORIC ART

1. See M. Berger, 1989.
2. Quoted in L. Lippard, 1967c, 26.
3. The allusions to prehistory would be quite different if Richard Long had stuck a picture of the Cerne Giant next to himself instead of the Wilmington Man. The Cerne Giant, another hill figure, has the biggest penis in public art (at least in the United Kingdom).
4. R. Long, 1972, in *Fragments of a Conversation I-VI*, in *Walking in Circles*, 38.

LAND ART AND CONSTANTIN BRANCUSI

1. H. Moore, in *The Listener*, 1937, quoted in H. Chipp, 595.
2. A. Goldsworthy, *Réfuges d'art*, 85.
3. A. Goldsworthy, *Sheepfolds*, 22-23.

LIGHT AND SPACE

1. Quoted in J. Butterfield, 161.

3 THE BIRTH OF LAND IN 1960S CULTURE

THE PRESENCE OF THE OBJECT: LAND ART, MINIMAL ART AND 'OBJECTHOOD'

1. C. Andre, 1978, 31.
2. See J. Yoshihara, in B. Bertozzi & K. Wolbert: *Gutai: Japanese Avant-Garde*, Darmstadt, 1991.
3. R. Morris, 1966, in G. Battock, 1995, 224.
4. R. Morris, 1966, 20-23. See also: P. Patton, 1983.

MINIMAL ART, POSTMINIMAL ART AND LAND ART

1. B. Rose, 1964, 41.
2. D. Judd: "Specific Objects", in G. de Vries, 1974, 128.

LAND ART AND CONCEPTUAL ART

1. "Mel Bochner on Malevich", 1974, 62.
2. R. Serra, in *Richard Serra, Interviews*, Hudson River Museum, New York, NY, 1980, 37.
3. D. Oppenheim, in 1992.

4. B. Flanagan, 1969.
5. J. Beuys, in *Documenta 7*, 2, Documenta, Kassel, 1982.
6. L. Weiner, in E. Lucie-Smith, 1987, 117.
7. L. Weiner: *Billowing Clouds...*, 1986, 86.2 x 17.5 in, Anthony d'Offay Gallery, London.
8. R. Long, 1985, 2, 24.

4 LAND ART, GENDER, SEXUALITY AND THE BODY

GENDER AND SCALE IN LAND ART

1. In A. Benjamin, 47.
2. "Donald Judd", *The New York Times*, Apl 1, 1977, C20.
3. L. Lippard, 1968, 42.
4. L. Lippard, 1979, 88.
5. See L. Anderson, 1973; *Mary Miss: Interior Works*, Bell Gallery, University of Rhode Island, Autumn, 1981.
6. See N. Holt, 1975, 1977; T. Castle, 1982.
7. See D. Judd, 1975; W. Agee, 1975, 40-49; P. Carlson, 1984, 114-8; D. Kuspit: "Donald Judd", 1985; B. Haskell, 1988; B. Smith, 1975.
8. Such as Tony Smith: *Die*, 1962, 72 x 72 x 72 in, Paula Cooper Gallery, New York, NY. See L. Lippard, 1972a; G. Baro, 1967; E. Greene: "Morphology of Tony Smith's Work", *Artforum*, April, 1974.
9. Such as Dan Flavin: *Untitled (to the "innovator" of Wheeling Peach-blow)*, 1968, Museum of Modern Art, New York; *Untitled*, 1976, pink, blue, green fluorescent light, Saatchi Collection, London. See W. Wilson: "Dan Flavin: Fiat Lux", *Art News*, Jan, 1970; J. Burnham, 1969; I. Licht, 1968.
10. Such as Richard Serra: *Clara-Clara*, 1983, Cor-Ten steel, installation, Jardin des Tuileries, Paris; *Prop*, 1968, 96in high, sheet 60 x 60 in, Whitney Museum of Art, New York. See R. Krauss, 1972; D. Crimp: "Richard Serra: Sculpture Exceeded", *October*, Fall, 1981.
11. See K. Baker, 1980, 88-94; D. Waldman, Oct, 1970, 60-62, 75-79; P. Tuchman, 1978, 29-33; E. Develing, 1969.

WOMEN SCULPTORS AND LAND ARTISTS

1. Other artists who have worked in postmodern, feminist modes include Cindy Sherman, Mary Kelly, Marie Yates, Yves Lomax, Martha Rosler, Sutapa Biswas, Mitra Tabrizian, Zarina Bhimji, Mona Hatoum, Lubaina Himid, Barbara Kruger, Jenny Holzer, Rose Garrard, Susan Hiller, Nancy Spero, Rosa Lee and Rachel Whiteread.
2. In C. Nemser, 62.

3. See B. Barrette: *Eva Hesse's Sculpture*: Catalogue Raisonné, New York, NY, 1989; R. Krauss & E. Hesse, 1979; C. Nemser, 1973, 12-13.
4. A. Chave, in H. Cooper, ed. *Eva Hesse*, Yale University Press, New Haven, CT, 1992, 100f.
5. Quoted in L. Lippard, ib., 6.
6. *Rosarium Philosophorum*, quoted in A. Mann, 87.

5 LAND ART AND RELIGION

1. M. Basho, *The Narrow Road to the Deep North and Other Travel Sketches*, tr. N. Yuasa, Penguin, London, 1966, 33.
2. M. Ueda: *Matsuo Basho*, Twayne, New York, NY, 1970, 167.
3. C. Andre, in *Carl Andre: Sculpture*, 1984.
4. M. Heizer, 1970.
5. Richard Long, 1985, part 1, 14.
6. R. Long, 1985, part 2, 22.
7. P. Redgrove, letter to the author, Apl 20, 1994.
8. R. Long, interview with R. Cork, in D. Sylvester.
9. M. Eliade: "Sacred Architecture and Symbolism", in *Eliade*, ed. C. Tacou, L'Herne, Paris, 1978, and in M. Eliade, 1988, 107.
10. A. Goldsworthy, *Hand to Earth*, 58.
11. A. Goldsworthy, sketchbook no. 22, 1988, *Hand To Earth*, 150.
12. Goldsworthy dislikes geometry being 'imposed upon nature' (HE, 162), though all his sculpture (like all art) can be seen as something 'imposed upon nature'. Even the most ephemeral and minuscule of Goldsworthy sculptures, such as the tiny flower or leafworks, are impositions and additions to the natural world. They are events which do not happen 'naturally'.
13. R. Long, 1985, 2, 17.

6 LAND ART AND BRITISH CULTURE

LAND ART AND BRITISH SCULPTURE

1. J. Roberts, 1990, 111f.

THE BRITISH LANDSCAPE TRADITION

1. R. Rosenblum, 1988, 7.
2. C. Andre, quoted in A. Causey, 1977, 126.

7 ROBERT SMITHSON

1. In C. Robins, 78.
2. Robert Smithson, in *Selected Writings*, 20, hereafter indicated as RS.
3. R. Hobbs, 12.
4. J.G. Ballard, in R. Smithson, 1997.
5. Smithson labelled pre-existing sites land artworks, non-sites, such as the pipes, boxes and walkways of an industrial zone in *Monuments of Passaic* (1967)
6. R. Smithson, "A Sedimentation of the Mind: Earth Projects", in *Selected Writings*, 85.
7. R. Smithson, "Discussion with Heizer, Oppenheim, Smithson", *Avalanche*, 1970, and in E. Johnson, 1982, 182.
8. C. Robins, 1984, 82.
9. In L. Lippard, 1973, 88.
10. J. Kounellis, in W. Sharp, 1972.
11. See M. Gimbutas, 1989.
12. R. Smithson: "The Spiral Jetty", unpublished MS, quoted in R. Krauss, 282. See R. Hobbs, 1981.
13. I. Sandler, 1990, 60.
14. *Selected Writings*, 37.
15. J. Coplans: "Robert Smithson: The Amarillo Ramp", in R. Hobbs, 53.
16. In R. Hobbs, 212.

8 CARL ANDRE

1. C. Andre, quoted in D. Bourdon: "The Razed Sites of Carl Andre", in G. Battock, 1995, 103.
2. Ib., 104.
3. L. Lippard, 1973, 157.
4. C. Andre, in *Carl Andre: Sculpture*, 1984
5. L. Lippard, 1965, 58.
6. C. Andre, 1970, 61.
7. In ib., 107.
8. D. Bourdon, 1978, 56. See M. Bochner, 1967, 39-43.
9. D. Bourdon, in G. Battock, 1995, 107.
10. R. Krauss, 1977, 271f.
11. M. Bochner, in G. Battock, 1995, 94.
12. C. Tomkins, 1989, 155.
13. C. Andre, in L. Lippard, 1970, 7.
14. Carl Andre, *Joint*, 1968, 183 units, each 14 x 18 x 36 in, installation at Windham College, Putney, Vermont.
15. A. Goldsworthy, *Time*, 180.
16. C. Andre, quoted in D. Bourdon, in G. Battock, 1995, 108.
17. T. Smith, quoted in M. Fried, 1967, in G. Battock, 1995, 131.

18. Ib., 131.
19. David Lee said that 'Andre repeats one thing in each piece; Smithson repeats one thing but increases its size' (1967, 44).

9 JAMES TURRELL

1. Dia Foundation, the McArthur Foundation, the National Endowment for the Arts, the Lannan Foundation, the Canon Company, the Bohen Foundation, the Martin Bucksbaum Family Foundation, Count Giuseppe Panza di Buimo, Dr Pentti Kouri, Jean Stein, plus other donors.
2. J. Turrell, in A. Benjamin, 47.
3. J. Turrell, 1987.

10 DENNIS OPPENHEIM

1. In D. Oppenheim, 1992.
2. L. Lippard, 1983, 52.
3. In M. Heizer, 1970.
4. D. Oppenheim, in M. Heizer, 1970.
5. In D. Oppenheim, 1978.

11 ROBERT MORRIS

1. R. Morris, quoted in M. Fried, 1967, in G. Battock, 1995, 126.
2. M. Friedman, 1966, 23.
3. D. Factor, 1966, 13.
4. In M. Compton, 1971, 16.
5. R. Morris, "Notes on Sculpture", 4, 51.
6. B. Rose, 1965.
7. D. Sylvester, 1996, 243.
8. J. Haldane, 1997, 56.

12 NANCY HOLT

1. N. Holt, "Sun Tunnels", 1977, 34.
2. In T. Castle, 1982, 88.
3. See N. Holt, 1975, 1977; T. Castle, 1982.
4. C. Robins, 1984, 10.

13 ALICE AYCOCK

1. H. Risatti, 37.
2. A. Aycock, quoted in E. Johnson, 1982, 223.
3. R. Smith, 1975, 68.
4. A. Aycock, quoted in N. Rosen: "A Sense of Place: Five

American Artists", *International Sculpture*, Merriewold West, 1975.
5. E. Johnson, 1982, 221.
6. A. Aycock, 1977.

14 MARY MISS

1. R. Onoratio, 1978, 32. See also R. Onoratio, 1979; K. Linker: "Mary Miss", *Mary Miss*, ICA, 1983.
2. See L. Anderson, 1973; M. Miss, 1981.

15 MICHAEL HEIZER

1. M. Heizer, 1970.
2. See A. Sonfist, 1983; J. Beardsley, 1984.
3. Sol LeWitt was sceptical of enormity: '[i]f it's so big that you can't really comprehend it except by its emotive force then I don't want it' (in F. Colpitt, 77). And Robert Morris wrote that 'beyond a certain size the object can overwhelm and the gigantic scale becomes the loaded term' (1966, 21).
4. See J. Brown, 1984; G. Müller, 42-45.
5. In H. Smagula, 1983, 286.
6. M. Heizer, in J. Bell: "Positive and Negative", *Arts Magazine*, Nov, 1974, 55.
7. R. Hughes, 1997, 571.
8. M. Miss, 1981, 6-7.
9. R. Hughes, 1991, 386.

16 WALTER DE MARIA

1. Walter de Maria proposed another shaft, *Olympic Mountain Project* (1970) – never made – which would have been 400 ft deep and 3 ft wide.
2. Quoted in H. Smagula, 289.
3. R. Smith, 1978, 104.
4. H. Rosenberg, 1972, 36.
5. See D. Bourdon, 1968, 39-43, 72; M. Winton, 1970, 18-19; R. Smith, 1978, 102-5.
6. K. Baker, 1988, 125-7.
7. W. de Maria, 1980.
8. See P. Redgrove: *The Black Goddess and the Sixth Sense*, Bloomsbury, London, 1987; *The Cyclopean Mistress*, H. Smagula, 290. De Maria himself thought that a lightning strike is a 'false climax' to the work, which really needs to be seen over a period of time to appreciate its qualities.

17 OTHER LAND ARTISTS IN THE U.S.A.

1. G. Matta-Clark, "Interview With *Avalanche*", *Avalanche*, Dec, 1974.
2. See L. Lippard, 1983, 49.
3. T. Murak, in B. Nemitz, 94.
4. D. Hollis, in B. Oakes, 107.

18 CHRIS DRURY

1. C. Drury, 2002, 91.
2. C. Drury, 2002, 72, 76.
3. C. Drury, 2002, 76, 84.
4. C. Drury, 2002, 90.
5. Statement, on C. Drury's website.
6. C. Drury, in 1998, 6.
7. C. Drury, 1998, 7.

19 DAVID NASH

1. See A. McPherson, 1978; H. Adams, 1979; D. Nash, 1980.
2. D. Nash: *Sea Hearth*, 1981, Isle of Bute, Scotland, *Wood Stove*, 1979, Maentwrog, Wales, *Slate Stove*, 1981, Blaenau Ffestiniog, Wales, *Snow Stove*, 1982, Kotoku, Japan.
3. At the University of Colorado, 1991.
4. D. Nash, in K. Martin, 1990, 66.
5. H. de Vries, in H. Gooding, 2002, 69.
6. D. Nash: *Fletched Over Ash Dome*, planted, 1979, Caen-y-Coed, Maentwrog, Wales.
7. D. Nash, in Welsh Sculpture Trust, 120.
8. In A. Causey.

20 RICHARD LONG

1. H. Thoreau, in *Walking*, 1861, in *The Portable Thoreau*, ed. C. Bode, Viking, New York, NY, 1980, 592.
2. A. Seymour, "Walking in Circles", 1.
3. R. Long, in *Walking In Circles*, 23.
4. R. Long, letter to the author, in W. Malpas, 1995.
5. *Old World, New World*, 54.
6. H. Fulton, in M. Auping, 1982.
7. R. Long, in *Walking In Circles*, 1986, 23.
8. R. Long, in ib., 224.
9. D. Reason: "Echo and Reflections", in S. Bann, 169.
10. R. Long, interview, Santa Fe, 1993, 236.
11. R. Long, in *An Interview With Richard Long*, R. Cork, in R. Long, *Walking In Circles*, 20.

12. J. Augoyard: *Pas a Pas. Essai sur le cheminement quotidien en milieu urbain*, Paris, 1979; C. Norberg-Schultz: *Existence, Space and Architecture*, London, 1971.
13. Kate Blacker, discussing Richard Long, Ian Hamilton Finlay and Stephen Willats wrote:

    I don't think Long ...reversed anything. They just weren't concerned with the same things as their predecessors were. Long went to St Martin's and was introduced to a very strict set of self-perpetuating rules. He seems to have spent no time considering what [Anthony] Caro or [Philip] King had to say. Instead he placed himself in another British tradition: that of landscape. Regardless of the format of how to display the sculpture, he was the first British artist to bring landscape indoors. It's no longer a framed picture, a window onto the landscape, as it was in Constable or the Norfolk School. He brings the sense of scale, the whole sensibility of that tradition, into three dimensions. (In P. de Monchaux, 1983, 92.)

14. R. Long, 1985, 2, 24.
15. R. Long, 1985, 1, 17.
16. In R. Long, interview, Santa Fe, 1993, 236.
17. R. Long, interview with G. Lobacheff, 1994, 6.
18. R. Long, interview, Santa Fe, 1993, 236.
19. Richard Long wrote: '[e]ven though it is necessary to get a good photograph, the photographs should be as simple as possible... the photographs have got to be fairly simple and straightforward, so that the feeling of the work somehow accurately comes through.' (In *An Interview With Richard Long*, R. Cork, in R. Long, *Walking In Circles*, 24).
20. R. Long, interview, Santa Fe, 1993, 236.
21. *An Interview with Richard Long*, Santa Fe.
22. R. Long, interview with G. Lobacheff, 1994, 8.
23. R. Long, 1985, 1, 12.

21 ANDY GOLDSWORTHY

1. Many of the big names in British sculpture have exhibited works at Goodwood, including Elisabeth Frink, David Mach, Phillip King, David Nash, Eduardo Paolozzi, Bill Woodrow, Tony Cragg, Ian Hamilton Finlay, Stephen Dilworth, Anthony Caro and Anthony Gormley.
2. A. Goldsworthy, *Time*, 82.
3. A. Goldsworthy, *Time,* 193.
4. J. Dibbets, in D. Ashton, ed. *20th Century Artists on Art*, Pantheon, New York, NY, 1985, 174.

5. A. Goldsworthy, in A. Causey, 1980.
6. A. Goldsworthy, in *Aspects*, 1986.
7. A. Goldsworthy, ib., *Hand To Earth*, 165.
8. A. Goldsworthy, *Sheepfolds*, 17.
9. A. Goldsworthy, *Réfuges d'Art*, 105.
10. Interview with T. Friedman, *Third Ear*, June, 1989 in *Hand To Earth*, 166.
11. A. Goldsworthy, *Stone*, 21.
12. A. Goldsworthy, *Stone*, 120.
13. R. Long, letter to the author, in W. Malpas, 1995.
14. A. Goldsworthy, *Hand To Earth*, 167.
15. K. Carter: "*Stone*", *New Welsh Review*, 27, Winter, 1994-95, 100.
16. A. Goldsworthy, *Wall*, 68-69.
17. A. Goldsworthy, *Réfuges d'Art*, 85.
18. 'My strongest work is so rooted in place that it cannot be separated from where it is made', Goldsworthy wrote in *Stone* (6).
19. A. Goldsworthy, *Hand To Earth*, 167.
20. A. Goldsworthy, *Stone*, 6.
21. In A. Papadakis, 1991, 250.
22. In J. Beardsley, 1984, 134.
23. A. Goldsworthy, *Midsummer Snowballs*, 31.
24. A. Goldsworthy, *Hand To Earth*, 165.
25. A. Goldsworthy, quoted in *Andy Goldsworthy*.
26. 'Urban living has always tended to produce a sentimental view of nature', wrote John Berger (*The White Bird: Writings by John Berger*, London, 1988, 7).
27. 'Nature for me is the clearest path to discover – *uncluttered by personalities* or associations – *it just is*', says Goldsworthy in a telling statement (my emphasis, sketchbook no. 19, 1988, *Hand To Earth*, 150).
28. A. Goldsworthy, *Time*, 112.
29. A. Goldsworthy, *Andy Goldsworthy*, Viking, London, 1990, no page numbers; and in N. Hedges, 67; *Hand To Earth*, 160-1.
30. A. Causey: "Environmental Sculptures", in *Hand To Earth*, 128.
31. A. Goldsworthy, *Third Ear*, BBC Radio 3, June 30, 1989, in *Hand To Earth*, 168.
32. 'Some works have qualities of snaking but are not snakes. The form is shaped through a similar response to environment' (*Andy Goldsworthy*).
33. A. Goldsworthy, *Réfuges d'Art*, 113.
34. Ib., 113.
35. In A. Davies, 1984, 151.
36. A. Causey, 1990, 128.
37. A. Goldsworthy, *Hand To Earth*, 163.

38. A. Goldsworthy, unpublished notes, 1988, in *Hand To Earth*, 134-5.
39. A. Goldsworthy, quoted in T. Friedman: "Monuments", in *Hand To Earth*, 154.
40. A. Goldsworthy, *Sheepfolds*, 12.
41. A. Goldsworthy, *Réfuges d'Art*, 111.
42. A. Goldsworthy, *Hand To Earth*, 19.
43. A. Goldsworthy, *Winter Harvest*; *Hand To Earth*, 162.
44. A. Goldsworthy, in M. Church; and *Stone*, 120.

22 LAND ARTISTS IN EUROPE

CHRISTO

1. J. Marck: *Wrapped Museum*, Museum of Contemporary Art, Chicago, 1969.
2. Christo, quoted in E. Johnson, 1982, 198.
3. See W. Spies: *The Running Fence Project, Christo*, Abrams, New York, NY, 1977.
4. Christo, in A. Haden-Guest, 40.

HANS HAACKE

1. H. Haacke, in J. Burnham, 1967.
2. H. Haacke, in ib.

HAMISH FULTON

1. H. Fulton, 1995.

OTHER LAND ARTISTS IN EUROPE

1. R. Martin, 31.
2. B. Nemitz, 78.
3. N. Pope, quoted in W. Strachan, 70.
4. R. Harris, quoted in D. Petherbridge, "Public commissions and the new concerns in sculpture", in P. de Monchaux, 136.
5. In W. Strachan, 179.
6. See R. Parker, 1987, 316; L. Lippard, 1976, 203.

Bibliography

H. Adams. "The Woodman", *Art and Artists*, 13, Apl, 1979
—. "Fabian Carlsson Gallery: London: Exhibit", *New Art Examiner*, 15, May, 1988
S. Adams & A. Robins, eds. *Gendering Landscape Art*, Manchester University Press, Manchester, 2000
C. Adcock. *James Turrell*, University of California Press, Berkeley, CA, 1990
W. C. Agee. "Unit, Series, Site: A Judd Lexicon", *Art in America*, May, 1975
L. Alloway. *Christo*, Abrams, New York, NY, 1969
—. "Robert Smithson", *Artforum*, 11, Nov, 1972
L. Anderson. "Mary Miss", *Artforum*, Nov, 1973
C. Andre. "Frank Stella: Preface to Stripe Painting", in D. Miller, 1959
—. "An Interview with Carl Andre", P. Tuchman, *Artforum*, 8, 10, June, 1970
—. *Carl Andre, Sculpture, 1958-1974*, Kunsthalle, Bern, 1975
—. "Object v Phenomenon", *Sculpture Today*, The International Sculpture Center, Toronto, 1978
—. *Carl Andre: Sculpture*, State University of New York Press, Albany, NY, 1984
—. *Carl-Andre: works on land*, Exhibitions International, 2001
J. Andrews. *The Sculpture of David Nash*, Lund Humphries, London, 1999
E. de Antonio & Mitch Tuchman. *Painters Painting*, Abbeville Press, New York, NY, 1984
M. Auping. *Common Ground*, John and Mable Ringling Museum of Art, Sarasota, 1982
—. "Hamish Fulton", *Art in America*, 71, Feb, 1983
A. Aycock. "Work", "Maze", 1975, in A. Sondheim, 1977
J. Baal-Teshuva, ed. *Christo: The Reichstag and Urban Projects*, Prestel Verlag, Munich, 1993
K. Baker. "Andre in Retrospect", *Art in America*, Apl, 1980a
—. "Reckoning with Notation: The Drawings of Pollock, Newman, and Louis", *Artforum*, 18, 10, Summer, 1980b
—. *Minimalism: Art of Circumstance*, Abbeville, New York, NY, 1988
S. Bann & W. Allen, eds. *Interpreting Contemporary Art*,

Reaktion Books, London, 1991
G. Baro. "Toward Speculation in Pure Form", *Art International*, Summer, 1967
—. "American Sculpture", *Studio International*, 172, 896, 1968
G. Battock, ed. *The New Art*, Dutton, New York, NY, 1966
—. ed. *Minimal Art: A Critical Anthology*, University of California Press, Berkeley, CA, 1995
J. Beardsley. *Probing the Earth: Contemporary Land Projects*, Smithsonian Press, Washington DC, 1977
—. *Art in Public Spaces*, Partners For Liveable Places, Washington DC, 1981
—. *Earthworks and Beyond: Contemporary Art in the Landscape*, Abbeville Press, New York, NY, 1984/ 1998
M.R. Beaumont. "Romantic Sculpture", in A. Papadakis, 1988
—. "Andy Goldsworthy", *Arts Review*, July 14, 1989
A. Benjamin, ed. *Installation Art, Art & Design*, 30, 1993
L. Bennett. *The Life and Work of Andy Goldsworthy*, Heinemann, London, 2005
N. Bennett, ed. *The British Art Show: Old Allegiances and New Directions, 1979-1984*, Arts Council/ Orbis, London, 1984
M. Berger. *Labyrinths: Robert Morris, Minimalism, and the 1960s*, Harper & Row, New York, NY, 1989
M. Bloem, ed. *Lawrence Weiner*, Stedelijk Museum, Amsterdam, 1989
Eugen Blume *et al. Richard Long: Berlin Circle*, 2011
M. Bochner. "Art in Process – Structures", *Arts Magazine*, 40, 9, 1966a
—. "Primary Structures", *Arts*, June, 1966b
—. "Systematic", *Arts Magazine*, 41, 1, Nov, 1966c
—. "Serial Art Systems: Solipsism", *Arts Magazine*, 41, 8, Summer, 1967
—. "Mel Bochner on Malevich", interview with J. Coplans, *Artforum*, June, 1974
S. Boettger. *Earthworks*, University of California Press, Berkeley, CA, 2002
D. Bourdon. "The Razed Sites of Carl Andre", *Artforum*, 5, 2, Oct, 1966
—. "Walter de Maria: The Singular Experience", *Art International*, Dec 20, 1968
—. "The Mini-Conceptual Age", *Village Voice*, Oct 17, 1974
—. "You Can't Tell a Painter By His Colors", *Village Voice*, Mch 24, 1975
—. *Carl Andre: Sculpture, 1959-1977*, Jaap Rietman, New York, NY, 1978
C. Brown. "Natural arts", *The Magazine*, July, 1987
D. Brown. "New British sculpture in Normandy", *Arts Review*, Feb 10, 1989
J. Brown *et al. Michael Heizer: Sculpture in Reverse*, see M.

Heizer, 1984
—. ed. *Occluding Front: James Turrell*, Lapis Press, Larkspur Landing, CA, 1985
D. Bruckner. "Earth works", *New York Times Book Review*, Jan, 1996
P. J. Burgard, ed. *Nietzsche and the Feminine*, University Press of Virginia, Charlottesville, VI, 1994
J. Burnham. *Beyond Modern Sculpture*, Braziller, New York, NY, 1968
—. "A Dan Flavin Retrospective in Ottawa", *Artforum*, 8, 4, Dec, 1969
—. "Robert Morris", *Artforum*, 8, 7, 1970
—. "Haacke's Cancelled Show at the Guggenheim", *Artforum*, June, 1971
—. *Great Western Salt Works*, Brazillier, New York, NY, 1974
—. "Hans Haacke: Wind and Water Sculpture", 1967, in A. Sonfist, 1983
K. Bussman & F. Matzner, eds. *Hans Haacke*, Cantz, Stuttgart, 1993
J. Butterfield. *The Art of Light and Space*, Abbeville Press, New York, NY, 1993
D. Cameron. "When is a door not a door?", *XLIII esposizione Internazionale d'Arte La Biennale di Venezia*, Edizioni La Biennale, Venice, 1988
—. "Art for the new year: who's worth catching?", *Art & Auction*, Jan, 1994
J. Campbell. *The Power of Myth*, with B. Moyers, ed. B. Flowers, Doubleday, New York, NY, 1988
P. Carlson. "Donald Judd's Equivocal Objects", *Art in America*, Jan, 1984
T. Castle. "Nancy Holt, Siteseer", *Art in America*, Mch, 1982
A. Causey. "Space and Time in British Land Art", *Studio International*, 193, 98, Feb, 1977
—. *Nature as Material: An Exhibition of Sculpture and Photographs Purchased For the Arts Council Collection*, Arts Council, London, 1980
—. "Environmental Sculptures", in A. Goldsworthy, *Hand to Earth*, 1990
—. *Sculpture Since 1945*, Oxford University Press, Oxford, 1998
G. Celant. "Introduction", *Arte Povera*, Praeger, New York, NY, 1969
—. *Conceptual Art, Arte Povera, Land Art*, Galeria Civica d'Arte Moderna, Turin, 1970
—. *Dennis Oppenheim*, Edizioni Charta Srl, 1997
A. Chave: "Minimalism and the Rhetoric of Power", *Arts*, Jan, 1990
H.B. Chipp, ed. *Theories of Modern Art*, University Press of California, LA, CA, 1968

M. Church. "A shower of stones, a flash in the river", *The Sunday Telegraph*, 10 April, 1994, 6

F. Colpitt. *Minimal Art: The Critical Perspective*, University of Washington Press, Seattle, WA, 1990

M. Compton. *Some Notes on the Work of Richard Long*, British Council, London, 1976

—. & D. Sylvester. *Robert Morris*, Tate Gallery, London, 1971

Concept Art, Minimal Art, Land Art, Edition Cantz, Stuttgart, 1990

L. Cooke. "Richard Long replies to a critic", *Art Monthly*, 68, July, 1983

—. "Between Image and Object: The "New British Sculpture"", in T. Neff, 1987

J. Coplans. "Serial Imagery", *Artforum*, 7, 2, Oct, 1968

—. "Robert Smithson", *Artforum*, Apl, 1974

T. Cragg. *Writings*, Editions Isy Brachot, Brussels, 1992

—. *Sculptures on the Page*, Henry Moore Institute, Leeds, Yorkshire, 1997

D. Crane. *The Transformation of the Avant Garde: The New York Art World, 1940-1985*, University of Chicago Press, Chicago, IL, 1987

P. Crowther, ed. *The Contemporary Sublime, Art & Design*, 40, 1995

A. Davies. "Richard Long and Hamish Fulton", *Art Monthly*, 25, April, 1979

H. Davies *et al*. *Blurring the Boundaries: Installation Art 1969-1996*, Museum of Contemporary Art, San Diego, CA, 1997

R. Davies & T. Knipe, eds. *A Sense of Place: Sculpture in Landscape*, London, 1984

W. de Maria. "The Lightning Field", *Artforum*, 18, 8, Apl, 1980

P. de Monchaux, *et al*, eds. *The Sculpture Show*, Arts Council of Great Britain, London, 1983

Amy Dempsey. *Destination Art: Land Art: Site-Specific Art: Sculpture Parks*, 2011

N. de Oliveira *et al*. *Installation Art*, Thames & Hudson, London, 1994

—. *et al*, eds. *Installation Art in the New Millennium*, Thames & Hudson, London, 2003

R. Deutsche *et al*. *Hans Haacke*, MIT Press, Cambridge, MA, 1986

E. Develing. *Carl Andre*, Gemeentenmeuseum, The Hague, 1969

—. & L. Lippard. *Minimal Art*, Stadtische Kunsthalle, Dusseldorf, 1969

J. Dibbets, in L. Bear & W. Sharp: "DIBBETTS", *Avalanche*, 1, Autumn, 1970.

R. Donnell. *Double Vision: Perspectives On Gender and the Visual Arts*, Farleigh Dickinson University Press, Rutherford, NJ, 1995

Molly Donovan & Tina Fiske. *The Andy Goldsworthy Project*, Thames & Hudson, London, 2010
L. Dougherty. "Art in nature: a new site for sculpture in Denmark", *Maquette*, Sept, 1994
C. Drury. *Shelters and Baskets*, Orchard Gallery, 1988
—. *Stones and Bundles*, Rebecca Hossack Gallery, London, 1995
—. *Silent Spaces*, Thames & Hudson, London, 1998/ 2004
—. Interview with W. Furlong, in M. Gooding, 2002
—. *Defying Gravity*, North Carolina Museum of Art, NC, 2003
—. *Heart of Stone*, Aberystwyth Art Gallery, Wales, 2003
M. Duncan. "On site: straddling the great divide", *Art in America*. 83, 3, Mch 1995
—. "Live from the Getty", *Art in America,* 86, 5, May, 1998
A. Dyson. *Richard Long: Sao Paulo Biennial 1994,* The British Council, 1994
J.C. Eade, ed. *Projecting the Landscape*, Humanities Research Centre, Canberra, 1987
M. Eliade. *Patterns in Comparative Religion*, Sheed & Ward, London, 1958
—. *Shamanism: Archaic Techniques of Ecstasy*, Princeton University Press, Princeton, NJ, 1972
—. *Myths, Dreams and Mysteries*, Harper & Row, New York, NY, 1975
—. *From Primitives to Zen: A Sourcebook*, Collins, London, 1977
—.*A History of Religious Ideas*, I, Collins, London, 1979
—. *Ordeal by Labyrinth*, University of Chicago Press, Chicago, IL, 1984
—.*Symbolism, the Sacred and the Arts*, Crossroad, New York, NY, 1988
Patrick Elliott. *Richard Long: Walking and Marking*, 2007
Ulrike Ezika. *Ready-made und Landschaft: Zur künstlerischen Verwendung der Natur bei Andy Goldsworthy*, 2010
D. Factor. "Los Angeles", *Artforum*, 4, 9, May, 1966
S. Farr. "Andy Goldsworthy: stone works in America", *Reflex*, 8, 6, Dec, 1995
S. Field. "Touching the Earth", *Art and Artists*, 8, Apl, 1973
J. Fineberg: *Art Since 1940: Strategies of Being*, Laurence King, London, 1995
P. Fingesten. *The Eclipse of Symbolism*, Columbia, 1970
A. Fisher & G. Gerster. *The Art of the Maze*, Weidenfeld & Nicholson, London, 1990
—. & J. Saward. *The British Maze Guide*, Minotaur Designs, London, 1991
—. & D. Kingham. *Mazes,* Shire Pulications, London, 1991
J. Fisher. "Richard Long", *Aspects*, 14, Spring, 1981
Tina Fiske & Andy Goldsworthy. *Andy Goldsworthy at Yorkshire*

 Sculpture Park, 2007
- B. Flanagan. "Sculpture made visible: Barry Flanagan in discussion with Gene Baro", *Studio International*, 178, 915, Oct, 1969
- S. Foley. *Unitary Forms: Minimal Structures by Carl Andre, Donald Judd, John McCracken, Tony Smith*, Museum of Modern Art, San Francisco, CA, 1970
- N. Foote. "Long Walks", *Artforum*, 18, Summer, 1980
- M. Fried. "Shape as Form: Frank Stella's New Paintings", *Artforum*, 5, 3, Nov, 1966
- —. "Art and Objecthood", *Artforum*, 5, Summer, 1967
- M. Friedman. "Robert Morris: Polemics and Cubes", *Art International*, 10, 10, Dec, 1966
- —. *14 Sculptors*, Walker Art Center, Minneapolis, MN, 1969
- E. Fry. *Alice Aycock*, University of South Florida Art Galleries, Tampa, FL, 1981
- —. "The Poetic Machines of Alice Aycock", *Portfolio*, Nov, 1981
- —. *et al. Robert Morris*, Museum of Contemporary Art, Chicago, IL, 1986
- R.H. Fuchs. "Memories of Passing: A Note on Richard Long", *Studio International*, 187, 965, Apl, 1974
- —. *Carl Andre*, Van Abenmuseum, Eindhoven, 1978
- —. *Richard Long*, text, in R. Long, 1986
- T. Fulgate-Wilcox. "Force Art: a New Direction", *Arts Magazine*, Mch, 1971
- P. Fuller. *Peter Fuller's Modern Painters: Reflections on British Art*, ed. J. McDonald, Methuen, London, 1993
- H. Fulton. *Hamish Fulton: Selected Walks, 1969-89*, Albright-Knox Art Gallery, Buffalo, New York, NY, 1990
- —. "Into a Walk Into Nature", *Thirty One Horrors*, Lenbachhaus, Munich, 1995
- —. *Walking Artist*, Annely Juda, London, 1998
- S. Gardiner. "Their medium is nature", *Landscape Architecture*, 80, Feb, 1990
- M. Garlake. "Andy Goldsworthy", *Art Monthly*, 93, Feb, 1986
- J. Gear. "Andy Goldsworthy", *Review*, Dec 1, 1996
- Gokce Gerekli. *Land Art on the Border between Topology and Atopology*, 2009
- J. Giovannini. *Mary Miss*, Architectural Association, London, 1987
- T. Godfrey, Tony. "Richard Wilson's watertable, Andy Goldsworthy", *Burlington Magazine*, 136, 1096, July, 1994
- —. *Conceptual Art*, Phaidon, London, 1998
- E. Goheen. *Wrapped Walk Ways*, Abrams, New York, NY, 1978
- A. Goldsworthy. *Andy Goldsworthy, Alan Rankle, Nigel Jepson*, Brampton Banks, Cumbria, 1982
- —. *Rain sun snow hail mist calm: Photoworks by Andy*

Goldsworthy, Henry Moore Centre for the Study of Sculpture, Leeds, Yorkshire, 1985
—. *Land Matters*, Blackfriars Arts Centre, Reed Press, 1986
—. & J. Fowles. *Winter Harvest*, Scottish Arts Council, 1987
—. *Mountain and Coast: Autumn Into Winter: Japan 1987*, Art Data, 1988
—. *Parkland*, Yorkshire Sculpture Park, West Bretton, 1988
—. *Touching North*, Fabian Carlsson, London, 1989
—. *Snowballs in Summer Installation*, Old Museum of Transport, Glasgow, 1989
—. *Leaves*, Common Ground, London, 1989
—. *Andy Goldsworthy*, Viking, London, 1990
—. *Hand to Earth: Andy Goldsworthy, Sculpture, 1976-1990*, Henry Moore Centre for Sculpture, Leeds, Yorkshire, 1990
—. Interview, *Third Ear*, BBC Radio 3, June 30, 1989, in 1990
—. "Geometry and Nature", interview, *Art & Design*, in A. Papadakis, 1991
—. *Sand Leaves*, Arts Club of Chicago, IL, 1991
—. *Ice and Snow Drawings*, Fruitmarket Gallery, Edinburgh, 1992
—. *Andy Goldsworthy: Breakdown*, Rose Art Museum, 1992
—. *Stone*, Viking, London, 1994
—. *Black Stones, Red Pools*, Pro Arte Foundation, 1995
—. *Wood*, Viking, London, 1996
—. *Sheepfolds*, Michael Hue-Williams Gallery, London, 1996
—. *Végètal*, Ballet Atlantique-Regine Chopinot, La Rochelle, France, 1996
—. *Alaska Works*, Anchorage Museum of History and Art, Anchorage, AK, 1996
—. *Andy Goldsworthy: A Collaboration With Nature*, Abrams, NY, 1996
—. *Andy Goldsworthy: Jack's Fold*, ed. Judy Glasman, University of Hertfordshire, 1996
—. *Hand to Earth: Andy Goldsworthy Sculpture*, T. Friedman, Thames and Hudson, London, 1997 & 2004
—. *Cairns*, Musée departemental de Digne, Reserve Geologique de haute Provence, 1997
—. *Andy Goldsworthy*, Musée d'art contemporain de Montréal, 1998
—. *Arch*, with D. Craig, Thames & Hudson, London, 1999
—. *Wall*, intr. K. Baker, Thames & Hudson, London, 2000
—. *Time*, Thames & Hudson, London, 2000
—. *Midsummer Snowballs*, intr. J. Collins, Abrams, New York, NY, 2001
—. *Andy Goldsworthy – Réfuges D'Art*, Editions Artha, 2002
—. *Passage*, Thames & Hudson, London, 2004
—. *Enclosure*, Thames & Hudson, London, 2007
M. Gooding & W. Furlong. *Song of the Earth,* Thames and Hud-

son, London, 2002
- A. Gopnik. "Basic Stuff: Robert Smithson, Myth, Science and Primitivism", *Art Magazine*, Mch, 1983
- J. Grande. *Balance: art and nature*, Black Rose Books, Montréal, 1994
- —. "Back to nature?", *Sculpture*, 13, 4 July/ Aug, 1994
- —. *Art Nature Dialogues*, State University of New York Press, NY, 2004
- N. Graydon. "Magic in the field", *Ritz*, 133, 1989
- B. Graziani. "Robert Smithson's Picturable Situation", *Critical Inquiry*, 20, 3, Spring, 1994
- C. Greenberg. *Art and Culture,* Beacon Press, Boston, MA, 1961
- G. Greig. "Circular Tours In the Name of Art", *Sunday Times*, June 16, 1991
- H. Gresty & D. Reason. *Landscape*, Kettle's Yard, Cambridge, 1986
- H. Haacke. *Framing and Being Framed*, New York University Press, New York, NY, 1975
- A. Haden-Guest. "The King of Wrap", *The Sunday Times Magazine*, Jan, 1994
- O. Hahn & P. Restany. *Christo*, Editioni Apollinaire, Milan, 1966
- J. Haldane. *A Road From the Past To the Future*, Crawford Arts Centre, St Andrews, 1997
- C. Hall. "Shared earth", *Arts Review*, 43, June 14, 1991
- —. "Site lines", *Arts Review*, 46, Oct, 1994
- A.M. Hammacher. *The Sculpture of Barbara Hepworth*, Abrams, New York, NY, 1968
- —. *The Evolution of Modern Sculpture: Tradition and Innovation*, Abrams, New York, NY, 1969
- C. Harrison. "Barry Flanagan's Sculpture", *Studio International*, 175, 900, May, 1968
- B. Haskell. *BLAM! The Explosion of Pop, Minimalism, and Performance, 1958-64*, Whitney Museum of American Art, New York, NY, 1984
- —. *Donald Judd*, Whitney Museum of American Art, New York, NY, 1988
- N. Hedges. "Growth, decay and the movement of change", *World Magazine*, 45, Jan, 1991
- M. Heizer, D. Oppenheim & R. Smithson. "Discussion", *Avalanche*, 1, Autumn, 1970
- —. *Sculpture in Reverse*, Museum of Contemporary Art, LA, CA, 1984
- A. Henri. *Environments and Happenings*, Thames & Hudson, London, 1974
- —. *Total Art*, Praeger, New York, NY, 1974
- J. Heslewood. *The History of Western Sculpture: A Young Person's Guide*, Belitha Press, London, 1994
- A. Hess. "Technology Exposed", *Landscape Architecture*, May,

1992

Galerie Max Hetzler. *Carl Andre, Gunther Forg, Hubert Kiecol, Richard Long, Meuser, Reinhard Mucha, Bruce Nauman and Ulrich Ruckreim*, Cologne, 1985

G. Hilty. *Recent British Sculpture*, Arts Council, London, 1993

R. Hobbs. *Robert Smithson: Sculpture,* Cornell University Press, Ithaca, NY, 1981

—. "Earthworks", *Art Journal*, 42, Fall, 1982

N. Hodges ed. *Art and the Natural Environment*, Art & Design, 36, 1994

—. ed. *The Contemporary Sublime, Art & Design,* 40, 1995

N. Holt. "Amarillo Ramp", *Avalanche*, Fall, 1973

—. "Hydra's Head", *Arts Magazine*, Jan, 1975

—. "Sun Tunnels", *Artforum*, Apl, 1977

K. Honnef. *Concept Art*, Phaidon, Oxford, 1971

P. Hovdenakk. *Christo: Complete Editions*, Schellman & Klüser, Munich, 1982

S. Hubbard, intr. *Sculpture At Goodwood: A Vision For 21st Century British Sculpture*, Sculpture At Goodwood, Sussex, 2002

R. Hughes. *Nothing If Not Critical: Selected Essays on Art and Artists*, Collins Harvill, London, 1990

—. *The Shock of the New*, Thames & Hudson, London, 1991

—. *American Visions: The Epic History of Art In America*, Knopf, New York, NY, 1997

L. Iizawa. "Earth work", *Studio Voice*, Mch, 1988

P. Inch. "Andy Goldsworthy", *Arts Review*, 42, July 13, 1990

R. Ingleby. "Visual arts: Andy Goldsworthy", *The Independent*, Nov 8, 1996

In Praise of Trees, Salisbury Festival, Wilts., 2002

G. Jeppson. *Richard Long*, Harvard College, Cambridge, MA, 1980

E.H. Johnson, *Modern Art and the Object*, Harper & Row, New York, NY, 1976

—. ed. *American Artist on Art*, Harper & Row, New York, NY, 1982

B. Jones. "A New Wave in Sculpture", *Artscribe*, 8, Sept, 1977

D. Judd. "Frank Stella", *Arts Magazine*, 36, Sept, 1962

—. "In the Galleries", *Arts Magazine*, 37, 10, Sept, 1963

—. "Local History", *Arts Yearbook 7*, 1964

—. "Black, White and Gray", *Arts Magazine*, 38, 6, Mch, 1964

—. "Specific Objects", *Arts Yearbook*, 8, Art Digest, New York, NY, 1965

—. "Barnett Newman", *Studio International*, 179, 919, Feb, 1970

—. *Complete Writings, 1959-1975*, Nova Scotia College of Art and Design, Halifax, Canada, 1975

—. *Complete Writings, 1975-1986*, Van Abbemuseum,

Netherlands, 1987
E. Juncosa. "Landscape as experience", *Lapiz*, 61 Oct, 1989
Philip Kaiser & Miwon Kwon. *Ends of the Earth: Art of the Land to 1974*, 2012
D. Karshan. *Conceptual Art and Conceptual Aspects,* Farleigh Dickinson University, 1970
J. Kastner, ed. *Land and Environmental Art,* Phaidon, London, 1998
S. Kemal & I. Gaskell, eds. *Landscape, natural beauty and the arts,* Cambridge University Press, Cambridge, 1993
G. Kepes, ed. *Arts of the Environment*, Brazillier, New York, NY, 1972
P. King *et al.* "Colour in Sculpture", *Studio International*, 177, 907, 1969
R.E. Krauss. "Richard Serra: Sculpture Redrawn", *Artforum*, May, 1972
—. "Sense and Sensibility: Reflection on Post '60s Sculpture", *Artforum*, 12, Nov, 1973
—. *Passages in Modern Sculpture,* Thames & Hudson, London, 1977
—. "Sculpture in the Expanded Field", *October*, 8, Spring, 1979
—. *Eva Hesse*, Whitechapel Art Gallery, London, 1979
—. *et al. Robert Morris*, Abrams, New York, NY, 1994
Z. Kraus, ed. *From Nature to Art, From Art to Nature*, Venice Biennale, Milan, 1978
D. Kuspit. "Robert Smithson's Drunken Boat", *Arts Magazine*, Oct, 1981
—. "Aycock's Dream Houses", *Art in America*, Sept, 1982
—. "Donald Judd", *Artforum*, 23, 5, Feb, 1985
I. Lamaitre. "Interview with Tony Cragg", *Artefactum*, 2, Dec, 1985
T. Lang. "News from the imagination", *Issues in Architecture, Art & Design*, 3, 1, 1993
Land Marks, Edith C. Blum Art Institute, Bard College, Annadale-on-Hudson, 1984
D. Laporte. *Christo*, Pantheon Books, New York, NY, 1985
B. Laws. "Where Art and Nature Meet", *The Telegraph Weekly*, Nov 12, 1988
D. Lee. "Serial Rights", *Art News*, 66, 8, Dec, 1967
—. "London Ecology Centre, Exhibit", *Arts Review*, 38, Jan 17, 1986
—. "Great art of the outdoors: bio-degrading sculptures", *Country Life*, 181, 35, Aug 27, 1987
—. "Pure, ephemeral spires", *The Times*, June 26, 1989
—. "Opinion: Richard Long and Hamish Fulton", *Arts Review*, July 26, 1991
—. "In profile: Goldsworthy", *Arts Review*, 47, Feb 1995
A. Legg, ed. *Sol LeWitt*, Museum of Modern Art, New York, NY,

1978
- P. Leider. "For Robert Smithson", *Art in America*, Nov, 1973
- K. Levin. "Reflections on Robert Smithson's *Spiral Jetty*", *Arts Magazine*, May, 1978
- —. "Robert Smithson", *Art News*, Sept, 1982
- F. Licht: *Sculpture, 19th and 20th Centuries*, Michael Joseph, London, 1967
- —. "Dan Flavin", *Artscanada*, Dec, 1968
- L. Lippard. "New York Letter: Apl-June, 1965", *Art International*, 9, 6, 1965
- —. "New York Letter: Recent Sculpture as Escape", *Art International*, Feb, 1966a
- —. "An Impure Situation", *Art International*, May 20, 1966b
- —. "The Silent Art", *Art in America*, 55, 1, Jan-Feb, 1967a
- —. "Sol LeWitt: Non-Visual Structures", *Artforum*, Apl, 1967b
- —. "Tony Smith", *Art International*, Summer, 1967c
- —. "Rebelliously Romantic?", *New York Times*, June 4, 1967d
- —. "Escalataion in Washington", *Art International*, 12, 1, Jan, 1968
- —. ed. *Surrealists on Art*, Prentice-Hall, Englewood Cliffs, NJ, 1970
- —. *Tony Smith*, Thames & Hudson, London, 1972a
- —. *Grids*, Philadelphia Institute of Contemporary Art, PA, 1972b
- —. *Six Years: The Dematerialization of the Art Object from 1966 to 1972*, Praeger, New York, NY, 1973
- —. *From the Center: feminist essays on women's art*, Dutton, New York, NY, 1976
- —. *Eva Hesse*, New York University Press, New York, NY, 1976
- —. "Complexities: Architectural Sculpture in Nature", *Art in America*, Feb, 1979
- —. *Overlay*, Pantheon, New York, NY, 1983
- C. Loeffier, ed. *Performance Anthology*, Contemporary Art Press, San Francisco, CA, 1979
- R. Long. *Touchstones*, Arnolfini, Bristol, 1983
- —. *Richard Long: In Conversation*, Parts 1 & 2, MW Press, Noordwijk, Holland, 1985-86
- —. *Richard Long*, text by R.H. Fuchs, Thames & Hudson, London, 1986
- —. *Old World New World*, Anthony d'Offay, London, 1988
- —. *Richard Long: Walking in Circles,* Hayward Gallery/ Thames & Hudson, London, 1992
- —. *Richard Long: Mountains and Water*, Anthony d'Offay, London, 1992
- —. *Circles, Cycles, Mud*, D. Friis-Hansen, Contemporary Arts Museum, 1996
- —. *From Time to Time*, DAP, 1997
- —. *Richard Long*, Hatje Cantz, 1997
- —. *A Walk Across England*, Thames & Hudson, London, 1997

—. *Mirage*, Phaidon, London, 1998
—. *Selected Walks, 1979-1996*, Morning Star Press, 1999
—. *Richard Long: a Moving World*, Tate Publishing, London, 2002
—. *Richard Long – Walking the Line*, Thames and Hudson, London, 2002
E. Lucie-Smith: *Sculpture Since 1945*, Phaidon, Oxford, 1987
N. Lynton. *David Nash: Sculpture, 1971-90*, Serpentine Gallery, London, 1990
R. Mabey. "Art and ecology", *Modern Painters*, 3, 4, Winter, 1990
D. Macmillan. "David Nash: Brancusi Joins the Garden Gang", *Art Monthly*, 65, Apl, 1983
L. MacRitchie. "Ancient Egypt", *Financial Times*, Dec 12, 1994
—. "Residency on earth", *Art in America*, 83, 4, Apl 1995
S. Madoff. "Andy Goldsworthy", *Garden Design*, 13, June, 1994
W. Malpas. *The Art of Richard Long*, Crescent Moon, 1995/ 1998/ 2008
—. *Andy Goldsworthy*, Crescent Moon, 1996/ 1998/ 2007
—. *The Art of Andy Goldsworthy*, Crescent Moon, 1998/ 2004/ 2007
—. *Land Art*, Crescent Moon, 1995/ 2008
A.T. Mann. *Sacred Architecture*, Element Books, Shaftesbury, Dorset, 1993
J. van der Marck. *Wrapped Museum*, Museum of Contemporary Art, Chicago, IL, 1969
—. *Herbert Bayer*, Dartmouth College Museum, Hanover, NH, 1977
M. Marmer. "James Turrell", *Art in America*, 69, May, 1981
R. Martin. *The Sculpted Forest: Sculpture in the Forest of Dean*, Redcliff, Bristol, 1990
B. Matilsky. *Fragile Economies*, Rizzoli, New York, NY, 1992
W.H. Matthews. *Mazes and Labyrinths*, Dover, New York, NY, 1970
J. May. "Landscape Fired by Ice", *Landscape*, Dec, 1987
B. McAvera. "Public art: site sensitivities", *Art Monthly*, 215, Apl, 1998
A. McPherson. "David Nash: interviewed by Allan McPherson", *Artscribe*, 12, June, 1978
K. McShine. *Primary Structures*, Jewish Museum, New York, NY, 1966
—. *Information*, Museum of Modern Art, New York, NY, 1970
—. *An International Survey of Recent Painting and Sculpture*, MOMA, New York, NY, 1984
H.C. Merillat: *Modern Sculpture: The New Old Masters*, Dod, Mead & Co, New York, NY, 1974
U. Meyer. *Conceptual Art*, Dutton, New York, NY, 1972
D.C. Miller, ed. *Sixteen Americans*, Museum of Modern Art,

New York, NY, 1959
- M. Miller. *The Garden as an Art*, State University of New York Press, Albany, NY, 1993
- M. Miss. *Mary Miss: Interior Works*, Bell Gallery, University of Rhode Island, Autumn, 1981
- J. Morland. *New Milestones: Sculpture, Community and the Land*, Common Ground, 1988
- H. Morphy & M. Boles, eds. *Art from the Land*, University of Washington Press, 2000
- R. Morris. "Notes on Sculpture", *Artforum*, Feb, 1966, Oct, 1966, June, 1967, Apl, 1969
- —. "Aligned with Nazca", *Artforum*, Oct, 1975
- —. *Robert Morris: Mirror Works, 1961-1978*, Leo Castelli Gallery, New York, NY, 1979
- —. et al. *Earthworks*, Seattle Art Museum, Seattle, WA, 1979
- —. *Selected Works*, Contemporary Arts Museum, Houston, TX, 1981
- —. *Continuous Project Altered Daily*, MIT Press, Cambridge, MA, 1993
- S. Morris. "A Rhetoric of Silence: Redefinitions of Sculpture in the 1960s and 1970s", in S. Nairne, 1981
- J. Morrison. "Landmatters", *British Journal of Photography*, 133, June 6, 1986
- A. Morgan. "Maze and labyrinth", *Sculpture*, 14, 4, July/ Aug, 1995
- D. Morse. "At Runnymede Farm, the crop is sculptures", *San Francisco Examiner*, May 2, 1997
- M. Mosser & G. Teyssot, eds. *The History of Garden Design*, Thames & Hudson, London, 1991
- A. Moszynska. *Abstract Art*, Thames & Hudson, London, 1990
- G. Müller. "Michael Heizer", *Arts Magazine*, Dec, 1969
- —. "The Earth, Subjected To Cataclysms, Is a Cruel Master", *Arts Magazine*, Nov, 1971
- S. Nairne & N. Serota. *British Sculpture in the Twentieth Century*, Whitechapel Art Gallery, London, 1981
- —. *State of the Art: Ideas & Images in the 1980s*, Chatto, London, 1987
- H. Nakamura. "Andy Goldsworthy and Anthony Green", *Ikebana Ryusei*, 38, Apl, 1988
- D. Nash. *Fletched Over Ash*, AIR Gallery, 1978
- —. "David Nash", *Aspects*, 10, Spring, 1980
- —. *Stoves and Hearths*, Duke Street Gallery, London, 1982
- T.A. Neff, ed. *A Quiet Revolution: British Sculpture Since 1965*, Thames & Hudson, London, 1987
- B. Nemitz. *Trans Plant: Living Vegetation in Contemporary Art*, Hatje Cantz, 2000
- C. Nemser. "An interview with Eva Hesse", *Artforum*, May, 1970

—. "My Memories of Eva Hesse", *Feminist Art Journal*, Winter, 1973

P. Nesbitt. "At Home with Nature: Andy Goldsworthy in Scotland", *Alba*, Spring, 1989

—. "A Landscape Touched by Gold", in G. Hughes, 1990

M. Newman. "New Sculpture in Britain", *Art in America*, Sept, 1982

I. Noguchi. *A Sculptor's World*, Harper & Row, New York, NY, 1968

A. Le Normand-Romain *et al*. *Sculpture: The Adventure of Modern Sculpture in the Nineteenth and Twentieth Centuries*, Skira, Geneva, 1986

J. Norrie. "Andy Goldsworthy", *Arts Review*, 3 July, 1987

B. Oakes, ed. *Sculpting the Environment*, Van Nostrand Reinhold, New York, NY, 1995

P. Oakes. "The Incomparable Andy Goldsworthy", *Country Living*, 48, Dec, 1989

R. Onoratio. "Illusive Spaces: The Art of Mary Miss", *Artforum*, Dec, 1978

—. *Mary Miss – Perimeters/ Pavilions/ Decoys*, Nassau County Museum, 1979

D. Oppenheim. *Dennis Oppenheim*, Musée d'Art Contemporain, Montréal, 1978

—. *Selected Works, 1967-1990*, Abrams, New York, NY, 1992

P. Osborne, ed. *Conceptual Art*, Phaidon, London, 2002

E. Osaka. *Andy Goldsworthy: Mountain and Coast: Autumn Into Winter*, Gallery Takagi, Nagoya, 1987

W. Packer. "Sculpture from the countryside", *Financial Times*, July 7, 1987

—. "Andy Goldsworthy's Transient Touch", *Sculpture*, July, 1989

A.C. Papadakis, ed. *The New Romantics*, Art & Design, 4, 11/12, Academy Group, 1988

—. *et al*, eds. *New Art*, Academy Group, London, 1991

R. Parker & G. Pollock. *Framing Feminism*, Pandora Press, London, 1987

D. Parr. "City focus: St. Louis: 'a different kind of energy'", Art News. 95, 3, Mch, 1996

J. Partridge. "Forest work", *Craft*, 81, July/ Aug, 1986

A. Patrizio. "Cube garden: sculpture at the Edinburgh Festival 1990", *Arts Review*, 42, July 27, 1990

P. Patton. "Robert Morris and the Fire Next Time", *Art News*, 82, 10, Dec, 1983

E. Pavese, ed. *Christo: Surrounded Islands*, Abrams, New York, NY, 1986

N. Pennick. *Mazes and Labyrinths*, Hale, London, 1990

J. Perreault. "A Minimal Future? Union-Made: Report on a Phenomenon", *Arts Magazine*, 41, Mch, 1967

J. Perrone. "Seeing Through Boxes", *Artforum*, 15, Nov, 1976

R. Pincus-Witten. *Postminimalism*, Out of London, New York, NY, 1977

—. *Post-Minimalism into Maximalism*, UMI Research Press, Ann Arbor, MI, 1987

J. Poetter. *Donald Judd*, Cantz, Stuttgart, 1989

L. Ponti. "Tony Cragg", *Domus*, 611, Nov, 1980

J.C. Powys. *Wolf Solent*, Penguin, London, 1964

—. *Autobiography*, Macdonald, London, 1967

A. Price. "A Conversation With Alice Aycock", *Architectural Design*, Apl, 1980

G. Prince. "With mud on their hands, growth, decay and the movement of change", *World Magazine,* Jan, 1991

E. Rankin. "Popularising public sculpture in Britain: from landscape gardens to forest trails", *de Arte*, 53, Apl 1996

C. Ratcliff. "The Compleat Smithson", *Art in America*, Jan, 1980

B. Redhead. *The Inspiration of Landscape: Artists in National Parks*, Phaidon, Oxford, 1989

H. Risatti. "The Sculpture of Alice Aycock", *Woman's Art Journal*, Summer, 1985

J. Roberts. *Postmodernism, Politics and Art*, Manchester University Press, Manchester, 1990

C. Robins. *The Pluralist Era: American Art, 1968-1981*, Harper & Row, New York, NY, 1984

Dieter Roelstraete. R*ichard Long (One Work) (Afterall)*, 2010

W. Romey. "The artist as geographer: Richard Long's Earth Art", *Professional Geographer*, 39, 4, 1987

B. Rose. "New York Letter", *Art International*, Feb 15, 1964

—. "Looking at American Sculpture", *Artforum*, 3, Feb, 1965a

—. "ABC Art", *Art in America*, 53, 5, Nov, 1965b

—. *Robert Morris*, Corcoran Gallery, Washington, DC, 1990

H. Rosenberg. *The De-Definition of Art*, Horizon Press, New York, NY, 1972

—. *The Tradition of the New*, Da Capo Press, New York, NY, 1994

R. Rosenblum. *Modern Painting and the Northern Romantic Tradition*, Thames & Hudson, London, 1978

—. *Jasper Johns' Paintings and Sculptures, 1954-1974*, Ann Arbor, Michigan, MI, 1985

—. "Romanticism and Retrospective: An Interview with Robert Rosenblum", in A. Papadakis, 1988

C. Ross. *Star Axis*, University of New Mexico Press, Albuqerque, NM, 1992

S. Ross. "Gardens, earthworks, and environmental art", in S. Kemal, 1993

—. *What Gardens Mean*, University of Chicago Press, Chicago, IL, 1998

M. Roth. "Robert Smithson on Duchamp", *Artforum*, Oct, 1969

—. ed. *The Amazing Decade: Women and Performance Art in America 1970-80*, Astro Artz, Los Angeles, CA, 1983

A. Saalfield. *Mary Miss*, Fogg Art Museum, Cambridge, MA, 1980

I. Sandler. *American Art of the 1960s*, Harper & Row, New York, NY, 1988

—. *Art of the Postmodern Era: From the 1960s to the Early 1990s*, HarperCollins, London, 1997

P. Schjeldahl. *Art in Our Time: The Saatchi Collection*, Lund Humphries, London, 1984

P. Schuck. "Interview: Earth, Water, Wind", *Contemporanea*, Apl, 1990

D. Schwartz. *Lawrence Weiner*, König, Cologne, 1989

W. Seitz. *The Art of Assemblage*, MOMA, New York, NY, 1961

P. Selz. *Directions in Kinetic Sculpture*, University of California Press, Berkeley, CA, 1966

—. *Art in Our Times: A Pictorial History 1890-1980*, Thames & Hudson, London, 1982

A. Seymour. "Walking in Circles", in R. Long, *Walking in Circles*

—. "Old World New World", in R. Long, *Old World New World*

G. Shapiro. *Earthworks: Robert Smithson and After Babel*, University of California Press, Berkeley, CA, 1995

W. Sharp *et al*. *Earth Art*, Andrew Dickson White Museum of Art, Cornell University, Ithaca, NY, 1969

—. "Structure and Sensibility", *Avalanche*, 5, Summer, 1972

N. Shulman. "Monday at the North Pole", *Arts Review*, June 2, 1989

P. Sims. *From Minimalism to Expressionism*, New York, NY, 1963

N. Sinden. "Interview: Art in Nature: Andy Goldsworthy", *Resurgence*, 129, Aug, 1988

H.J. Smagula. *Currents: Contemporary Directions in the Visual Arts*, Prentice-Hall, Englewood Cliffs, NJ, 1983

D. Smith. *Sculpture and Drawings*, ed. J. Merkert, Prestel-Verlag, Munich, 1986

R. Smith. "Review", *Artforum*, Dec, 1975

—. "De Maria: Elements", *Art in America*, May, 1978

R. Smithson. "Entropy and the New Monuments", *Artforum*, 4, 10, June, 1966

—. "Incidents of Mirror-Travel in the Yucatan", *Artforum*, Sept, 1967

—. "The Monuments of Passaic", *Artforum*, Dec, 1967

—. "Toward the Development of an Air Terminal Site", *Artforum*, Summer, 1967

—. "A Museum of Language in the Vicinity of Art", *Art International*, 12, 3, Mch, 1968

—. *The Writings of Robert Smithson*, ed. N. Holt, New York University Press, New York, NY, 1979
—. *Robert Smithson*, ed. J. Flam, University of California Press, Berkeley, CA, 1996
—. *Robert Smithson: A Collection of Writings*, Pierogi Galery New York, NY, 1997
T. Sokolowski *et al*. *Robert Morris*, New York University Press, New York, NY, 1989
A. Sondheim, ed. *Post-Movement Art in America*, Dutton, New York, NY, 1977
A. Sonfist. *Alan Sonfist*, Neuberger Museum, New York, NY, 1978
—. ed. *Art in the Land: A Critical Anthology of Environmental Art*, Dutton, New York, NY, 1983
W. Spies. *The Running Fence Project, Christo*, Abrams, New York, NY, 1977
J. Stathatos. "Andy Goldsworthy's Evidences", *Creative Camera*, 255, Mch, 1986
F. Stella. *Working Space*, Harvard University Press, Cambridge, MA, 1986
—. *Frank Stella*, Madrid, 1995
N. Stewart. "Richard Long, Lines of Thought: A Conversation with Nick Stewart", *Circa*, Nov, 1984
K. Stiles & P. Selz, eds. *Theories & Documents of Contemporary Art: A Sourcebook of Artists' Writings*, University of California Press, Berkeley, CA, 1996
S.L. Stoops. *Andy Goldsworthy: Breakdown*, Rose Art Museum, 1992
W.J. Strachan. *Towards Sculpture: Maquettes and Sketches from Rodin to Oldenburg*, Thames & Hudson, London, 1976
Roy Strong *et al*. *Close: Landscape Design and Land Art in Scotland*, 2010
G. Sutton. "Land art", *Landskab*, Dec, 1989
D. Sylvester. *About Modern Art*, Chatto & Windus, London, 1996
G. Tiberghien. *Land Art*, Art Data, London, 1995
Lisa Tickner. "The Body Politic: Female Sexuality and Women Artists Since 1970", *Art History*, 1, 2, June 1978, 236-51
S. Tillim. "Earthworks and the New Picturesque", *Artforum*, Dec, 1968
C. Tomkins. *Post- to Neo-: The Art World of the 1980s*, Penguin, London, 1989
M. Treib. "Frame, moment and sequence: the photographic book and the designed landscape", *Journal of Garden History*, 15, 2, Summer, 1995
E. Tsai. *Robert Smithson Unearthed*, Columbia University Press, New York, NY, 1991
M. Tuchman. *American Sculpture of the Sixties*, Los Angeles County Museum of Art, CA, 1967

P. Tuchman. "Background of a Minimalist: Carl Andre", *Artforum*, Mch, 1978

J. Turrell. *Mapping Spaces*, Peter Blum, New York, NY, 1987

—. Interview, in B. Oakes, 1995

G. de Vries, ed. *On Art: Artists' Writings on the Changed Notion of Art After 1965*, Cologne, 1974

D. Waldman. *Carl Andre*, Guggenheim, New York, NY, 1970a

—. "Holding the Floor", *Art News*, Oct, 1970b

Clarrie Wallis. *Richard Long: Heaven and Earth*, Tate, London, 2009

J. Watkins. "In the artist's studio: Andy Goldsworthy: touching North", *Art International*, 9, Winter, 1989

M. Webster. "Andy Goldsworthy at San Jose Museum of Art", *ArtWeek*. 26, 4, Apl, 1995

U. Weilacher *et al. Between Landscape Architecture and Land Art*, Birkhauser Verlag AG, 1999

L. Weiner. *Lawrence Weiner, Works*, Anatol AV und Filmproduktion Hamburg, 1977

Welsh Sculpture Trust. *Sculpture in a Country Park*, Welsh Sculpture Trust, 1983

C. West. "From genesis to box", *Modern Painters*, 5, 4, Winter, 1992

D. Wheeler. *Art Since Mid-Century: 1945 to the Present*, Thames & Hudson, London, 1991

J. White. *The Birth and Rebirth of Pictorial Space*, Faber, London, 1981

O. Wick *et al. James Turrell*, Turske & Turske Gallery, Zurich, 1990

A. Wildermuth. *Richard Long*, Galerie Buchmann, Basel, 1985

A. Wilding: *Alison Wilding*, with M. Tooby, Tate Gallery, St Ives, Cornwall, 1994

C. van Winkel. "The Crooked Path, Patterns of Kinetic Energy", *Parkett*, 33, 1992

M. Winton. "Sculptures That Blow Away", *Ark*, Spring, 1970

S. Wrede & W. Adams. *Denatured Visions: Landscape and Culture in the 20th Century*, Abrams, New York, NY, 1991

S. Yard. *Christo: Oceanfront*, Princeton University Press, Princeton, NJ, 1975

—. *Sitings*, La Jolla Museum of Contemporary Art, La Jolla, CA, 1986

M. Yule. "Andy Goldsworthy, a Lake District photowork", *National Art-Collections Fund Review*, 88, 1992

du Zeitschrift für kultur, *Walking Into Existence*, no. 756, 2005

L. Zelevansky. "Richard Long", *Art News*, 83, 8, Oct, 1984

WEBSITES

Robert Smithson   <www.robertsmithson.com>
   <spiraljetty.org>
Mary Miss   <www.marymiss.com>
Alice Aycock   <aaycock.com>
Donna Dennis   <donnadennisart.com>
Yvette Martin   >yvettemartin.co.uk>
Walter de Maria   <www.lightningfield.org>
Christo   <www.christojeanneclaude.net>
James Turrell   <www.rodencrater.org>
Chris Drury   <www.chrisdrury.co.uk>
Donald Judd   <www.chinati.org>   <juddfoundation.org>
Dennis Oppenheim   <dennis-oppenheim.com>
Michael Heizer   <doublenegative.tarasen.net>
Sjoerd Buisman   <sjoerdbuisman.nl>
Nikolaj Recke   <nikolajrecke.dk>
Andy Goldsworthy, Sheepfolds site: <www.sheepfolds.org>
Andy Goldsworthy, *Rivers and Tides* DVD
   <www.skyline.uk.com/riversandtides>
Richard Long   <www.richardlong.org>
Richard Long Newsletter   <therichardlongnewsletter.org>
Hamish Fulton   <www.hamish-fulton.com>

Earthworks   <www.earthworks.org>
The Artists: <www.the-artists.org>
Sacred Sites   <sacredsites.com>
Sculpture at Goodwood, CASS: <www.sculpture.org.uk>
Crescent Moon Publishing: <www.crmoon.com>

ARTS, PAINTING, SCULPTURE

The Art of Andy Goldsworthy
Andy Goldsworthy: Touching Nature
Andy Goldsworthy in Close-Up
Andy Goldsworthy: Pocket Guide
Andy Goldsworthy In America
Land Art: A Complete Guide
The Art of Richard Long
Richard Long: Pocket Guide
Land Art In Great Britain
Land Art in Close-Up
Land Art In the U.S.A.
Land Art: Pocket Guide
Installation Art in Close-Up
Minimal Art and Artists In the 1960s and After
Colourfield Painting
Land Art DVD, TV documentary
Andy Goldsworthy DVD, TV documentary
The Erotic Object: Sexuality in Sculpture From Prehistory to the Present Day
Sex in Art: Pornography and Pleasure in Painting and Sculpture
Postwar Art
Sacred Gardens: The Garden in Myth, Religion and Art
Glorification: Religious Abstraction in Renaissance and 20th Century Art
Early Netherlandish Painting
Jasper Johns
Brice MardenLeonardo da Vinci
Piero della Francesca
Giovanni Bellini
Fra Angelico: Art and Religion in the Renaissance
Mark Rothko: The Art of Transcendence
Frank Stella: American Abstract Artist
Alison Wilding: The Embrace of Sculpture
Vincent van Gogh: Visionary Landscapes
Eric Gill: Nuptials of God
Constantin Brancusi: Sculpting the Essence of Things
Max Beckmann
Gustave Moreau
Caravaggio
Egon Schiele: Sex and Death In Purple Stockings
Delizioso Fotografico Fervore: Works In Process 1
Sacro Cuore: Works In Process 2
The Light Eternal: J.M.W. Turner
The Madonna Glorified: Karen Arthurs

LITERATURE

J.R.R. Tolkien: The Books, The Films, The Whole Cultural Phenomenon
J.R.R. Tolkien: Pocket Guide
Beauties, Beasts and Enchantment: Classic French Fairy Tales
Tolkien's Heroic Quest
Brothers Grimm: German Popular Stories
Sexing Hardy: Thomas Hardy and Feminism
Thomas Hardy's *Tess of the d'Urbervilles*
Thomas Hardy's *Jude the Obscure*
Thomas Hardy: The Tragic Novels
Love and Tragedy: Thomas Hardy
The Poetry of Landscape in Hardy
Wessex Revisited: Thomas Hardy and John Cowper Powys
Wolfgang Iser: Essays and Interviews
Petrarch, Dante and the Troubadours
Maurice Sendak and the Art of Children's Book Illustration
Andrea Dworkin
Cixous, Irigaray, Kristeva: The *Jouissance* of French Feminism
Julia Kristeva: Art, Love, Melancholy, Philosophy, Semiotics and Psychoanalysis
Hélene Cixous I Love You: The *Jouissance* of Writing
Luce Irigaray: Lips, Kissing, and the Politics of Sexual Difference
Peter Redgrove: Here Comes the Flood
Peter Redgrove: Sex-Magic-Poetry-Cornwall
Lawrence Durrell: Between Love and Death, East and West
Love, Culture & Poetry: Lawrence Durrell
Cavafy: Anatomy of a Soul
German Romantic Poetry: Goethe, Novalis, Heine, Hölderlin
Novalis: *Hymns To the Night*
Feminism and Shakespeare
Shakespeare: *The Sonnets*
Shakespeare: Love, Poetry & Magic
The Passion of D.H. Lawrence
D.H. Lawrence: Symbolic Landscapes
D.H. Lawrence: Infinite Sensual Violence
The Ecstasies of John Cowper Powys
Sensualism and Mythology: The Wessex Novels of John Cowper Powys
Amorous Life: John Cowper Powys (H.W. Fawkner)
Postmodern Powys: New Essays on John Cowper Powys (Joe Boulter)
Rethinking Powys: Critical Essays on John Cowper Powys
Paul Bowles & Bernardo Bertolucci
Rainer Maria Rilke
Joseph Conrad: *Heart of Darkness*
In the Dim Void: Samuel Beckett
Samuel Beckett Goes into the Silence
André Gide: Fiction and Fervour
Jackie Collins and the Blockbuster Novel
Blinded By Her Light: The Love-Poetry of Robert Graves

POETRY

Ursula Le Guin: *Walking In Cornwall*
Peter Redgrove: Here Comes The Flood
Peter Redgrove: Sex-Magic-Poetry-Cornwall
Dante: Selections From the *Vita Nuova*
Petrarch, Dante and the Troubadours
William Shakespeare: *The Sonnets*
William Shakespeare: Complete Poems

Blinded By Her Light: The Love-Poetry of Robert Graves
Emily Dickinson: Selected Poems
Emily Brontë: Poems
Thomas Hardy: Selected Poems
Percy Bysshe Shelley: Poems
John Keats: Selected Poems
John Keats: Poems of 1820
D.H. Lawrence: Selected Poems
Edmund Spenser: Poems
Edmund Spenser: *Amoretti*
John Donne: Poems
Henry Vaughan: Poems
Sir Thomas Wyatt: Poems
Robert Herrick: Selected Poems

Rilke: Space, Essence and Angels in the Poetry of Rainer Maria Rilke
Rainer Maria Rilke: Selected Poems
Friedrich Hölderlin: Selected Poems
Arseny Tarkovsky: Selected Poems
Paul Verlaine: Selected Poems
Novalis: *Hymns To the Night*
Arthur Rimbaud: Selected Poems
Arthur Rimbaud: *A Season in Hell*
Arthur Rimbaud and the Magic of Poetry
D.J. Enright: By-Blows
Jeremy Reed: *Brigitte's Blue Heart*
Jeremy Reed: *Claudia Schiffer's Red Shoes*
Gorgeous Little Orpheus
Radiance: New Poems

Crescent Moon Book of Nature Poetry
Crescent Moon Book of Love Poetry
Crescent Moon Book of Mystical Poetry
Crescent Moon Book of Elizabethan Love Poetry
Crescent Moon Book of Metaphysical Poetry
Crescent Moon Book of Romantic Poetry
Pagan America: New American Poetry

MEDIA, CINEMA, FEMINISM and CULTURAL STUDIES

J.R.R. Tolkien: The Books, The Films, The Whole Cultural Phenomenon
J.R.R. Tolkien: Pocket Guide
The *Lord of the Rings* Movies: Pocket Guide
The Ghost Dance: The Origins of Religion
The Cinema of Hayao Miyazaki
Hayao Miyazaki: *Princess Mononoke*: Pocket Movie Guide
Hayao Miyazaki: *Spirited Away*: Pocket Movie Guide
The Peyote Cult
Cixous, Irigaray, Kristeva: The *Jouissance* of French Feminism
Julia Kristeva: Art, Love, Melancholy, Philosophy, Semiotics and Psychoanalysis
Luce Irigaray: Lips, Kissing, and the Politics of Sexual Difference
Hélene Cixous I Love You: The *Jouissance* of Writing
Andrea Dworkin
'Cosmo Woman': The World of Women's Magazines
Women in Pop Music
Discovering the Goddess (Geoffrey Ashe)
The Poetry of Cinema
The Sacred Cinema of Andrei Tarkovsky
Andrei Tarkovsky: Pocket Guide
Andrei Tarkovsky: *Mirror*: Pocket Movie Guide
Walerian Borowczyk: Cinema of Erotic Dreams
Jean-Luc Godard: The Passion of Cinema
Jean-Luc Godard: Pocket Guide
John Hughes and Eighties Cinema
Ferris Buller's Day Off: Pocket Movie Guide
The Cinema of Richard Linklater
Liv Tyler: Star In Ascendance
Blade Runner and the Films of Philip K. Dick
Paul Bowles and Bernardo Bertolucci
Media Hell: Radio, TV and the Press
Detonation Britain: Nuclear War in the UK
Feminism and Shakespeare
Wild Zones: Pornography, Art and Feminism
Sex in Art: Pornography and Pleasure in Painting and Sculpture
Sexing Hardy: Thomas Hardy and Feminism

The Light Eternal is a model monograph, an exemplary job. The subject matter of the book beautifully organised and dead on beam. (Lawrence Durrell)

It is amazing for me to see my work treated with such passion and respect. (Andrea Dwor

Sex-Magic-Poetry-Cornwall is a very rich essay... It is like a brightly-lighted box. (Peter Redgre

CRESCENT MOON PUBLISHING P.O. Box 1312, Maidstone, Kent, ME14 5XU, Englan
0044-1622-729593   cresmopub@yahoo.co.uk   www.crmoon.com

www.ingramcontent.com/pod-product-compliance
Lightning Source LLC
Chambersburg PA
CBHW031611210526
45464CB00004B/1526